London 2000

1924

EXPLODING LONDON

1960

2000?

London Transport

British Railways

LONDON 2000

Peter Hall

Professor of Geography
University of Reading

FABER AND FABER LIMITED
24 Russell Square, London

First published in 1963
by Faber and Faber Limited
24 Russell Square, London, W.C.1
Second edition 1969
Printed in Great Britain by
Western Printing Services Ltd., Bristol
All rights reserved

SBN 571 046 746

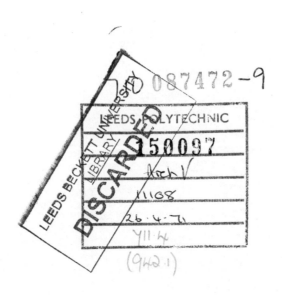

TO JOHN VAIZEY

Contents

Illustrations

PLATES

11

ILLUSTRATIONS

MAPS

12

Preface

This book is an exercise in academic polemic. I have tried to use research, my own and others', to uncover the problems that lie before us in reshaping London; the limitations that the facts of economy and society place upon the range of our possible actions; the choices that are open to us, and the courses we ought to follow.

As far as possible I have tried to be exact. I have made, or borrowed, precise estimates of jobs, population, houses, costs. But in some places I have had to guess, intuit, suggest; for in planning London, time will not wait for us to satisfy every academic scruple.

I have also tried to be positive. One cannot write on planning, one cannot scan through its enormous literature, without being conscious of a great pitfall. It is so easy and so sterile to be virtuous and vague. Every newspaper article now tells us that we want to re-invigorate the industrial areas of the north to counter the attractions of London; that we ought to be building more New Towns; that we must redevelop our city centres comprehensively. I have tried to go beyond these generalities; to ask questions like: can we re-invigorate the north, and is it worth it? How many New Towns, and where? How exactly can we achieve this comprehensive development?

I have not tried here to provide a comprehensive blueprint for a new London; that is beyond the capacity of any one man. But I have tried to concentrate on presenting material towards that blueprint. And I have preferred always to provoke rather than to peddle banalities. If in consequence I give my critics a good day at the fair, we shall all have enjoyed ourselves.

The writer on town planning has to try to be that impossible being, the master-of-all-trades. He fails, of course; but the failure is perhaps less abject than it might be, because he can rely to such an extraordinary extent upon the specialist wisdom of others, freely given. Here I want to acknowledge very particularly the help of the following people:

13

PREFACE

Professor Michael Wise, for his suggestions on Chapters 1–4.

Wyndham Thomas, Director of the Town and Country Planning Association, for reading and commenting upon the opening chapters.

Gerald Manners and Michael Chisholm, for stimulating conversation after the symposium on contemporary economic geography at the Institute of British Geographers Conference at Liverpool, January 1962, where an early version of Chapter 3 was presented.

Research Officers of the Ministry of Housing and Local Government, in particular Dr. Christie Willatts, Geoffrey Powell and Ronald White, who have generously commented on various points. I must add the usual rider: 'their contribution was personal and in no wise reflects official endorsement'.

Barry Cullingworth, for commenting closely on Chapter 3.

P. A. Stone, for permission to use his material in Chapter 4.

Christopher Foster, for great help with Chapter 5.

All members of the *Socialist Commentary* study groups on town planning (which produced *The Face of Britain*, September 1961) and on transport (which produced *Transport is Everyone's Problem*, April 1963). Many essential ideas in this book were evolved and defined in discussion within these groups.

Lewis Keeble and Betty Trevena, for help with the technicalities of the 'Third Schedule'.

My 'lay readers', who made many valuable comments on style and presentation: John Hall and Carla Wartenberg.

Lastly I owe a very special debt to John Vaizey who first suggested the idea of this book and who commented on successive drafts throughout. His contribution on economic matters—especially on the complex problems of Chapter 8—was quite invaluable. And much of the general philosophy of the book was evolved in discussions which started in Cambridge nearly ten years ago. I dedicate it to him.

PETER HALL

Preface to Second Edition

Nathaniel Lichfield reviewed this book, and questioned my claim that it was academic polemic; it was, he said, academic journalism. I think both of us were right. Now both journalism and polemic are of their time, and nothing else; translated into another age, the interest becomes merely historic or literary. That is what has happened, in six short years, to *London 2000*.

It is not merely that the details are dated; those could be changed. It is that the whole point of the book belongs to the past. It was written when people who made decisions, and moulded opinion, had to be told of the necessity to plan. Now they need not be told. We have had more plans, and more activity leading to plans, in London this last half decade than in any previous similar period. And I do not except those feverish years of Barlow, Uthwatt, Reith and Abercrombie.

Therefore I would have been happy to see the book die, turning up occasionally as a curiosity on the second-hand stalls, until the year of judgement came and people could judge for themselves the rightness or the absurdity of my predictions. But my publishers prevailed on me that people still wanted to buy the book. I resisted all temptation to alter the text. Instead, I agreed to add postscripts to each chapter setting out the bare facts of how the problems and the plans and the ideas had changed.

When I finished, I had completed a text nearly one-third as long as the original book. This could mean that I had become a good deal more prolix than when the first edition was written. I prefer to think it is a measure of the extraordinary activity that has seized London in the years since the book was published. It would be flattering to think that the book itself had something to do with it; but wrong. Rather, the book itself was a symptom of the mood that produced the effort. It now promises to produce a *London 2000* far closer to my vision than I ever dared think. May the promise be fulfilled.

Part I · POSING THE PROBLEM

CHAPTER 1

London's Problems

The first problem with London is to define it. London has never taken kindly to attempts at delimitation, whether by people who wanted to govern it, or by those who just wanted to fix it statistically; every time this was done, London promptly outgrew its administration or its figures. The Census, in 1961, still gives figures for a *Greater London Conurbation*. This is an area 720 square miles in size, within a ring of radius about 15 miles from Charing Cross; very roughly, it resembles the area which according to present plans will be administered, from April 1965 onwards, by the Greater London Council. Again very roughly, it represents the built-up London of 1938, and it is surrounded by the Metropolitan Green Belt, an idea fixed by legislation in that year[1] in a vain attempt to halt the spread of the capital into the fields of surrounding England, and realized after the Second World War.

Within the Conurbation is a much smaller area, 117 square miles in extent, the area of the old *London County Council*. Very approximately indeed, it represents the built-up London of 1888: the year the L.C.C. was established. Again according to present plans, it is destined to disappear from the statistics and from the administrative maps (save as a unit of school management) in April 1965. And within this again is the minute core of London, only 677 acres in extent: the *City of London*, which (again very roughly) represents the Roman and medieval origins of the city of today. Despite its many critics, the City has survived the centuries as a powerful administrative entity; and it looks like surviving the holocaust of April 1965.

But just as the L.C.C. area became inadequate as a definition of London almost as soon as it was in being, so, ironically, the Conurbation is inadequate even before its successor the G.L.C. begins to function. For between 1951 and 1961 the Conurbation as a whole, and most of its constituent local authority areas—except the very outermost ones—actually declined in population; while in contrast, the belt thirty miles wide around the Conurbation (that is, fifteen to forty-five miles from

[1] *Green Belt Act*, 1938. Cf. Ministry of Housing and Local Government, *The Green Belts* (1962), 2.

19

Charing Cross), which includes the greater part of the Green Belt, increased its population by no less than 964,000 in ten years. Some of this enormous increase—probably less than a quarter—represents new people, the excess of births over deaths. The rest is migration, and most of it has almost certainly come from the Conurbation. In addition, a large part of the births—how many, we cannot exactly say—are to ex-London parents. The *Outer Ring*, then, must now be regarded as part of London too.[1] So Greater London is no longer great enough: it is necessary to talk instead of a *London Region*, about forty miles in radius from Charing Cross (Map 1). It stretches to Royston on the north-east, beyond Southend on the east, to Maidstone on the south-east, nearly to Brighton on the south and to Basingstoke on the south-west, far beyond Aylesbury on the north-west. It covers over 4,400 square miles, $7\frac{1}{2}$ per cent of the land area of England and Wales. The London Region is the London of this book. It has four great concentric rings (Map 1).

		Area, square miles	Population 1961
LONDON REGION		4,412	12,453,300
Outer Ring		3,690	4,281,500
Suburban Ring	} Conurbation	605	4,976,800
Inner Ring } L.C.C.		107	2,925,100 approx.
Central Area		10	270,000 approx.

This London Region, like any other geographical region, has a large element of the arbitrary about it. One could write a book in itself on the scientific definition of London,[2] though at the present rate of growth it might be seriously out-of-date by the time it was published. Of the present definition one can only say that it has been evolved by practical planners on the basis of close study of population trends; and that if anything it errs on the generous side, so that it will remain a workable unit for some years to come. That is why it is used here.

Planning for Londoners

Accepting the definition, there are in 1962 some twelve and a half million Londoners. Their city has been in existence about two thousand years. But apart from the earliest Roman city, few traces of which survive today, only in the last fifteen of these years has London been effectively a planned city: that is a city subject to overall

[1] A. G. Powell first drew attention to this fact. 'The Recent Development of Greater London', *The Advancement of Science*, 17 (1960–1), 76–86.

[2] Since this was written, American researchers have defined a London 'Metropolitan Region' with a population of 10,490,690 in 1956. Leo F. Schnore, 'Metropolitan Development in the United Kingdom', *Economic Geography*, 38 (1962), 215–33. This area excludes four other 'Metropolitan Areas' (Reading, Luton, Aldershot/Farnborough, Rochester/Chatham/Gillingham) which are contiguous with the London area, and which are included in the 'London Region' of this book; total 1956 population, 726,950.

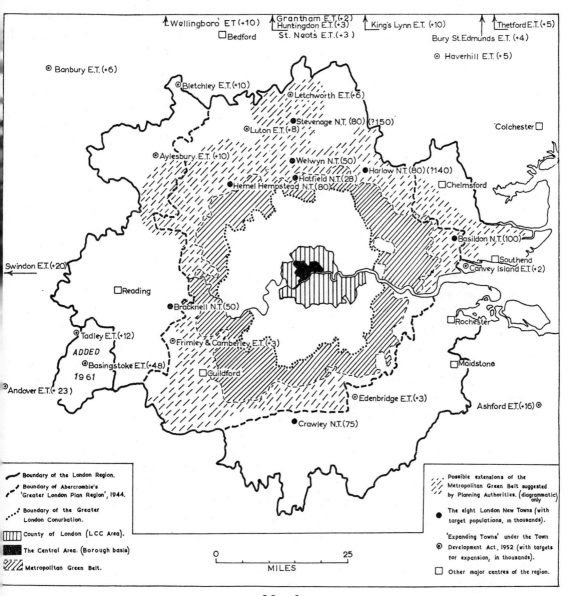

Map 1

THE LONDON REGION

planning control by an official agency or agencies. This book is about the planning of London. Its main object is to look at the lessons of these fifteen years' planning, and to use them for the next forty years, to see how we can most effectively remake our London for the year A.D 2000. Throughout, the book poses these questions. How well, since 1945, has planning worked in the London region? What has been happening since 1945 in the region, demographically, economically, socially? How far did the planners foresee and plan for these trends, or adapt themselves to them? Will they continue, or should any of them, can any of them, be reversed? If they continue, what sort of London will we have by the year 2000? Can planning affect the sort of London we have, and if so how far and in what ways? What is inevitable, and what is the area of human choice where planning can operate? Within the area of choice, what are the choices?

Planning in this book is a shorthand word to mean what used to be called town and country planning, and which is better called physical planning: building a physical environment, in terms of housing and shops and factories and offices and railways and roads and parks and pubs and libraries, which is better to live in and work in than the alternative which would have grown up without a plan. The first object of this book, the object of this chapter, must be to judge the quality of our physical planning so far. In this, two steps are necessary.

The first is to look and feel. Not to explain, not to analyse, not to render in statistics; that comes later. To look around; to see what we have done, since 1945, with London. And to look critically. The positive achievements of planning in London do not go unheralded; neither the Government of the day, whatever its complexion, nor the L.C.C., ails for lack of effective self-publicity. So we must be concerned to point up, in the paragraphs that follow, the shortcomings.

The second step is to compare, baldly, with the original objects of the planners. London, and all the country of which it is capital, are physically planned because of a great burst of creative and intellectual endeavour in the wartime and immediate postwar years, roughly from 1940 to 1947. In these years the Coalition and Labour Governments created the postwar planning machinery of Britain, which with modifications has survived. They did so on the basis of advice contained in a great series of interlinked official reports, which contained very large assumptions and made very sweeping proposals. The failures of planning since 1945 are failures in terms of this machinery and this advice. The machinery has not worked as was hoped; or the advice has not been taken; or the assumptions have been falsified. These are the possibilities.

I want to stress that detailed analysis of the mistakes must come later. Indeed, it is the main burden of the book. If the following paragraphs seem confused and bewildering, I shall have succeeded in my aim. I shall light upon concrete examples in the massive London City-Region of 1963, and I cannot hope that the examples will be familiar to all. But I hope that the problems they illustrate will; and that everyone can substitute his own illustration. And I shall compare my examples with reports and recommendations of commissions and committees, names, acts, pieces of administrative machinery, many of which form the essential jargon, the language of physical planning. These names like Barlow and Uthwatt and Abercrombie, Development of Industry Act and New Towns Act, Development Control and Development Charge, will become familiar as they are expounded and analysed in the course of this book. If the changing face of London is like a play constantly in performance, these reports and acts are like the original text against which the performance must be judged. But the best way of introduction to the text is to look in, even briefly, at the performance.

Hypertrophy at the Middle: Oxford Street

Looking west from Oxford Circus, Oxford Street in late 1962 presents an extraordinary scene of destruction and renewal. Here were until recently late Victorian shops, dating from the eighties and nineties of last century; the period when the department store and popular fashion shop began to develop, and with them the fortunes of Oxford Street as a fashion centre. In the ever-faster building investment cycle of central London they are already obsolescent after eighty years. They have been torn down, and in their place arise buildings to house the representative central area functions of the London of today: new and bigger department stores, specialized shops, a technical college. Functions like these helped to add about 150,000 to the working force of central London in the nineteen-fifties; and these 150,000 were a major element, in turn, in the net increase of employment of some 500,000 in the London Region as a whole in the same period. Some of the 150,000 are at this very moment part of the immense crowd—it is 9.0 a.m.—which is trying to squeeze through the narrow exits of Oxford Circus tube station, or are stuck in the queue of buses in Oxford Street itself. Here is an extraordinarily dramatic contrast. As were the old buildings, both the station and the street are seriously obsolescent: Oxford Circus station has not been materially enlarged since the Bakerloo line arrived there in 1906, and Oxford Street has not changed much since it was built by the Romans to carry their legionaries to Silchester—for which purpose, presumably, it was adequate. But while private enterprise finds it profitable to renew the buildings, no one finds it profitable to renew the means of getting the workers to them. After seven years of disputation London Transport have at last persuaded the Government that Oxford Circus shall have a new tube line and a new station, though they will lose money; but the engineers are only just making their preliminary surveys, and the work will not be finished till 1968. While no one has any plans for Oxford Street, except for the short-term palliative of making it a one-way street; which suggestion the shopkeepers are fighting tooth and nail.

In the buildings to house the new arrivals, the old London Building Acts, which for centuries fixed rigid limits to the heights of buildings, have been abandoned since 1945 in favour of a new planning principle; to achieve maximum daylight on

23

small ground areas, very low structures alternate with very tall ones. Elsewhere, as in the Fitzrovia district north and east of Oxford Circus, uniformity has been maintained, and a new London is appearing that in purely aesthetic terms is an acceptable twentieth-century equivalent to the harmony and good manners of Georgian town architecture. But *functionally*, whatever their height, the new buildings are curiously less suited to the needs of their age than the Georgian town houses were to theirs, Those houses had front doors entering on to a street, which was just wide enough to give daylight and to carry the essential carriage traffic that would use it. At the back, quite segregated from the carriage street, they had mews facilities for loading and unloading goods and for the various services the house needed. You will look in vain for such an admirably rational distribution of functions in the new blocks. True, the planners have insisted on internal car parks and loading bays for goods. But each shop or office block is conceived by itself, not at all in relation to the system of circulation around it. It faces a busy traffic street; shoppers, or office workers, must reach their destinations across streams of fuming, roaring traffic. Complete planning would have planned the circulation system, too, so that traffic could flow, pedestrians could walk and sit and stare, without mutual frustration and inconvenience.

The area round Oxford Circus is only a slightly extreme example of what is taking place all over the ten-square-mile central business area of London. It poses these questions.

First: why has employment grown so fast at the centre? The plans of the era 1940–7 said that it should not. In 1940 the *Barlow Report*[1] had urged that immediate measures be taken to stop the drift of population to London and the Home Counties. Working on this basis, the two *Abercrombie Plans*[2] for London in 1943–4 assumed that the total working force of London would not grow at all; and that there would be a massive decentralization of jobs out of the central and inner districts into the Outer Ring. The *Distribution of Industry Act* in 1945 was intended specifically to give the central Government the power to divert the growth of employment away from London and towards the depressed industrial areas of the inter-war period.[3] Given that these plans have been falsified, what can we do for the future? Is this growth in the small central area an inevitable feature of the growth of London? Should we seek to find more effective ways of curbing the growth of London as a whole, as Barlow and Abercrombie assumed? If this is impossible, or undesirable, should we and could we find some way of diverting some or all of the growth out of the central area?

---

[1] *Report of the Royal Commission on the Distribution of the Industrial Population*, Cmd. 6153 (H.M.S.O. 1940). Generally known after its Chairman, Sir Anderson Montague-Barlow (1868–1951).

[2] *County of London Plan*, 1943 (with J. H. Forshaw) and *Greater London Plan* 1944 (H.M.S.O. 1945). Named after their author, Professor Sir Leslie Patrick Abercrombie (1879–1957).

[3] And the Town and Country Planning Act, 1947, put teeth into that power by making the grant of planning permission for new factories or extensions dependent, in practice, on the possession of an 'Industrial Development Certificate' from the Board of Trade.

Second: if there continues to be even *some* growth at the centre, while the resident population does not grow, how do we deal with the resulting commuter problem? Even for a declining labour force in the central area, the *Abercrombie Plans* postulated massive and very expensive transport improvements: new tubes, better integration with the surface railways, radical reconstruction of the road system. These have not materialized; indeed, until the very end of the nineteen-fifties, there was no major investment in improvements to the road or underground system in the central area. For the future, the question is: does this have to continue? Or could we end the paradox of private affluence and public squalor, which Oxford Street and the tube station represent? Where could London find the money to improve its transport system? Providing it could provide the means, how should it improve the system, and how should the improved system be managed to give the maximum welfare to the travelling public?

Third: whether employment at the centre continues to grow or not, the centre will go on being rebuilt rapidly; that is the nature of any flourishing city centre business district. How then can we ensure that it is rebuilt on better principles? In planning jargon, how do we ensure *comprehensive redevelopment*: that is, rebuilding to an overall master plan which rebuilds the pattern of circulation as well as the individual buildings? In 1947 there was passed the *Town and Country Planning Act*, the most important piece of postwar planning machinery in Britain, and still probably the most advanced and comprehensive piece of planning control in any advanced industrial country. The central feature of this machinery, which has become an established part of British life, is the system of planning through *development control*. The entire land area of Britain is subject to planning control through bodies big enough to be efficient: the Counties and County Boroughs.[1] Each authority has a statutory duty to prepare (and periodically revise) a Development Plan for its area, showing first the changes necessary to remedy defective layout and low standards (the County and Town Maps) but also a staged programme for carrying out the changes (the Programme Map). No development can take place except according to the plan, so that anyone wanting to build or rebuild has, with certain minor exceptions, to apply for permission to the planning authority; and that authority is given considerable power to initiate comprehensive development itself. But in fact only a very small proportion of London, or of any British city, has been rebuilt on comprehensive principles; and the system of individual planning permissions has produced the sort of inadequate piecemeal redevelopment around Oxford Circus, which will merely put back the proper replanning of the area until the time the new buildings in their turn are ripe to come down, in another eighty years.

The questions that arise here, then, are: was there a failure in conception in the 1947 Act, in that it provided for comprehensive development but did not provide adequate ways of making it the rule? Or has there been a failure in execution, either at central or local level? What changes are needed for the future? Legislative? Administrative? Financial?

---

[1] Eighteen in the London Region: thirteen Counties and five County Boroughs.

There is a fourth question, which has loomed large in the public consciousness in recent years. These new developments, many of them, are speculative, and put huge sums in capital gains into the pockets of a few. Yet in 1942 one of the great wartime reports—the *Uthwatt Report*[1]—had recommended that an attempt be be made to take some of these gains for the community, whose actions had at least in part created them; and in 1947 the *financial provisions of the Town and Country Planning Act* had made such an attempt, though not the one Uthwatt had recommended. Under the system of development control instituted by the 1947 Act, the right to develop was in effect nationalized, and anyone wishing to develop had to pay the community for the privilege. The payment was made on the grant of permission to develop, and was called a *Development Charge*. In practice the Development Charge proved difficult to operate, and it was abolished by the Conservative Government in the 1953 Town and Country Planning Act without any alternative being put in its place. The questions here are: was the Development Charge system really unworkable? If it could have been made to work, was it really the best way of taking some of the development gains for the community? Why did Uthwatt propose a different solution, and why did the Labour Government in 1947 reject Uthwatt? What other possible solutions are there? What is best on the grounds of simplicity? of effectiveness? of political feasibility?

These are only some of the major questions suggested by the rapid renewal of London's City and West End since the end of building licensing in 1954. They fall naturally under different chapters. I consider the question of the growth of employment in London, and particularly at the centre, in Chapters 2 and 3; the problems of traffic congestion and journey to work in Chapter 5; the techniques of renewal in Chapters 7 and 8; and the problem of gains in value in Chapter 8.

Internal Decay: Paddington and North Kensington

Two to three miles north and west of London's West End is London's West Side. In London as in New York, in recent decades an abrupt reversal of geographical fortunes has taken place. Since 1945, as the bombed East End has been torn down and rebuilt under comprehensive redevelopment procedures, the West Side has become London's belt of poverty and social problems. Here Harrow Road started life as an Anglo-Saxon field track, snaking its course round the corners of open-field strips, long before the urban tide of London washed over it. In the first half of the nineteenth century, two new lines of communication, the Grand Union Canal and the Great Western Railway, were built parallel and close to the old road. Along this belt of movement, a mean type of ribbon development sprawled out in the eighteen-fifties; cramped terrace houses, hastily built, as speculative ventures for

---

[1] *Final Report of the Expert Committee on Compensation and Betterment*, Cmd. 6386 (H.M.S.O. 1942). Generally known after its Chairman, Augustus Andrewes Uthwatt (later Lord Uthwatt) (1879–1949).

middle-class families who failed to arrive. Rapidly, they became divided into flats and even one-room apartments, though their sanitary facilities were barely adequate even for the original household. Traditionally, North Kensington was a working-class area, which attracted new immigrants: labourers in the Acton brickfields, long since built over, whose wives took in laundry for the big houses to the south. But unlike the East End, as a community it failed to settle down; those who waxed prosperous moved out westwards, to new working-class suburbs in Feltham or Southall or Hayes; their places were taken by new unskilled immigrants, from Dublin and Cork, Trinidad and the Barbados.

Our definition of slum is still an inadequate one, which covers the insanitary, fast-disappearing two-storey rows of Limehouse and Bow Common, but not the decaying stuccoed terraces of West Paddington and North Kensington. They are euphemistically described as 'dwellings in multi-occupation'. This is a description to the House of Lords by Earl Jellicoe, then Joint Parliamentary Secretary to the Ministry of Housing and Local Government, of what the term often means. It was not drawn necessarily from West London, but it would adequately describe too many of the houses in this belt.

'. . . basement areas used as common refuse dumps, roofs used for garbage disposal, entrance halls bearing the marks, if I may use the term, of a common pissoir, with contraceptives strewn in the rickety Dickensian staircases, often with the plaster peeled off and the bare lattice boards exposed; broken window panes, exposed and dangerous electric fittings, and common lavatories and bathrooms of almost indescribable sordidness.'[1]

The first question for areas like these, then, is: can we speed up the rate of renewal, and if so how? It is a large problem, the size of which I try to estimate in Chapter 4. Areas like Paddington and North Kensington can be multiplied all over inner Victorian London. There is hardly one of the twenty-eight Metropolitan Boroughs which cannot offer up examples; and several areas just outside the County of London have very serious areas of urban decay also. Is their elimination merely a matter of political decision: a question of the amount of money that the community, through its elected government, chooses to spend on this piece of welfare in opposition to other sorts of government spending? Or are there legal or financial measures which would speed up the process of renewal?

But secondly: provided we can achieve a satisfactory rate of renewal, how to assure that we rebuild properly? The essential is to plan the individual new homes, whether they are houses or maisonettes or tall blocks of flats, in relation to the lives that the people have to live outside their homes. Every day, some of them will go to work; others to school; others will shop, hang out washing, talk to neighbours. So the housing must be planned in intimate relation to roads and tube stations, schools and playing fields and parks and swimming-baths, shops and libraries and

[1] *Lords Hansard*, 11 July 1961, Col. 93, in a debate on the 1961 Housing Act, which gives local authorities greater powers over such houses.

launderettes and pubs. And the overriding objective must be to cope with the problem of traffic. People need transport as their willing servant, not—as too often in any city—a tyrannical master. They have to be able to join the fast-moving streams of traffic outside if they want to, while noticing its existence as little as possible at all other times. In London, the traffic is too often obtrusive and moving slowly; the two are connected.

Abercrombie understood these things, and his plans for London showed one solution; in rebuilding, people were to be grouped in precincts, with access to the traffic streams around but sealed off from them. This demanded comprehensive rebuilding of large areas—at the very minimum, the areas within the main traffic roads—in such a way that the systems of circulation within the blocks, both for for vehicles and pedestrians, were rationalized and civilized. And the 1947 Act, as already seen, provided the procedures for this sort of redevelopment.

Unfortunately the years since 1947, in London as elsewhere, have seen far too few schemes of comprehensive redevelopment and far too many small-scale housing schemes which, like the piecemeal renewal of the central area, combine to frustrate the purposes of good planning. The questions arise: why have the ideas of Abercrombie and the 1947 Act been so largely put aside? Were they inadequately thought through, or have they been weakly administered? What changes are possible for the future? Are the new techniques we need the same as those we need to rebuild the centres? These are questions I discuss in Chapters 7 and 8.

Congestion of the Arteries: Finchley Road

Whether they need wholesale renewal or no, the inner Victorian districts of London—the ring roughly two to six miles from the centre—suffer from one overwhelming problem, which I have already touched upon in writing about Harrow Road. This is the ever-increasing burden of traffic along the main radial and cross roads, and its effects upon the lives of the people who live alongside them and near them.

Finchley Road is the most dramatic illustration of this problem, because the vocal inhabitants of Hampstead have ensured it publicity. But the same conditions, and eventually the same dilemma, confront us along any one of the score of main arterial approaches into central London: Harrow Road, Holloway Road, Hackney Road, Lee High Road, Brixton Road, Holland Park Avenue, all would serve as illustrations.

These roads had different origins and have in consequence slightly different physiognomies. Finchley Road, built in the early nineteenth century as a turnpike, is straighter than some, and less burdened with ribbon shopping centres. But it has two such, at Swiss Cottage and Golders Green, and the first of these is on the section of the road which forms part of the main traffic route from London to the Birmingham motorway. Since 1957 this shopping centre has been rebuilt by the Hampstead Borough Council, on plans approved by the L.C.C. planners. Commercial considerations of the narrowest sort dictated that the rebuilt shops should continue to front on to the main traffic street. (As a concession to the twentieth century, the shops have back-loading facilities.) Despite waiting prohibitions, the dense traffic generated by the shops reduces through traffic to a day-long crawl. The solution proposed by the L.C.C.—roads as well as planning authority—is to turn the road into a six-lane super-highway, narrowing the pavements so that the traffic will pass a few feet from the shop-windows; the pedestrian will navigate the road by means of a few subways; at junctions traffic flow will still be impeded by traffic lights.

The Finchley Road scheme has been universally condemned. It represents what can too easily happen: the triumph of cheap, short-cut solutions to the growing traffic problem, which in the not very long term prove bad value for money as well as bad planning. The questions it poses are many.

First: traffic grows, and with it delays and frustration multiply, for vehicles and pedestrians alike. Is it possible simply to go on providing for the extra traffic that will be arriving, not merely now, but in twenty or forty years' time? How is society to decide how much it wants to spend on road improvements? Is our present system based on any rational consideration of needs or priorities? If not, how can one be devised? Is it true that, as increasing numbers of people are asserting, we cannot go on providing all the road-space for all the people who want to use it? What might we suggest as an alternative, and how would we seek to persuade people to use the alternative?

In 1943 and 1944, when Abercrombie made his transport proposals for London, these problems were less obtrusive. For this reason, the dilemma illustrated by Finchley Road was less acute. In his County of London Plan, many of the main arterial roads are the existing roads, which are widened and straightened and sealed off for long distances from side roads. Yet for trying to do this, the L.C.C. is now condemned. Abercrombie's solution went further, though: it was to take the local uses—such as shops—away from the main roads. But in practice the L.C.C. cannot afford to do this. It receives a grant from the Ministry of Transport only to widen the road, but not to deal with the problems of planning thus created. To buy out the commercial interests along the road, which are already established there, would mean enormous sums in compensation; so the L.C.C. makes the best of a bad job. In these circumstances, are our concepts of road planning out of date? Would it not be better, cheaper, to society in the long run to build a new road pattern first? To build, for instance, parallel to Finchley Road, a new motorway, so that Finchley Road itself could become a purely local road? The question is vitally related, of course, to the problems of urban renewal represented along Harrow Road. For Abercrombie, the precinct and the arterial road were two halves of the same operation: comprehensive redevelopment. The plan to widen Finchley Road is bad because it is not comprehensive redevelopment. An effective road plan for London, then, demands not mere analysis of traffic demands and how they can be met at lowest social cost (Chapter 5), but leads straight on to the wider question of

29

comprehensive urban renewal (Chapter 7) and the legal and financial changes necessary to make comprehensive redevelopment the rule (Chapter 8).

The Chronic Problem of the Suburbs

The problems of the centre, and of the inner Victorian ring, are acute. They are serious threats to London's well-being and, given drastic surgery, they are capable of cure. With the interwar suburbs the diagnosis is different. Here the story is almost everywhere the same. At some date between 1918 and 1939, the tube or the Southern Electric arrived; within five years, the former fields around the station had been covered with speculative-built detached and semi-detached. So, within these twenty years, the suburbs spread over the vast belt between six and fifteen miles from central London, multiplying the area of London about four times.

Planners and architects, as they sit snug in their Canonbury conversions, are apt to mock the suburbs, or prepare Utopian plans for their removal, or confess whimsical attachment to them. The truth is that none of these attitudes is justified. For all their defects, most suburban houses represented better mass housing than the world had ever known before; the vast majority of them have elementary sanitary facilities, which millions of British homes still deplorably lack; and because they are mostly (as I write) between twenty and forty-five years old, they probably have at least half a century of useful life in them.

The problem of the suburbs is chronic and, in the short term, incurable. It is that they wasted land on such an epic scale. They were mostly built at very low densities, of twelve to the acre or less—in extreme cases they run down to one or two per acre—and ill-conceived bye-laws imposed ugly and wasteful street patterns on them. In addition, their road systems show some of the very worst features of the roads of the inner Victorian ring: ribbon shopping centres along main traffic roads, for instance. Abercrombie's Greater London Plan saw these defects, and provided the only answer: London was to have no more suburbs. The existing suburbs were to be ringed by the Green Belt; and the area outside the Green Belt was to be developed with self-sufficient and self-contained towns. Today we have the Green Belt and the towns, but most of them are far from self-contained, and becoming less so year by year. As a result, more and more long-distance commuters are having to cross the ten-mile cordon of the suburbs as well as five miles or more of the Green Belt, every morning and night, to earn their living. They have good reason to mutter imprecations against the builders who let the suburbs sprawl. But as a society with scarce resources, that is about the limit of our protest. It will not be till A.D. 2000, or later, that we can start usefully considering how to rebuild our suburbs.

London's Offspring

Up to 1939, London was a fairly well-defined organic whole. The map showed a central business area; a densely built-up Victorian ring with houses of all sorts, very poor to very rich; the low-density interwar suburbs, running outwards on average about fifteen miles from the centre, but extending finger-like much farther along the main roads and railways. Since 1945 London has continued to grow, but not of itself; it has reared and nurtured offspring. The map today[1] shows, first, the built-up area of 1939. It terminates abruptly, almost without post-1945 additions, at the edge of the Metropolitan Green Belt. Outside the belt, though within the area of later extensions to it, development control under the 1947 Act has ensured a pattern very unlike the old sprawl. Growth now takes place in communities which are rigidly defined and of limited size: the largest of them, which were big before 1945—like Reading and its suburbs, or Southend and the neighbouring areas—have less than 250,000 people, and these are exceptions. Each is separated from its neighbours by considerable tracts of still undeveloped land.

These communities fall into two types. One is the *New Towns*, established under the *New Towns Act 1946*, following recommendations of a committee under Lord Reith. There are eight New Towns in the belt twenty to thirty-five miles around London, all established in the period 1946-9.

The first point about the New Towns is that they were hardly ever new. There was always a small nucleus, generally a village, but sometimes (as at Hemel Hempstead) a quite considerable market town. The two essential New Town features were first their administration—they were built by Development Corporations modelled on the B.B.C. (Reith's influence)—and second their self-contained quality, which they drew from Abercrombie. People and work must move out from inner London together; the New Towns must not become, as earlier garden cities like Welwyn had become, mere dormitory suburbs for London. This objective has been maintained in the New Towns: though the commuters' belt has moved into the New Town belt, few of them live in the New Towns themselves.

In physiognomy the New Towns differ less from their Garden City prototypes. Today, to a latter generation of architects, they represent 'prairie planning': the roads are too wide, the spaces too open, the cottage-type architecture too often anaemic. But the fact remains that not only were the New Towns superior to almost any previous mass building; they are superior to most equivalent building *since*.

Since 1951, there has been no official plan for any more New Towns in the London region, save for the very original proposal of the L.C.C. for a New Town of their own at Hook in Hampshire, which had to be dropped after local opposition. Nor is there rumour of any plan in preparation. The tremendous growth of population in the 'Outer Ring' of the region has therefore gone perforce into expansions of existing towns. A few of these are planned schemes for the reception of overspill population, the so-called *Expanding Towns* which Abercrombie called for in his 1944 Report and which were finally provided for by the *Town Development Act* in 1952. But most people have gone spontaneously and individually; and the town

[1] The best is Map 5 accompanying the *Report of the Royal Commission on Local Government in Greater London*, Cmnd. 1164 (H.M.S.O. 1960).

expansions which have accommodated them, though planned in the sense that they needed planning approval, mostly represent speculative private housing on the outskirts of existing towns.

Many of these towns have old and distinguished histories. One of them, Guildford, claims a thousand years of urban life. Other examples are High Wycombe, Reading, Luton, Aylesbury, Bishop's Stortford, Chelmsford, and Maidstone. Up till 1939 they were mainly market centres for the agricultural areas surrounding them, with local industries depending on local raw materials (brewing at Guildford and Maidstone, chairs at High Wycombe, hats at Luton) or serving the local population. Their contacts with London were slim; the capital was a place you might visit for a shopping expedition, two or three times a year. But since 1930, and especially since 1945, their character has changed out of recognition.

In the first place, these towns are now numbered among the fastest-expanding industrial centres of Britain. The reason is that there is no land left for expansion in the Conurbation itself; industrial expansion has leap-frogged the Green Belt. Secondly, for the same reason, commuters have come there to look for homes. And thirdly, both sorts of expansion have a multiplier effect; the traditional market and service function of the town grows out of proportion.

The casual visitor will find any of these places much more sympathetic and attractive than the equivalent interwar suburbs. As he stands in the main street of Wycombe or Guildford he will know immediately, as he will not in Wembley or Carshalton, that here is a town, one that remains a place with its own identity, a place its citizens feel they belong to, even if they spend their working days at City or West End office desks. The modern southern Englander is sophisticated enough for double loyalties: he can be a Londoner and a citizen of Guildford too.

But a closer look is disturbing. The local planning officers and committees—most of these towns have some planning powers delegated to them by their County Councils, even when they are not planning authorities themselves—are conscious enough of their civic responsibilities. But in one of the handsomest of these towns, a local councillor is quoted as saying:

'Millions of pounds of building work has been put through in the last few years, but we have not had a proper committee to do the planning. At present there is no time for town planning.'[1]

And even for the doughtiest planning committee, the problems are overwhelming. In the first place the shopping centre is invariably bursting at the seams. The planning authority is bombarded by applications for redevelopment as the multiple stores take over more and more of the shop fronts in the High Street. More and more of the shoppers, and more and more of the working population of the centre, are using private transport; the result is a traffic and parking problem of vast proportions. In addition, some of these town centres are still having to carry through

---

[1] Alderman R. E. Darby at a High Wycombe Council meeting, quoted by L. K. Watson, *Planning Wycombe* (High Wycombe, 1961), p. 1.

traffic. The most notorious case is probably Wycombe, where all the traffic between London, Oxford and South Wales judders along the narrow main shopping street. All these problems create in these towns almost irresistible pressures for demolition and reconstruction. There must be new shop fronts, new storage space, new public buildings, acres of new car parks; an inner relief road must be driven through the medieval lanes behind the High Street. How to achieve this, and still maintain the character that make these places worth living in, is one of the most delicate problems a planner can hope to find. And it is repeated scores of times in the zone twenty to fifty miles round London.

Most of these towns have superb natural settings, hardly excelled elsewhere in England, in gaps through the chalk ridges which nearly encircle London. The original medieval market towns enhanced these settings; they are still models of organic growth, good to see, pleasant to work or relax in. But not only is there the problem of maintaining this character at the centre; there is the responsibility to see that the new is as good as the old. And the newest parts of these towns, the estates that in the years since 1950 have spilled out over the hillsides of the Chilterns and North Downs, are often unworthy of their heritage. In a sense, the 1947 system of control ensures that these outgrowths are planned. There is a County Development Plan, which says where houses can go, and where not; which says how many houses can go on how many acres; which gives the planning authority complete freedom, subject only to right of appeal, to veto proposed plans, whether for the layout of an estate or for the design of an individual house. Yet bad design and poor layouts still multiply. Rape of superb natural landscapes, maladroit use of available space, layouts which cause maximum inconvenience to the inhabitants and are ugly to boot, the multiplication of brick and asphalt deserts; these are the rule rather than the exception, over the face of the Home Counties. Is this a failure of the powers in the 1947 Act? Or a failure of administration at local planning level? In any case, what can we now do about it? Do the planning authorities need new powers? Or do we need a completely new concept of speculative building, perhaps with new agencies? These are questions that need answering quickly, if the face of southern England is not to be irretrievably blighted.

In all these towns, many of the houses—as I write, no up-to-date statistics exist to say how many—are being bought by people who have come to live here, thirty or forty miles from their work in central London, because nowhere nearer can they find a house they like at a price they can afford.[1] As a result, they may spend well over an hour getting to their work in the morning, and as much getting home at night: perhaps one-fifth of their working life spent in transit. Partly this is the effect of the misuse of land in the suburbs between 1918 and 1939; partly it is the effect of Green Belt policy, which placed a cordon round London; but primarily it is due to

[1] Cf. any sample of advertisements from the London evening papers, or the revealing series in *The Observer* (Autumn 1962) called 'Commuter Country', which featured areas like Hayward's Heath in Sussex (38 miles from London) and Fleet in Hampshire (36 miles from London).

the fundamental problem, which we also saw operating right at the centre: the continued growth of London. South-east England has been since 1945, as before 1939, the boom region of Britain, despite all the planners did to limit its growth. Boom attracts people, and makes many of them rich enough to demand homes of their own; the process will go on, unless something drastic is done to stop it; and towns like Wycombe and Luton and Maidstone will not be the end of the commuter's road.

These towns, then, pose some of the most important questions of planning in the London of today. Can anything be done to stop their continued growth? Which means first, can anything be done to stop the growth of the region, and would it be desirable? If not, could the increase of population be accommodated elsewhere? Should there be more New Towns? Or can we house the extra people by putting more of them on to every acre of the older parts of London—the built-up area of 1939? Are we content to see people commuting over longer and longer distances, in direct contradiction to the Abercrombie policy of moving homes and work together? Is commuting an unmitigated evil? If so, how can we bring work to the workers? Given that this policy has worked in New Towns, can it only work there? Or can it be repeated in the expanding market towns? These are questions which I try to answer throughout this book—in Chapter 3 on jobs, in Chapter 4 on population growth and housing, in Chapter 6 on new and expanding towns, and in Chapter 8 on methods of development.

The Central Problem

In this rapid tour across the London region, some problems recurred; others turned up in new disguises. The fact is that all the major problems of the London region—the growth at the centre, the decay in the inner ring, the congestion of the major traffic arteries, the unseemly growth of the Outer Ring—are closely related; for they all revolve around one central problem. *Shall London Grow?* Upon our answer to this question will depend the way we phrase the other questions, and the answers we give to them. Barlow in 1940, Abercrombie in 1944, the apparatus of control set up under the 1947 Act: all worked on the fundamental assumption that London would not grow. But it has; and we need to look again at the growth, and ask two questions.

First: why do we want to stop London growing? The answer to this is set out in the very careful analysis of the Barlow Report in 1940. We need to re-examine Barlow's arguments, and those of other critics. This I do in Chapter 2.

Secondly, and independently: is it in any case possible to stop London growing? As Barlow recognized, this means: is it possible to stop (or greatly limit) the growth of employment in London? This is what we have been trying to do, on Barlow's advice, since 1945; and we have not succeeded. This suggests that Barlow's analysis of economic history, which forms the first part of the report, may have been wrong. In Chapter 3, where I deal with employment, I re-examine the Barlow thesis.

LONDON'S PROBLEMS
Postscript, 1969

The promised reform of London government, as everyone knows, did take place. With it went a minor change in the definition of the Greater London conurbation, which now corresponds to the area of the Greater London Council—a useful convention. The 1966 Census showed that the population of the London region was little more than the 1961 total, though the sample enumeration may have missed some people:

	Area, square miles	Population 1966
LONDON REGION (Metropolitan Area)	4,412	12,577,290
Outer Ring (Outer Metropolitan Area)	3,792	4,906,070
Suburban Ring ⎫	503	4,671,230
Inner Ring ⎬ GLC	107	2,758,670
Central Area ⎭	10	241,320

The tour across London from centre to edge, written in 1962, was supposed to present a picture of chaos. It would be good to report that the same tour in 1968 would show less chaos. In fact, if anything it would show the same chaos, slightly intensified. Two melancholy comments on details only: the new tube at Oxford Circus, due to have been open in 1968, was delayed until 1969; some of the main road traffic was still juddering through High Wycombe, because the by-pass has been delayed, in the early months of 1969. In March 1969, relief came at last on both counts.

CHAPTER 2

Anti- and Pro-London

In this chapter I wish to argue that London, and its continued growth, are in themselves not necessarily a bad thing. The lay Londoner may think this thesis so obvious as to need no proof. But among professional planners it is not so. The whole basis of post-1945 British planning has had a strong anti-metropolitan bias, both explicit and implicit. The main reason for this is a report, which appeared at the very end of the interwar era, and which attacked with great power the whole concept of the giant metropolis; which first became the basis of official postwar planning policy, and which then passed almost into the folk-consciousness of a whole generation of planners, so that its precepts have become accepted virtually as tablets of planning law. This is the Report of the Royal Commission on the Distribution of the Industrial Population, generally known after the Commission's chairman, Sir Anderson Montague-Barlow, which appeared in January 1940.[1]

Modern British town and country planning, it can fairly be said, was conceived out of Barlow. It remains, as I write, the official guide to the regional planning of jobs, and through them population. However unsuccessful Governments may have been in putting the Barlow precepts into practice, they have joined in paying their formal respects to them. It is more than time to re-examine the orthodoxy of planning embodied here: to ask, nearly a quarter of a century after the appearance of the Report: how far were its conclusions justified then? How far have they ceased to be relevant?

Barlow versus London: The Social Case

This was Barlow's conclusion on London:

'It is not possible from the evidence submitted to us to avoid the conclusion

[1] *Report of the Royal Commission on the Distribution of the Industrial Population*, Cmd. 6153 (H.M.S.O. 1940).

that the disadvantages in many, if not in most of the great industrial concentrations, alike on the strategical, the social, and the economic side, do constitute serious handicaps and even in some respects dangers to the nation's life and development, and we are of opinion that definite action should be taken by the Government towards remedying them. . . . The continued drift of the industrial population to London and the Home Counties constitutes a social, economic and strategical problem which demands immediate attention.'[1]

What were these disadvantages, 'social, economic and strategical'? One of the most important, which occupied the Commission a great deal in their sittings, was *public health*. From the Ministry of Health the Commission got a great deal of evidence to show that health was poorer in the big conurbations. But even then, in 1938, London was, on average, healthier than the rest of the country, if the statistics are any guide; since then, the revolutionary improvement in public health—a product of higher living standards and better welfare services—has given Barlow's conclusions a strangely archaic air. These, for instance, are the infantile mortality figures per thousand live births (which are generally regarded as an effective general index of public health) for Stepney: 1921–30, 76; 1931–8, 72; 1951–60, 23. Similar trends are observable throughout inner London, especially in the poorer areas, in this as in all other general medical indices of health; and the figures for these poorer areas are commonly better than the national average. (The infantile mortality rate for England and Wales in 1951–60 was 25.) Nor is it true, as sometimes asserted, that as physical health has improved, mental breakdown has followed. Statistics, such as they are (and they are few), show that the easiest place to go out of one's mind is in a small or medium-sized town. The rate of first admission to mental hospitals for all causes per thousand population is much higher in towns of under 100,000 population than in Greater London or than in conurbations in general.[2]

When the Barlow Commissioners sat, London suffered from the worst problem of *overcrowding* in the country. The standard measure is the proportion of the population living at 2 persons and over per room. At the 1931 Census, this was 6·9 per cent for England and Wales; 13·1 per cent for the County of London; 23·6 per cent for Stepney and Bethnal Green; and 29·1 per cent for Shoreditch. Yet only eleven years after the Commission reported, bombing and postwar redevelopment had made the problem almost statistically negligible: the 1951 Census gave the proportions 2·2 per cent for the country, 2·5 per cent for the County of London, 2·8 per cent for Bethnal Green, 3·5 per cent for Shoreditch, 3·4 per cent for Stepney; Paddington (by then the worst) had 5·2 per cent.[3]

[1] *Ibid.*, paras. 413, 428.
[2] Registrar-General's Statistical Review of England and Wales, *Supplement on Mental Health*, 1954–6 (H.M.S.O. 1960).
[3] For the 1961 Census the standard was revised: it was the proportion of persons living at more than 1·5 persons per room. The figure was 11·5 per cent for the L.C.C. area, 12·4 for Bethnal Green, 13·6 for Shoreditch, 16·2 for Stepney, and 20·9 per cent for Paddington—still the most

Barlow pointed out one social disadvantage of life in London that is still too potently with us: *air pollution*. London is still 'The Smoke'. In the year 1959, *one and a half hundredweights* of impurities were deposited out of the air *per acre* in parts of central London.[1] Yet even here, the Clean Air Act of 1956 has been prosecuted with incomparably greater energy by the Metropolitan Boroughs than by their provincial counterparts. By end-1963 nearly 40,000 acres, or 55 per cent of the County of London, should be in smoke control areas.[2] Most metropolitan boroughs' programmes provide for clean air by the late sixties; Walsall and West Bromwich will wait until 1980. By 1970, for London, this Barlow conclusion should have passed into history too.

The Economic Case

These were social factors. But the Barlow Commissioners based their case against London also on economic factors with social implications: the problem of social capital, the problem of land values, the problem of the journey to work and the problem of traffic congestion.

The concept of *social capital* really grew out of the special circumstances of the nineteen-thirties, but it has gone on being used in an era when it has lost most of its validity.[3] It says that in the stagnant or decaying industrial towns of the north, a great amount of capital has been invested by society, which is ancillary to the productive process: streets, houses, public buildings, shops, schools, cinemas and football grounds. It represents economic waste to let this lie under-used, while the same capital is being reproduced in south-east England for the population that migrates there. This was perhaps true even as late as 1939, in a society which could not afford to consider the *quality* of social capital. But today, it is a matter of common observation that many of the towns of the Industrial Revolution—the Lancashire cotton towns, ports like Liverpool—were developed rapidly within a relatively short period of time between 1820 and 1870, so that part—possibly a large part—of their social capital needs almost simultaneous renewal. Liverpool, an extreme case, had 80,000 houses—almost two-fifths of the city's dwellings—*technically* classed as slums in 1961; a figure that almost certainly falls short of the real amount of obsolescence. It is notable that enthusiastic supporters of the social capital argument are also eager advocates of massive renewal programmes for the same places. However much the argument is sophisticated, it is difficult to believe that it justifies the indefinite freezing of the economic geography of Britain in the form it happened to have assumed when Barlow reported. That way lies economic stagnation. Even Professor

overcrowded borough in London. In parts of Paddington and Kensington there is evidence of worse overcrowding in 1961 than in 1951; elsewhere there has been steady improvement. *Census 1961*, County Report: *London*, Table 3.

[1] Based on figures in City of Westminster, *Report of the Medical Officer of Health for 1959*.

[2] Ministry of Housing and Local Government, *Smoke Control (England and Wales), 1962–1966* (Cmnd. 1890, H.M.S.O. 1962).

[3] Most recently by Douglas Jay, *Socialism in the New Society* (1962), 171.

Sykes, a leading advocate of the social capital argument, concedes finally that 'where localised unemployment is structural in origin, and employment elsewhere is high, the case for migration is strong.'[1]

The other economic problems have remained since 1939, and if anything have magnified. *Land and property values* rose faster, in the nineteen-fifties, than the general level of prices or incomes. While the general rise in house prices in 1960 was 10 per cent, in London it was 16 per cent and in parts of Essex one-third.[2] The average length of *journey to work* has almost certainly increased markedly since the last complete survey was made for the 1951 Census, as is evidenced by the increase of 104,000 in arrivals at main line stations in central London between 1953 and 1961. Traffic congestion, as measured by the falling average speed of traffic on central London streets, rose steadily throughout the fifties.[3]

But the important thing about these problems is that they are not necessary features of the big metropolis; they are merely contingent features of the contemporary London scene, arising from our inability to plan for a satisfactory arrangement of functions *within* the Region. To confuse the two, and argue from that against the Metropolis *per se*, is very elementary, but quite misleading. Thus in the Outer Ring of the London Region, where the biggest growth of employment took place in the fifties, there is little evidence that journey to work is a serious problem, though it may yet become one; traffic congestion is largely limited to the centres of the older towns, and is curable by better traffic planning; and the big rises in house and land values have resulted from a quite artificial land shortage, due to planning restrictions which were based on faulty predictions of future population. Within the London Region, the central problems remain those of the growth at the centre, and it is these that the planner should be trying to cure.

For the Barlow Commissioners, London was also a *strategic* liability. This conclusion was based on evidence heard in camera; in the war-scared atmosphere of summer 1939, when the report was being written, it may have proved decisive. Today, like many of the social arguments, it has a strangely archaic ring. Whether to be in Greater London while it was blown up by a 100-megaton bomb,[4] or in Birmingham, Manchester or Cardiff while they were obliterated by more minor weapons, seems an aridly academic question.

National Balance and Provincial Culture

Finally, though, Barlow went much wider, and vaguer. They accepted implicitly the London County Council's testimony that Greater London 'is already larger than is desirable either on proper planning principles or in the interests of the popula-

[1] J. Sykes, 'Remedies for Localised Unemployment', *The Manchester School*, 19 (1951), 86.
[2] *The Observer*, 14 May 1961. [3] See later, Chapter 5.
[4] A 100-megaton bomb would destroy *by blast* virtually all the buildings in the Greater London Conurbation. (John Maddox in *The Guardian*, 19 September 1961.)

tion of the county of London':[1] a view based upon the fundamentalist dogma that the right-sized London was that within the L.C.C. boundaries. Twenty years later, the Herbert Commission on London Local Government proved more politically sophisticated on this point than the Barlow Commissioners.

But in accepting this argument the Barlow Commission seem to have rested on a principle that underlay much of their thinking about London: the concept of *National Balance*.

'The concentration in one area of such a large proportion of the national population as is contained in Greater London, and the attraction to the Metropolis of the best industrial, financial, commercial and general ability represent a serious drain on the rest of the country.'[2] Now it is true that there is a long-term, continuous drift of the more able people out of smaller provincial towns, in search of the higher forms of professional or technical training; that most of these people never return;[3] and that in consequence these small towns are often very moribund places. But do the people left in such towns ever *feel* impoverished? Do their able sons and daughters not find that they get more out of life, put more into it, contribute infinitely more to general economic and social progress, in the centres to which they migrate? The answer must be subjective; I would suggest that the strong presumption is that the process is to society's net advantage, and that it is up to those who would stop it to prove otherwise.

Through arguments like the Commission's it is possible to divine a curious strand of English thought, that runs in a devious line from William Morris: a strand that elevates, to an almost mystical status, provincial folk-culture, as it was supposedly practised fifty or a hundred years ago in the back streets of Leeds or in the South Wales valleys.[4] But if it did exist—and there is plenty of evidence, from a novel like *Middlemarch*, that too often it failed abysmally to develop at all—it flourished because it had an economic and social base. Coal attracted entrepreneurship; entrepreneurship meant ability, perhaps creativity to spare; thus a provincial middle-class culture. Society was intensely parochial, education was limited, geographical and social mobility were low, bright talents shone in obscure places; thus a working-class folk-culture. These things are no more; should we regret the fact? Surely not; and still less should we try only to interfere with economic trends on shadowy social grounds, until we know far more about these trends than we do now. To this point I return in the next chapter.

Pro-London

The fact remains that people prefer London. Into the London Region, between 1951 and 1961, there was a net migration of about a quarter of a million people,

[1] Barlow Report, *op. cit.*, para. 171.   [2] *Ibid.*
[3] On this point see A. H. Birch, *Small-Town Politics* (Oxford 1959), Ch. 3.
[4] For an effective attack on the whole notion of folk-culture, see R. Wollheim, *Socialism and Culture* (Fabian Tract, No. 331, 1961), 10–15.

of whom a large part came from the older industrial districts of Lancashire, South Wales or the North-east. Were they so ill-informed, or irrational? Was their choice distorted? The outer parts of the London Region get 23–25 inches of rain a year, about 1,500 hours of bright sunshine; Burnley gets 47 inches and 1,056 hours. In towns like Burnley or Rochdale there is no serious theatre; a visiting orchestra may appear a few times a year for a popular concert; a continental cinema may show last year's Cannes prizewinner with the aid of a salacious poster. In a typical month, there were in London 186 musical performances (concerts, recitals and operas) and in the whole of the provinces, including Scotland and Wales, 196. Of film programmes 'of special interest to film enthusiasts' the London region had 144, the whole of the rest of the United Kingdom 86; the south-east Lancashire conurbation (population, two and a half million) had three.[1] This state of affairs might be met by subsidizing the arts in the provinces very heavily. But only partially; for it is the very concentration of the market in London that allows the proliferation of performances for specialized tastes.

The anti-metropolitans' answer to this is automatic devaluation: metropolitan culture is a purely acquisitive culture, 'the princely ritual of conspicuous expenditure' in the words of Lewis Mumford, high priest of the movement. For Mumford, the metropolitan 'stage, the motion picture screen, the radio, no less than the newspaper and the printed book . . . create an image of a valuable life than can be satisfied only by a ruthless concentration of human interest upon pecuniary standards and pecuniary results: the clothes of the metropolis, the jewels of the metropolis, the dull expensive life of Park Avenue and the Kurfürstendamm, Piccadilly and the Champs Elysées, become the goals of vulgar ambition.'[2] This view, it seems to me, is based on a profound misunderstanding of modern economic and social history. As men get richer, their wants grow larger and more various, and the economic machine becomes capable of more easily satisfying them. As members of rich societies, we can legitimately criticize some of the ways our extra wealth is spent: we may think more ought to be given to help poorer societies than ours, or reinvested, or spent on welfare; but to argue—as Mumford essentially does—that it is immoral to spend more on personal gratification, is surely reactionary, presumptuous, arrogant and quite irrelevant to planning.

Yet even Mumford, at the end of his demoniac indictment of the metropolis, comes to recognize its essential central place:

'In laying down the foundations of a new regional order, based on the culture of life, the metropolis nevertheless has a proud part to play. At present the world cities, through the very fact of monopoly, contain many of the best elements in man's heritage.'[3]

And he goes on to argue for a re-ordering of metropolitan functions; for a diffusion of metropolitan advantages over a wider area. This also is a central argument of the

[1] Based on programmes listed in *Music and Musicians* and *Films and Filming*.
[2] *The Culture of Cities*, edition of 1940, 230. [3] *Ibid.*, 297.

present book. I have tried to argue in this chapter that to plan London effectively, it is necessary to accept it, and if necessary to accept its continued growth; but to plan to resort and regroup its functions within the wide metropolitan region, so as to make it a more efficient and a happier place to work in. This will demand no apocalyptic word-picture of the coming disintegration of Megalopolis; but a cool, pragmatic approach. We need to estimate likely increases in jobs, and population, over the coming forty years; to consider where these jobs should be provided, in closer relation to homes and transport than they have been in the past; to ask what demands this will make on the building industry and where; and to see what legal, administrative and financial changes will be needed to make the plans effective. This I try to do in the chapters that follow.

Postscript, 1969

This chapter largely deals with past facts of history and past arguments; and it would look little different if it were written anew today. The pro-Londoners and the anti-Londoners have moved perhaps a little closer together, in their common recognition of two facts. First, that large parts of Britain are less prosperous than the South East, and face problems of massive re-adaptation of their economics with the threatened run-down of the coal industry in the 1970s; they therefore demand some degree of help. Secondly, that the continued growth of London cannot and will not be stemmed; first because it so largely arises from natural increase of the region's own population, secondly because it is based on the continual growth of jobs that are intimately related to the national and international functions of the metropolitan region. London's Airport is a good example; it has grown from negligible beginnings in 1946 to employ 42,000 people directly today; taking into account indirectly-generated employment and the dependents of the employees, it probably supports a quarter of a million people in the western part of Greater London and the adjacent parts of the Outer Metropolitan Area.

Perhaps one new fact has emerged. Two detailed surveys, one of London office workers,[1] the other of migration,[2] have thrown up the same results: that a substantial proportion of London workers would consider moving elsewhere if they could get suitable employment, but that the traditional Development Area is almost the last place they would consider. On the other hand, there is remarkable enthusiasm for the South West of England—much of which also happens to be a Development Area. If the Government really wanted to create an effective counter-magnet in a Development Area, it could do worse than think of a new city in the Cornish Riviera.

[1] *Commuters to the London Office: A Survey.* (Location of Offices Bureau, London 1966), pp. 2–3.
[2] Government Social Survey, *Labour Mobility in Great Britain* (S.S. 333, H.M.S.O. 1966), Table 31, p. 28.

Part II · GUIDING GROWTH

CHAPTER 3

Jobs 2000

In this chapter I wish to argue two basic propositions. The first, which I hope to prove, is that planners are not free to manipulate the geography of employment as they please; but that this follows economic laws which, though difficult to analyse in detail, cannot be broken with impunity; that in planning for the future, we need to start with a new respect for economic forces, with a belief that we may bend them but we cannot break them, and a determination to find out, by research and by gentle trial and error, just how far they can be bent.

Secondly I want to argue from this that, because of the very strength of these forces, we can predict in broad terms what is likely to be the pattern of the economy forty years on. This, it may be argued, is strictly an occupation for the foolhardy. I disagree profoundly. On the contrary, I believe that to fail to make the prediction is a form of obtuseness, which has already cost us dear. Is it really possible to argue that we could not, in 1921, have assembled a team of economists, economic geographers and industrialists who could have made a broad prediction for the 1960s which would have stood the test of time? The economic and social trends of our age were all present then. Our 'growth industries' were disproportionately located in London. London was growing faster than the rest of the country in employment. Within London the search for space, both for industry and homes, had long been manifest. Railways were being electrified, the tubes were being extended out into the open fields; suburbia was already spreading, as with steadily rising living standards in southern England, it was bound to. Why then was Britain surprised when, in 1940, the Barlow Report told it what was happening? Why, today, do we seem surprised that our post-Barlow planning machine has not done quite what we asked of it? It is time for a new prediction of the built-in inevitabilities in the economic mechanism, and of the possibilities open to us of regulating it.

There is a rather better objection to prediction. It is that our tools are very rapidly getting better. With the methods of regional analysis being developed in this country and in the United States, we may well be able, by 1970, to make increasingly accurate and detailed models of the course of development of the London regional economy.[1] Prediction of this sort should be a first task of the National Economic Development Council. But meanwhile, for broad planning purposes I hope to show that it will be useful to make a more generalized, cruder prediction by simple extrapolation of the trends of the last forty years.

To these trends I now turn. I wish to analyse first the trends of the interwar period, 1918–39, which the Barlow Commission studied and on which the machinery of postwar employment planning was based; secondly, the trends of the postwar era.

The Interwar Years

At the end of their analysis of the growth of employment in the interwar years,[2] the Barlow Commission concluded:

'in the absence of some restrictive legislation by the Government, we find no reason for supposing that the trend to the South-East will be permanently checked.'[3] Paradoxically, in this they were right, though they had been extremely ill-served with the facts of the situation. The 1931 Census was seven years old; the Ministry of Labour statistics were then incomplete in coverage. Probably because of this limitation, the Commission's analysis does not always clearly distinguish between *all* industry (including services) and *manufacturing* industry alone. And it makes no distinction at all within the London region; it is impossible to tell, for instance, what part of any change took place within the Greater London Conurbation.

It was in fact over a decade after publication of the report that the 1951 Census industry tables at last made possible a complete analysis of the changes that had taken place during the thirty-year period since 1921. The first important point which they bring out is that total employment in England and Wales had increased by 19 per cent between 1921 and 1951 (Barlow estimated 22·3 per cent for the period 1923–37 alone) and in London and the Home Counties by 30 per cent (Barlow 43 per cent for 1923–37). The Commission therefore over-estimated the long-term increase and the London differential. But their most striking finding is substantially confirmed: that while London and the Home Counties had only 25 per cent of national employment in 1921, they had 40 per cent of the increase between 1921 and 1951 (Barlow for 1923–37, 43 per cent).

The second important conclusion concerns the nature of the industrial growth of London and the Home Counties. Here the 1951 figures show that the analysis which J. H. Jones made for the Commission[4] was substantially right: London and Home

---

[1] See (e.g.) W. Isard and others, *Methods of Regional Analysis: An Introduction to Regional Science* (1960).

[2] *Barlow Report* (Report of the Royal Commission on the Distribution of the Industrial Population), Cmd. 6153 (H.M.S.O. 1940).

[3] *Ibid.*, para. 104.   [4] Barlow Report, *op. cit.*, Appendix 2.

Counties grew so fast, *not* because their 'growth industries'[1] were growing faster than elsewhere, but because these industries were so heavily weighted in the region in 1921 that the same (or even a lower) percentage growth meant a large absolute increase, and hence a large relative increase in *total* employment. Between the wars, six industries were of overwhelming importance in the growth of employment, both in England and Wales and in London and Home Counties: two were manufactures (engineering, vehicles), and four services (building, distribution, administration, professional services). In 1921 only one of these was less important, relatively, in London than in the country; and together the six industries made up 41 per cent of total employment in London and Home Counties, compared with 35 per cent in England and Wales as a whole. Between 1921 and 1951 they accounted for only 77 per cent of total net growth in London and Home Counties compared with 103 per cent[2] in the whole country; this was a result of the fact that in the whole country the expansion of the growth industries was offset by a great contraction in contracting industries, like agriculture, mining and textiles, which were much less important in London and Home Counties in 1921. *Service* trades as a whole increased about as fast in London as in the whole country between 1921 and 1951; *manufacturing* faster.

The last important point about the interwar growth is that relatively little of it took place outside the Greater London Conurbation: only 12 per cent. Manufacturing industry as a whole grew as fast in the outer ring as in the Conurbation. But of the important growth manufactures engineering grew much more slowly; vehicles grew at about the same pace. Three of the four services grew more slowly in the outer ring; the sole exception was administration. The figures available to the Barlow Commission had made no distinction within the London Region.

For this smaller Conurbation area, an instructive comparison can be made over a longer period. Between 1921 and 1951, employment grew there at an average annual rate of 0·9 per cent, compared with 0·5 per cent for England and Wales; corresponding figures for 1861–1921 were 1·3 per cent for Greater London, 1·0 per cent for England and Wales. The Conurbation accounted for 36 per cent of net increase of employment in England and Wales during 1921–51, compared with 23 per cent in 1861–1921. So the interwar growth of Greater London's labour force was no new phenomenon; indeed it was slower than in the Victorian period; but it took a larger share of national total, mainly because—as already shown—that national increase was limited by the inclusion of depressed industries and areas.[3]

The Barlow Commissioners, then, were right in thinking that employment in London and the Home Counties had been growing much faster than elsewhere. They were right in stressing the importance of certain 'growth industries' in this rapid development. But they failed to put sufficient stress on the growth of service

[1] i.e., industries which in the national economy were growing faster than average.

[2] More than 100 per cent, because there was a net *decline* in all other employment.

[3] For a fuller analysis of the figures see my *The Industries of London since 1861* (1962), 21–2. For technical reasons, figures in this section refer only to employment classified to industries.

industries, because the statistics before them under-estimated employment in these industries. And they failed to emphasize that the development of the region was largely concentrated in the restricted area of the Greater London Conurbation, within fifteen miles of Charing Cross; where it was merely a continuation of a trend that had been taking place in Victorian times.

Barlow Policy in Action

Employment in London, said Barlow, would continue to grow unless the Government restricted it. But the Government should restrict it, because of the supposed disadvantages—social, economic and strategic—which this growth brought in train: disadvantages which, I have argued in Chapter 2, were illusory then or irrelevant today.

Beyond that point, the Commission divided over the apparatus of control; in the event, the postwar machinery for the control of industrial location was modelled on the radical recommendations of the Barlow Commission minority. The Town and Country Planning Act, 1947,[1] gave the Board of Trade power to regulate the establishment of new industrial undertakings or the extension of existing ones, through the issue or refusal of Industrial Development Certificates. This power was limited. It extended to factories only; it excluded new factories of less than 5,000 square feet or extensions of less than 10 per cent of existing space. This power the Board of Trade have used to direct new industrial development away from London and the South-east towards areas like Tyneside and South Wales. The local planning machinery established under the Town and Country Planning Act, 1947, was empowered to control the location of all employment through the licensing of new premises or extensions: there were in principle no limitations as to size or type of activity, though in practice there were.[2] In the administration of local planning policy the guiding principle has remained that laid down by Abercrombie in his advisory plan for Greater London in 1944:[3] the wholesale planned decentralization of over a million people and over a quarter of a million jobs out of the congested inner areas of the Conurbation, not into the Suburban Ring (which was to remain static), but into the Outer Ring beyond the Green Belt, and even beyond the boundaries of the Region altogether.

In these plans there was one extraordinary lacuna: no machinery was postulated for controlling office employment. The County of London Plan ignored it, the Greater London Plan dealt in pious hopes: decentralization of business firms was 'very desirable', and firms which had moved out during the war should be encouraged to

---

[1] Section 14 (4).

[2] E. J. L. Griffith, 'Moving Industry from London', *Town Planning Review*, 26 (1955–6), 60.

[3] *Greater London Plan* 1944 (H.M.S.O. 1945), 5, 50. The 'Greater London' of this plan was not the Conurbation, but a larger area, intermediate in size between the Conurbation and the 'London Region' of this book. Cf. Map 1.

stay out. Possibly this failure stemmed from the fundamental confusion which runs through the Barlow Report, between *all* industry (including services) and *factory* industry alone. In the event, the 1947 Town and Country Planning Act gave the planning authorities the power to control the growth of office jobs through the granting or refusal of permission to develop. But evidently, the concentration of these jobs in the centre of London is far more than the County of London's problem. It is at very least a regional problem, and—because no effective regional government exists—by default a national one. Yet the Board of Trade have resolutely refused to recognize any national responsibility here. As late as 1958 they told the Herbert Commission on Local Government in Greater London:

'The planning authorities are in possession of powers to control office building and there is no obvious basis on which the Board's present powers could be extended to cover office premises, even if it were thought desirable to do so.'[1]

So the distribution of office jobs has never been considered officially even throughout the Greater London Conurbation, let alone the wider London Region.

Despite this loophole in the machinery, the basic premises of Barlow–Abercrombie policy are quite explicit. One is set out in the Barlow recommendation on the power of its proposed National Board:

'As the drift of the industrial population to London and the Home Counties (Beds., Bucks., Essex, Herts., Kent, Middx., and Surrey) constitutes a social, economic and strategical problem which demands immediate action, the Board to be vested from the outset with powers to regulate the establishment within that area of additional industrial undertakings. The Board to have power to refuse consent to the establishment of such additional undertakings except in cases where the intending undertaker establishes to the Board's satisfaction that the proposed undertaking could not be conducted on an economic basis elsewhere than in the area in question.'[2]

The other is set out in the Assumptions of the Greater London Plan:

'Inseparable from consideration of London's industrial future is the question of decentralization of persons and industry from the congested centre. . . . The numbers in the centre will decrease, those in the outer areas will grow, though no longer at a spectacular rate, nor in a sporadic way.'[3]

The Geography of Postwar Growth

How far have these aims been realized? Ministry of Labour employment figures for the period 1952–8[4] give the simple arithmetic of growth in the nineteen-fifties; they are set out in Tables 1a and 1b. During these six years, employment in England and

[1] *Royal Commission on Local Government in Greater London, Memoranda of Evidence from Government Departments* (H.M.S.O. 1959), 159.

[2] Barlow Report, *op. cit.*, para. 432. [3] *Greater London Plan* 1944, *op. cit.*, 5.

[4] 1952–8 presents the best time-span for comparison for technical reasons. There are imperfections in the Ministry of Labour figures for small areas, which make it difficult to state the changes in (e.g.) the Central Area, with any precision.

EMPLOYMENT STRUCTURE AND CHANGES, 1952–8

Source: Ministry of Labour.

Industry	Employment, 1952			
	England and Wales		London Region	
	total	per cent of total	total	per cent of total
Primary Industry	**1,424,130**	**7·6**	**95,515**	**1·7**
Engineering, Electrical	1,737,200	9·3	545,077	9·8
General Engineering*	936,600	5·0	269,350	4·8
Electrical Engineering	589,230	3·2	255,128	4·6
Vehicles	1,005,890	5·4	264,823	4·8
All other Manufacturing	5,045,330	27·0	1,324,826	23·8
All Manufacturing	**7,788,420**	**41·7**	**2,134,726**	**38·4**
Distributive Trades	1,927,000	10·3	650,748	11·7
Professional Services	1,344,100	7·2	473,823	8·5
All other Services	6,202,670	33·2	2,208,031	39·7
All Services	**9,473,770**	**50·7**	**3,332,602**	**59·9**
Miscellaneous	**11,170**	**0·1**	**2,594**	**0·0**
All Employment	**18,697,490**	**100·0**	**5,565,437**	**100·0**

Industry	Changes in Employment, 1952–8 (plus unless indicated)			
	England and Wales		London Region	
	total change	per cent of total net change	total change	per cent of total net change
Primary Industry	**–112,230**	**–11·4**	**–14,812**	**–4·7**
Engineering, Electrical	205,520	21·0	82,119	26·2
General Engineering*	88,270	9·0	38,676	12·3
Electrical Engineering	113,030	11·5	44,857	14·2
Vehicles	139,860	14·3	46,375	14·7
All other Manufacturing	185,690	19·0	69,697	22·1
All Manufacturing	**531,070**	**54·3**	**198,191**	**62·9**
Distributive Trades	307,770	31·5	104,848	33·3
Professional Services	257,050	26·3	99,233	31·5
All other Services	–3,480	–0·3	–71,598	–22·7
All Services	**561,340**	**57·4**	**132,483**	**42·0**
Miscellaneous	**–1,670**	**–0·2**	**–708**	**–0·2**
All Employment	**978,510**	**100·0**	**315,154**	**100·0**

Industry	Employment, 1958			
	England and Wales		London Region	
	total	per cent of total	total	per cent of total
Primary Industry	**1,311,900**	**6·7**	**80,703**	**1·4**
Engineering, Electrical	1,942,720	9·9	627,196	10·7
General Engineering*	1,024,870	5·2	308,026	5·2
Electrical Engineering	702,260	3·6	299,985	5·1
Vehicles	1,145,750	5·8	311,198	5·3
All other Manufacturing	5,231,020	26·6	1,394,523	23·7
All Manufacturing	**8,319,490**	**42·3**	**2,332,917**	**39·7**
Distributive Trades	2,234,770	11·4	755,596	12·8
Professional Services	1,601,150	8·1	573,056	9·7
All other Services	6,199,190	31·5	2,136,433	36·3
All Services	**10,035,110**	**51·0**	**3,465,085**	**58·9**
Miscellaneous	**9,500**	**0·0**	**1,886**	**0·0**
All Employment	**19,676,000**	**100·0**	**5,880,591**	**100·0**

TABLE 1B

PERCENTAGE EMPLOYMENT CHANGES, 1952–8

Source: Ministry of Labour.

	1958 as per cent of 1952		London Region as per cent of England and Wales		
	England and Wales	London Region	1952	1952–8	1958
Primary Industry	**92**	**85**	**7**	**13**	**6**
Engineering, Electrical	112	115	31	40	32
General Engineering*	109	114	27	41	30
Electrical Engineering	119	118	43	40	43
Vehicles	114	118	26	33	27
All other Manufacturing	104	105	26	38	27
All Manufacturing	**107**	**109**	**27**	**37**	**28**
Distributive Trades	116	116	34	34	34
Professional Services	119	121	35	39	36
All other Services	100	97	36	—	34
All Services	**106**	**104**	**35**	**24**	**35**
All Employment	**105**	**106**	**30**	**32**	**30**

* Excluding Shipbuilding and Marine Engineering, for which figures are not separately shown.

51

Wales grew by 978,500. But of this increase, London Region had 315,000: 53,000 a year, or half-a-million a decade. This increase, however, has to be seen in the wider context of the great growth of employment in South-east England, south and east of the Solent–Wash line. Between 1952 and 1958, employment in this zone rose by 494,000, of which 178,000 was outside the London Region altogether.

Thus between 1952 and 1958 the South-east portion of England attracted no less than half the net national employment growth. Between 1921 and 1951, the same south-eastern quadrant had attracted 74 per cent. But what was really happening was that while the South-east was growing at about the same rate as between the wars, the rest of the country—virtually stagnant between the wars—was now growing at very nearly the national rate. If between 1921 and 1951 employment in the rest of the country had increased as fast as it did there in 1952–8, while the South-east had grown at the same rate, the share of the South-east would have fallen from 74 to 49 per cent; almost exactly the same share as in the fifties. There is a strong suspicion, then, that the attraction of South-east England was virtually the same as it was between the wars; it is merely that the depressed areas were no longer as depressed.

Within the South-east, London Region attracted 32 per cent of the net national increase between 1952 and 1958, compared with 40 per cent for the slightly bigger London and Home Counties region between 1921 and 1951. If we repeat the assumption about rates of growth made in the last paragraph, then the share of the London Region would be slightly bigger in 1952–8 than in 1921–51.

Both in the country as a whole and in London Region, the industrial growth of 1952–8 was dominated to a quite exceptional extent by only four major industry groups: two manufactures (engineering including electrical, vehicles) and two services (distributive and professional services). But in the nineteen-fifties, as compared with the twenties and thirties, there was an interesting geographical reversal of fortunes. Between 1921 and 1951, employment in much of England and Wales, outside the London Region, had stagnated because any increases in the 'growth industries' were offset by declines in the older staples like coal, ships and textiles. In the fifties the increases in London were being offset by declines in two of its older staple industries—administration and miscellaneous services—but not so seriously as to impede the general industrial growth of the Region.

Table 1 confirms for the London Region the truth of Professor Sykes' conclusions,[1] based on study of employment changes by standard regions during 1949–57; that in the postwar period, in contradistinction to the interwar years, regional employment changes over a period of time are not to be explained merely in terms of a more or less favourable industrial structure at the beginning of that period. The chief factor is that in the faster-growing areas, the growth industries themselves have grown at a faster rate than in the slower-growing areas. In 1952, engineering was about as important in London Region's economy as in the country's (but general engineering

[1] J. Sykes, 'Employment and Unemployment in Regions and in the Development Areas', *Scottish Journal of Political Economy*, 6 (1959–60), 193–210.

less and electrical much more); vehicles were less important, distribution and professional services more. But these groups expanded as fast or faster, between 1952 and 1958, in London Region than in England and Wales as a whole. (Electrical engineering was the sole exception.)

Within the four main rings of the London Region, there have been very different patterns of postwar growth. These have not been tabulated in Table 1 because some of the figures are tentative estimates. Of the net increase of 315,000 within the Region, the Outer Ring, outside the Conurbation, accounted for three-fifths (190,000 in six years). Of this 190,000, almost three-quarters (141,000) was in manufacturing industry: half was in the two leading 'growth manufactures' alone, 55,000 in engineering of all sorts (including electrical goods), 37,000 in vehicles.

In the Suburban Ring of the Conurbation—the zone of rapid interwar development, outside the County of London—the growth in employment was roughly 100,000 in six years. Of this total again, exactly three-quarters—75,000—was in manufacturing, and two-fifths in the two 'growth manufactures': 30,000 in engineering and 12,000 in vehicles. The growth of employment in this ring during the fifties seems to have been rather less than half the interwar (1921–51) rate. The biggest increases took place in relatively small zones, already highly industrialized in 1945: especially the great industrial zone of West Middlesex, which added perhaps 50,000 workers in the decade.

Clearly, the great expansion of employment that has taken place outside the County of London has been dominated by *manufacturing* industry. Again, this was only part of the wider growth in the South-east England region. Between 1952 and 1958, manufacturing employment in this region rose by 302,000: of this figure 104,000 was outside the London Region altogether; 141,000 in the Outer Ring; and only 57,000 in the Conurbation (75,000 in the Suburban Ring; – 18,000 in the L.C.C. area). So that of the net increase of manufacturing employment in South-east England over these years, over four-fifths occurred outside the Greater London Conurbation.

Maps 2A and 2B show that the detailed patterns of growth of the two great 'growth manufactures' have been very different. Whereas that in engineering has been widely distributed among a number of centres, that in vehicles has been extremely concentrated in a few places where the large plants are situated. These patterns probably reflect differences in the scale of production in those branches of the industries most important in the London Region. But this difference apart, the 'growth manufactures' are similar in their location needs: they both need space, to get the greatest possible advantage from flow methods of production; and they are constantly pushed farther from the centre of London by the pressure of competing uses on scarce land. This process was already observable in London by the early nineteenth century.[1] Between the wars it drove manufacturing industry into the Suburban Ring; since 1950, as that Ring was filled up, the major part of the growth was naturally diverted over the Green Belt into the Outer Ring.

[1] See my *The Industries of London since 1861* (1962), Chapter 9.

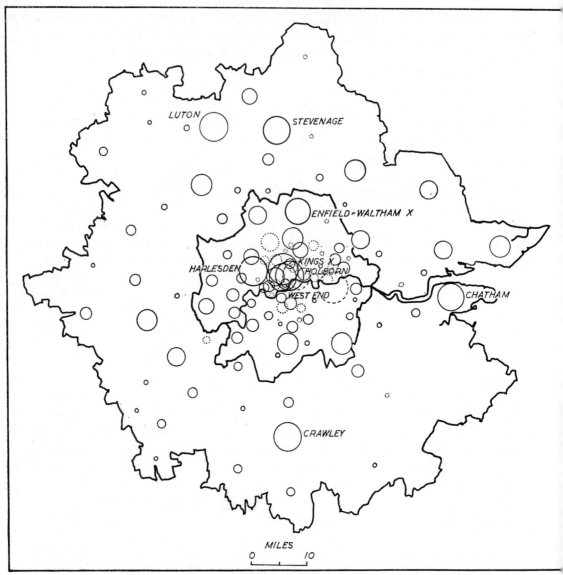

Map 2. *Major Industries: Employment Changes, 1952–8*
A. ENGINEERING (INCLUDING ELECTRICAL)

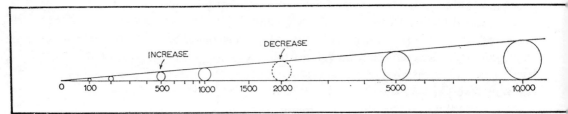

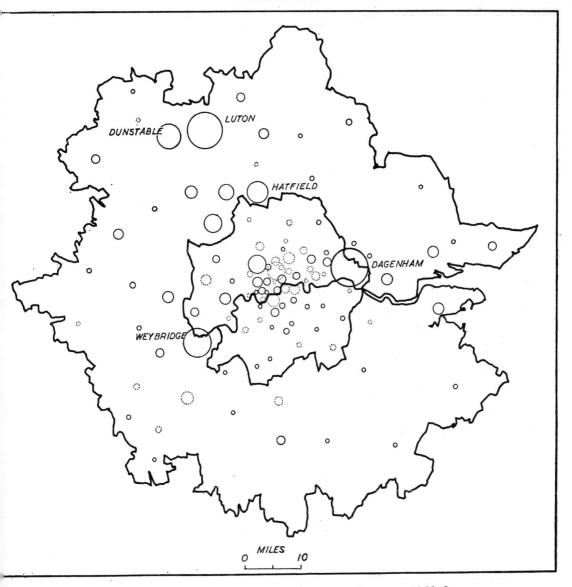

Map 2. Major Industries: Employment Changes, 1952–8

B. VEHICLES

Boundaries are those of London Region and Conurbation area. They differ slightly from other maps because they are based on Employment Exchange and National Insurance Office Areas.

55

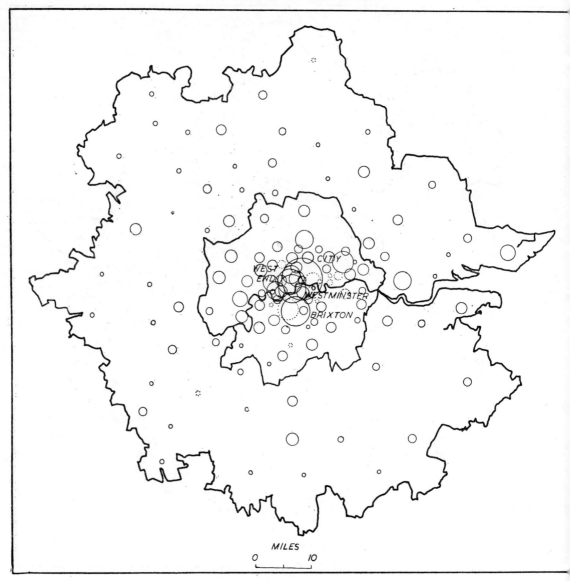

Map 2. Major Industries: Employment Changes, 1952–8
C. DISTRIBUTIVE TRADES

See scale and note on pages 54–5

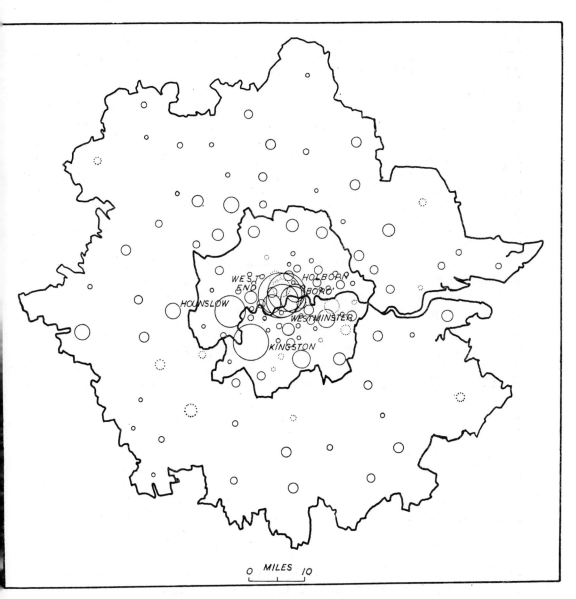

Map 2. Major Industries: Employment Changes, 1952–8
D. Professional Services

The Inner Urban Ring—that part of the County of London outside the very small central area—lost workers very heavily in the nineteen-fifties. The exact figure is impossible to state with certainty; probably between 50,000 and 70,000 in the period 1952–8, that is 10,000 a year, of whom about 5,000 were in manufacturing. This rate of decline is much too slow to achieve the decentralization targets of the Abercrombie or the County of London Development Plans in any reasonable time.

Lastly, the minute Central Area, only some ten square miles in extent, had a very large increase. Again, the exact figure is impossible to state precisely, but between 1952 and 1958 it was probably between 70,000 and 90,000: say 13–15,000 a year, 130–150,000 during the nineteen-fifties. Of the 1952–8 increase, some 15,000 were in distributive trades, 25,000 in professional services, and 20,000 in other services. The increase in 'growth manufactures' was negligible; 'other manufacturing' (chiefly printing and publishing and clothing) rose by 17,000. Here, then, as in the Suburban and Outer Rings, a little under half of the total increase in employment was in two 'growth industries'; but in this zone they were the service industries. (Maps 2C and 2D.)

Evidently, the increase of the service trades at the centre parallels the growth in manufacturing at the edge, as the other great economic phenomenon of the post-war London Region. Two-fifths of the total net growth of employment in the service trades within the Region—60,000 out of 132,000—was in the central area. The rest was very evenly distributed within the other zones, and tended to follow the same trends as the growth or decline of manufacturing employment. The distinction here, of course, is between the 'local services' which spring up to serve an existing popula-tion: corner shops, suburban shopping centres, local schoolteachers, doctors, den-tists—and the extremely concentrated regional, national or international central area services: certain types of distributive trading, both wholesale and retail; banking, insurance and finance; administration; certain professional services.

A very large part of the increase in service trades at the centre has been in office jobs. The precise figure is difficult to calculate. The L.C.C. has estimated for each major service industry group, and for all productive industry, the proportion of office workers to total workers in the central area in 1951.[1] For all industries this was 49·3 per cent; but for the industry groups which have dominated the increase of the fifties, the proportions were bigger: 53·9 per cent for distributive trades and 64·0 per cent for professional services. Applying ratios for these main expanding industries and for the residual groups, the increase of office workers in the central area between 1952 and 1958 may have been between 40,000 and 45,000—perhaps 70,000 in a decade; it is impossible to be more precise.

This trend has attracted so much attention, and so much ill-informed criticism, that it is important to be clear about its nature. The largest single group of increases in office workers has been in the category 'professional services'; and within this group

[1] *L.C.C. Development Plan*, First Review 1960; Country Planning Report, Vol. II: Statistics, Table 4. The definition of 'central area' used there differs slightly from that used here.

the fastest-increasing sub-headings, both in the whole London Region and at the centre, have been *education*—the product of the great postwar expansion of higher and further education of all sorts, much of it right in the centre of London—and the residual head 'Other professional and business services' which includes professions like *architecture*, *surveying*, *journalism*, and *professional organizations* such as the Royal Institute of British Architects, the Town Planning Institute, the Town and Country Planning Association, the Royal Institute of Public Administration and thousands of others. It is ironic, but the literal truth, that the sort of people who have called most insistently for a halt to office growth have been among its main causes.

Agglomeration

These are the trends. To use them as a basis for employment planning, it is first necessary to understand the economic forces that have produced them. Why has employment in the London Region continued to grow so fast? What explains the different patterns of change in different parts of the Region? The factors in any individual change are very complex, and to some extent unique. But one broad principle underlies most of the patterns within London Region: that of *agglomeration*, depending on *external economies*. It was Alfred Marshall who, in a famous passage, first developed the significance of external economies:

'When an industry has thus chosen a locality for itself, it is likely to stay there long: so great are the advantages which people following the same skilled trade get from near neighbourhood to one another. The mysteries of the trade become no mysteries; but are as it were in the air, and children learn many of them unconsciously. Good work is rightly appreciated, inventions and improvements in machinery, in processes and the general organization of the business have their merits promptly discussed: if one man starts a new idea, it is taken up by others and combined with suggestions of their own; and thus it becomes the source of further new ideas. And presently subsidiary trades grow up in the neighbourhood, supplying it with implements and materials, organizing its traffic, and in many ways conducing to the economy of its material.'[1]

The German economists, Alfred Weber[2] and August Lösch,[3] later developed the concept of external economies into a complete theory of agglomeration. The more complex type of agglomeration arises, Weber said, when several enterprises gather at the same location, for one cause or another: better servicing facilities, superior forms of labour organization, better marketing facilities, both for materials and product; lower general overhead costs of the social capital necessary for the efficient functioning of industry—gas and water mains, streets, refuse disposal. Contrary to these forces of agglomeration, Weber argued, are what appear to be forces of

[1] A. Marshall, *Principles of Economics* (8th Edition, 1920), 271.
[2] A. Weber, *Theory of the Location of Industries*, tr. C. J. Friedrich (Chicago 1929), Ch. 5.
[3] A. Lösch, *The Economics of Location*, tr. W. H. Woglom (New Haven 1954), Ch. 6.

deglomeration. But in reality these are not forces in themselves: merely anti-agglomerative forces. They arise from competition for land in areas of agglomeration, which forces certain enterprises out; so that agglomeration may be said to contain the seeds of its own decay, though these may never come to fruition.

From Weber's general theory, Lösch argued that there were two forms of agglomeration: agglomerations of similar enterprises and agglomerations of different interrelated enterprises. The first type is that illustrated in Marshall's passage: it can also be called agglomeration through *specific* external economies. The second, or general type, arises from the common needs of various industries for various services; from the general advantage of association of people in a place (a common market, a common culture) and from advantages of pure proximity, especially for the parasitic trades or local service industries. This type can also be called agglomeration through *general* external economies.

Clearly, in a metropolitan complex like London both sorts of agglomeration occur. The first sort is best illustrated on a *regional* scale by the tendency of many 'growth industries' to cluster in the metropolitan region; on the *local* scale by the many extremely localized 'industrial quarters' of the older manufacturing areas of inner London. The other sort is illustrated by the whole phenomenon of the modern metropolis, in which each part of the economic machine depends on a thousand others. But increasingly, in twentieth-century London, the anti-agglomerative tendencies manifest themselves. The *scale* of agglomeration is greatly increased, due to increasing competition for space plus the increased mobility of industry; the traditional manufacturing quarter declines, and the industrial City-Region, an interlinked industrial complex eighty miles across, takes its place.

Diverting Employment Growth

Bearing in mind the principle of agglomeration, the critical questions we need to ask about the patterns of growth since 1921 are these.

1. How far could employment growth have been diverted out of the London Region (and South-east England) altogether? How far should it?

2. How far could the internal pattern of employment growth within the region have been different? How far could increases in some parts have been diverted into other parts? How far should they?

It is very important to keep these two questions separate. But I propose to analyse them in the same way: I shall first consider the costs in different locations for the individual enterprises (*private* costs); then I shall ask whether there are any extra *social* costs which the community, and not the individual enterprise, bears if economic activity locates in one place rather than another.

There is one imponderable feature in the future growth of London which I believe no planner can yet take account of. That is the future pattern of growth of industry and population in Western Europe, as it may be influenced by the existence of the

European Economic Community. It has been claimed that the continued growth of London and South-east England is only part of a wider European phenomenon: the development of a 'Golden Triangle' between Birmingham, Paris and the Ruhr, in which industry and population are increasingly concentrated; a tendency which will operate with increased force as the economies of the E.E.C. countries are gradually integrated. Closer analysis shows that this picture is over-simplified: in the nineteen-fifties, the actual areas of biggest growth were the metropolitan zones of London, Paris, the Western Netherlands and the Rhine–Ruhr cities of Federal Germany. In other words, the pattern of population growth is still to be interpreted in *national* terms.[1] This may change; but on the future development of the European Economic Community it is almost impossible to speculate. Clearly the E.E.C. Commission's 'Second Stage Action Programme'[2] foresees a total integration of the national economies into a continental system within a relatively short time. But there are powerful forces in the Community, as now constituted, which will resist this move. Should it occur, the long-term effect might be to shift the area of maximum growth to the neighbourhood of a new European metropolis. But it is impossible to guess what form this metropolis might take or where it might be. Brussels, the present effective centre of the Community, has shown little evidence of exceptional magnetism in the decade up to 1961.

Diversion to the Provinces?

In discussing the private costs of the individual firm, it is first necessary to reckon with the way that industry actually grows within a region. As long ago as the thirties, the Surveys of Industrial Development by the Board of Trade made it quite clear that industry was growing in London first because of new firms, and second because of extensions of existing firms; migration of firms into London was negligible. Study of entrepreneurial history makes the process of growth clearer. A typical London engineering firm[3] might have started in inner London in the early nineteenth century, making printing machinery for the central London market; then, through technological innovation and commercial acumen, it might have moved into motor-car manufacture for West End buyers; then, during the 1914–18 War, into aeroplane manufacture for the Government; more recently still into rocket propulsion. The details vary, but certain features are constant. First, close contact with the evolving needs of the metropolitan market. This factor of *contact* recurs constantly in studies of industrial location in contemporary Britain. The Toothill Report's penetrating

[1] Peter Hall, 'How Europe is Growing', *New Society*, 28 March 1963.

[2] European Economic Community Commission, *Action Programme of the Community for the Second Stage* (Brussels, 1962).

[3] The history is actually that of D. Napier and Son, told by C. H. Wilson and W. Reader: *Men and Machines* (1958).

analysis of the competitive weaknesses of the Scottish economy[1] listed these advantages of contact for firms in South-east England: contact with the *market* ('since the rest of the organisation is seen as having to go along with sales'[2] in an industry producing standardized goods in large quantities); contact with the main current of scientific and industrial *research*, which is essential for technological advance; contact with *Government*, which itself buys research and research-based products; contact with the *labour market* for highly trained personnel—research scientists and highly trained engineers for example. 'These considerations lead us to conclude', the report admits, 'that further impetus will be given to the centripetal pull already exerted by London and the south-east quadrant, unless in future marketing from Scotland becomes demonstrably easier.'[3] Second, and allied with it, a very high rate of technological innovation and adaptation, which London industry shares with the other boom area of contemporary industrial England—the West Midlands. Third, a typical history of shifts of location over short distances within the region as the scale of production extended.[4] In general, a move right out of the region would be feasible only if a completely separate branch factory were established using key personnel from the old factory.

Because of this last fact, it is extremely difficult to get any general and accurate picture of costs in alternative locations, even for manufacturing firms in the 'growth industries'. There is one analysis, for 1951, of the radio industry.[5] This tried to establish the effect on firms' costs when they had moved all or some (i.e. a branch) of their activity to a Development Area as a result of Government pressure after 1945. It compared costs in the Development Area with the hypothetical costs in the alternative London factory. It showed that transport costs were higher; that service costs were marginally lower; that managerial and administrative costs were slightly higher. In labour costs there was no clear indication of higher costs either way, but there was evidence of lack of skilled labour in the Development Areas. The final conclusion was that cost differentials were small; but that most London firms thought the remoteness of the Development Area a handicap, because—once again—of the importance of close *contact* with technical developments and the whims of the market; a factor which it was impossible to express satisfactorily in cost terms. The advantages of agglomeration, or external economies, then, proved critical. The smaller the average unit of production, the less the experience of the average entrepreneur, the greater the advantages of agglomeration in the existing centre of growth.

A more comprehensive study of costs in alternative locations was made between

---

[1] Scottish Council (Development and Industry), *Inquiry into the Scottish Economy 1960–61* (Edinburgh 1961), Ch. 3.

[2] *Ibid.*, 35.

[3] *Ibid.*, 36.

[4] Cf. the evidence in my *The Industries of London since 1861* (1962), Fig. 22.

[5] D. C. Hague and J. H. Dunning, 'Costs in Alternative Locations: the Radio Industry', *Review of Economic Studies* 22 (1954–5), 203–13.

1949 and 1957 by a group under W. F. Luttrell.[1] Because it deals with a large sample of firms in different industries, it represents the most important advance for many years in our understanding of the costs of location. Ninety-eight cases were studied; 85 formed the main study of branches established by firms away from the parent factory in the early postwar period. Luttrell's main conclusions were that there were high initial costs of establishing the branch; but that after ten years at most, costs had tended to settle down at about the same level as the parent plant. Extra transport costs, which are often cited in discussions about decentralization, proved to be of negligible importance. Small subsidiary branches, duplicating a process carried on in the parent factory, and without full managerial staff, found advantage in a site not more than 30–35 miles from the parent factory—roughly the distance of the New Towns from central London. But self-contained new factories, with their own managerial and technical personnel, could afford to move several hundred miles, the distance from London to a Development Area. The main difficulty was to get key workers to move, especially to areas that looked unattractive. And the firm might have continuing trouble with inadequate facilities for technical training where such training was important.

Despite the scale of the Luttrell study, even it has clear limitations. The most important, which is inherent in all comparative studies, is that the main study dealt only with the establishment of branches.[2] In fact, it is clear that industry grows in regions partly, or even mainly, by firms spawning off other firms, in that a manager or technician in a firm will break away and set up in business on his own account. The growth of an existing firm can be diverted successfully, in some cases, into a distant branch factory; that the Luttrell study proves. But the other sort of growth, which is essential for the continued vigour of the economy, is much more difficult to divert, even impossible. For the new entrepreneur by definition usually lacks the experience, and even the risk capital, to set up his works in an unfamiliar area.

From this unavoidable fact, one school of planning has argued that new provincial centres of agglomeration—'counter-magnets'—should be created, into which many of London's activities, including the central area services, would be decentralized.[3] By definition, there are no cases to prove or disprove the wisdom of this course. There is, though, a foreign parallel: postwar Federal Germany, a country with a population size and an economic and social structure very like ours. Before the war in Germany, and increasingly under the Nazi régime, all administrative, financial and cultural institutions were progressively concentrated in Berlin. Since 1949, though, Western Germany has been reorganized on the basis of a small 'political' capital and a number of big provincial capitals, among which some degree of

[1] W. F. Luttrell, *Factory Location and Industrial Movement* (National Institute of Economic and Social Research, 1962. 2 vols.).

[2] A subsidiary study dealt with complete moves of existing factories.

[3] The latest statement is in *Land Use in an Urban Environment* (*Town Planning Review* special number, 1961), 243–64.

specialization has developed: Cologne has become the insurance centre, Frankfurt the banking and finance centre, Düsseldorf the centre for industrial administration.[1] To put it mildly, this system has proved itself economically viable; but before we rush to follow, some qualifications must be made. First, prewar Berlin was never the centre of a Commonwealth of nations or a great financial block, like London. Second, Berlin was truncated from the main body of Western Germany by administrative fiat; and the structure of the West German economy was then built up from scratch. The same thing could not be done for an economy in motion without the most fearful dislocation. It is clearly impossible to prove that the result would work better than our present arrangements; it would be done almost purely on social grounds, to convey some supposed benefit on the citizens of provincial England, which they show no real sign of wanting for themselves.

Beyond this point, the advocates of provincial decentralization point to social costs. Agglomeration is a sort of social benefit, enjoyed by industry as an unearned bonus. This, it is argued, is offset by enormous external diseconomies in the metropolitan machine, which are paid for not by those who create them, but by society as a whole. In fact, nearly all of these diseconomies are what the Barlow Commission analysed in 1940 under the head of social disadvantages; in those days sophistication had not advanced to the point of costing social evils.[2] Most of these disadvantages, I have already argued in Chapter 2, are irrelevant today; those which remain—traffic congestion, journey to work, the rising land values—could largely be ameliorated, if not cured, by better *internal* planning of the metropolis. An important part of this planning would be a more rational distribution of jobs and homes within the region, and a closer relation between the two. To this internal problem I turn in the next section.

If there is one single index which effectively expresses the regional balance sheet of costs and benefits, both private and social, it is regional productivity per head. Here the pioneer work of F. A. Leeming[3] has shown that per capita output in London and the South-Eastern Region is considerably higher than that of (say) Scotland or the East and West Ridings, not only for manufacturing output as a whole but for most individual manufacturing groups. Though there are many pitfalls in the interpretation of these statistics, not least the size of the regions involved and the possible differences within them, they do establish a prima facie case for believing that the growth regions are also, industry for industry, the high-productivity regions; and that any attempt to divert growth out of them may result in net economic loss.

[1] Cf. L. C. Kitching, 'Problems of London's Green Belt', *Journal of the Town Planning Institute*, 47 (1961), 34.

[2] More correctly, to asserting that they could be costed; the science of calculating social costs and benefits is yet in its infancy.

[3] F. A. Leeming, 'Problems in the Evaluation of Local Outputs in the United Kingdom', *Transactions and Papers, Institute of British Geographers*, Publication No. 30 (1962), 45–58.

Diversion within the Region?

Within the London region the problems can be limited, and defined, at the outset. There is no object in considering further the costs of the factories which have located or extended themselves, in such large numbers, in the Outer Ring since 1945. Had they not located here, they should have gone outside the London Region altogether; and this, I have just argued, is an extremely doubtful proposition. The problems to consider are nearer the centre. First: should factory jobs have expanded so fast in the Suburban Ring? Second: is the rate of decline in the Inner Ring the sort of rate we want? Third, and almost certainly most important: should jobs, and especially jobs in service occupations, have expanded so fast in the centre? For all three problems it is necessary to ask: looking at what has happened in the nineteen-fifties, was it necessary? If not, how far was it undesirable, on social grounds?

First, the suburban growth. This has been of the order of 170,000 extra jobs in a decade—an increase certainly not foreseen by Barlow or Abercrombie. In the troubled postwar situation, the overriding needs of export trade and defence have simply triumphed over planning considerations. In addition, the Board of Trade have openly admitted that in administering the machinery of control, the decentralization of industry within the London Region came 'very much as a second best'[1] to that of getting factories into the unemployment areas. In any case, much of the expansion that did take place occurred through new small factories and repeated small extensions, which did not need Board of Trade permission at all. Partly then the growth has gone uncontrolled, partly the machinery of control has connived at it for very good practical reasons. But is it, in fact, so socially reprehensible? Are the social costs involved so unduly high? It has increased journey to work, true: the resident population of the Suburban Ring has actually fallen during the fifties, and journeys across the Green Belt must have increased sharply. But these journeys have been distributed among a number of different centres; and a substantial number must have been across or against the main rush-hour trends, thus evening out to some extent the burden on the public transport system.[2] Again, most of the industrial development in this zone is concentrated in relatively compact and homogeneous industrial areas, which do not raise serious problems of non-conforming industry. If the suburban growth does give rise to planning problems, then, they are among the less serious London has to face; nevertheless, the aim in the future should be to get a much larger part of this growth into the Outer Ring.

Secondly, the decline in the Inner Ring. A rate of 10,000 a year—it may be much less than this—is almost negligible compared with the total figure for employment in the zone of about 1·5 million in 1958, and compared more particularly with the terrible problem of slum workshops in this ring. The situation is even worse than the statistics show; for the decline has been highly selective. The 'growth industries'

[1] *Royal Commission on Local Government in Greater London, Minutes of Evidence*, Q. 15216.
[2] This cannot be proved before the publication of the relevant 1961 Census figures.

have moved out most readily, and have made most of the long-distance moves to the Outer Ring; while the traditional 'industrial quarter' industries, which present the worst planning problems of non-conforming industry, bad working conditions and traffic congestion, have been most reluctant to go. In redevelopment schemes, it has been found impossible to persuade more than 10–20 per cent of the workshops to move outside the County area. Such firms may find it financially difficult even to move to new flatted factories within the quarter. The basic fact about the Inner Ring is that it is a zone of obsolescence. The economic enterprises of the Ring—whether workshops or corner retail shops—are often small firms that can only eke out an existence on the basis of low-rent premises.[1] The problem then is to ensure a more rapid rate of renewal of capital of all sorts. At present, to speed up the process of planned renewal would mean paying very large sums indeed to owners of vacated premises: E. J. L. Griffith has estimated £50–70 million to achieve the targets set in the 1951 L.C.C. Development Plan.[2] This money is unlikely to be forthcoming; there are too many other worthy candidates in the queue of claimants on the public purse. An urgent need, therefore, is to find a means of speeding up the renewal of obsolescent property without putting the burden on the community's limited funds.[3]

At the same time it must be recognized that many of the small industrial plants of inner London are extremely dependent upon the external economies which they derive from agglomerating in their specialized industrial 'quarters'; if the effect of planning is in any way to break these quarters up, and thereby costs are raised, that must be reckoned against the social benefits which accrue. We are only just beginning to learn the facts of economic life in inner London, through research done since 1955;[4] it shows the quite extraordinary strength and complexity of the ties which bind any one small plant to a host of others within five miles of central London. We should not presume to interfere too roughly with the working of that delicate mechanism until we are quite sure of the effects of our action.

But by common consent the most serious planning problem of all is the continued increase of office jobs at the centre. Surprisingly, it seems to have taken the planners —central and local—almost by surprise, though the dangers have been pointed out since 1954,[5] when the process was starting. Since about 1953 it has been official Ministry policy to hold residential uses in the central area, and to provide for office overspill in the plans of receiving authorities (for instance Middlesex, who were encouraged to plan for the development of offices outside the North Circular Road). But by a blunder of central Government policy, the effect of the third Schedule

---

[1] J. E. Martin pointed this out in his paper on 'Industry in Inner London', *Town and Country Planning*, 25 (1957), 125–8.

[2] E. J. L. Griffith, 'Moving Industry from London', *Town Planning Review*, 26 (1955–6), 51, 61.

[3] See below, Chapter 8.

[4] Cf. my *The Industries of London since 1861* (1962), Chapters 4–7; and the contributions of J. E. Martin and myself to J. T. Coppock (ed.), *Greater London* (1964).

[5] W. F. Manthorpe, 'The Limitation of Employment in Central London with particular reference to Employment in Offices', *Journal of the Royal Institution of Chartered Surveyors*, 34 (1954–5), 390.

of the 1947 Town and Country Planning Act was that developers were able to claim an extra 10 per cent cubic capacity on being granted permission to redevelop office accommodation. This overlooked the fact that modern office blocks are designed with much lower ceilings, so that even the same cubic content means great increase in floor accommodation, and 10 per cent extra cubic space means something like 40 per cent extra floor accommodation. Partly as a result, between 1948 and 1959 the L.C.C. licensed no less than 50 million square feet of new office space for all purposes (new, replacement, change of use) in the central area. Between 1956 and 1959, it found itself sanctioning an average annual increase of 3·5 million square feet a year, compared with the 2 million square feet which would be a realistic estimate of replacement needs.[1]

In these circumstances—needless to say—there has been little official consideration of the central question: how far could the increase have been diverted elsewhere? The debate on factory decentralization out of London, I have already tried to show, has taken place in a partial factual vacuum. But that on office decentralization within London is taking place within a virtually complete one. We know that the 'once-for-all' costs of an office move are negligible, since there is very little heavy machinery to be moved. The chief advantage of the out-of-London site is the lower rent. In 1962 these were representative:

Central: Mayfair, Victoria, St. James's, Knightsbridge, 40s.–50s. per square foot; City (centre), 35s.–40s.

Central Fringe: Marylebone Road, South Bank, Barbican, 27s. 6d.–35s.

Inner Urban: Earl's Court, Southwark, 25s.–30s.

Suburban: Woolwich, Ilford, Ealing, 15s.–17s. 6d.

Outer Ring: Guildford, Redhill, Hemel Hempstead, 12s. 6d.–15s.[2]

Wage rates in the suburbs and county towns are also lower; on average, about five-sixths central London rates. On the basis of wages and rents, the Town and Country Planning Association estimated in 1962 that the saving in a New Town as compared with central London would be, at an extremely conservative estimate, £140 per year per employee.[3]

But most important, and least calculable, are the higher costs of location outside the centre. Mostly these are concealed costs, paid in lower efficiency. As the American economist, R. M. Haig, said as long ago as 1926, in a central business district, 'What is all-important is transportation of intelligence';[4] and where that good must be personally transported its costs of transportation are unduly high. Thus routine and

[1] Town and Country Planning Association, *The Paper Metropolis* (1962), 27–8, 30–1. The Town and Country Planning Bill, 1963, belatedly recognizes this fact and attempts to counter it for the future. It provides that local planning authorities shall be under no liability to pay compensation if they refuse to allow an increase in *floorspace* of more than 10 per cent of the amount devoted to a particular use in any building which is being redeveloped.

[2] *Ibid.*, 48–9.   [3] *Ibid.*, 51.

[4] R. M. Haig, 'Toward an Understanding of the Metropolis', *Quarterly Journal of Economics*, 40 (1925–6), 427.

research work can most easily move; insurance companies can move routine operations, but have to keep a small city head office for contacts with brokers, commodity markets, shipowners, exchanges and banks. Yet only in large offices is this separation feasible; and these account, it is estimated, for less than 25 per cent of total office employment in the City.[1]

Even for work that can be decentralized, contact with the centre is thought vital. So it is not generally possible to persuade firms to go more than an hour's journey from London; the New Towns (about one and a half hours' journey) are generally at a distinct disadvantage in competition with locations on the fringe of the Conurbation. Mechanical communications—especially the telephone—are markedly more expensive outside the local call range from Central London, and this extends only just beyond the edge of the Conurbation; from central London 2d. buys three minutes on S.T.D. to Watford, only thirty seconds to the Hertfordshire New Towns. A survey of 60 decentralized firms in 1961 showed that 48 were within 25 miles of central London. The most popular locations were locations with good road and rail access, in service centres in the suburbs or in sizeable towns just outside.[2]

These are factors which affect private costs. They do not take into account—save in the most indirect way—the social costs of location in central London. Of all the postwar changes in the employment pattern of London Region, the growth in central area employment has raised the problem of social costs in the most acute form. The most important of these is probably the increased distance, cost and strain of the journey to work. Between 1951 and 1961, while employment in the central area rose by perhaps 150,000, the resident population of the whole area within a circle roughly 15 miles round the centre—the Greater London Conurbation—fell by 176,000. It goes without saying that commuting across the Green Belt, from the zone between 25 and 40 miles from the centre, must have increased markedly, because this is where the resident population has grown fastest. At the same time rail services have improved on many lines in speed and comfort, so we should not assume that strain has increased proportionately. But certainly costs have; and they are likely to rise even more dramatically up to 1970, if present trends continue. As late as 1960, it appears that British Railways' commuter services were still just breaking even, even though some of them were cross-subsidized from other services.[3] But this state of affairs will certainly not continue if—as seems certain—costly extra capacity has to be installed to deal with the thousands of extra commuters who may be arriving at central London termini by 1970. Fares over the whole commuter system will go up even more sharply, or travel conditions will worsen immeasurably, or very probably a combination of both will happen. To some extent, it is true, the market mechanism should operate to deal with the situation: commuters

[1] 'Office Location in London Region', *Town and Country Planning*, 26 (1958), 342–4.
[2] *The Paper Metropolis, op. cit.,* 37–8.
[3] *Report from the Select Committee on Nationalised Industries: British Railways* (H.M.S.O. 1960), xxv, xxxiv. Cf. British Transport Commission, *Annual Report 1961*, 4, and *The Reshaping of British Railways* (H.M.S.O. 1963), 20.

will be goaded to press salary claims, costs of central London locations will go up relative to peripheral ones, employers will be tempted to make a move. But in this there are several snags. First, employees cannot easily put an adequate cost on steadily worsening traffic conditions: so these are unlikely to be passed on in higher salaries. Second, even if they are, they are likely to be absorbed and passed on, somewhere along the line, in higher costs to consumers, as part of an inflationary spiral; which economic planning is now trying to prevent. Third, and most important, if no one considers now the implications of what is likely to happen, the result is quite likely to be a system that works less efficiently, in purely *economic* terms, than if social costs were considered by planners, and if they took action to ensure in time that individuals took notice of these social costs. It is no good if the market mechanism persuades employers to decentralize in 1972 in order to avoid the higher costs of the rail facilities that have by that time been provided. We need to consider *now* whether it is in society's interest to provide these facilities.

But we need more than a generalized argument for decentralization, and a generalized plan to bring it about: we need to consider in detail where to put the decentralized offices, within an employment plan for the whole London Region. In particular, we should be looking at sites for office development within the older parts of the London Region, which are ripe for urban renewal: the Victorian shopping centres of the Inner Ring, and the outworn centres of the suburban market towns which were swallowed up in the growth of the Suburban Ring between 1918 and 1939. Here, it is most useful to look at the trends which have naturally occurred, with the connivance of the planners or in despite of them, since 1955.

Croydon provides perhaps the most spectacular example so far of suburban office decentralization. Here is an old-established market, shopping and transport centre, a planning authority in its own right: the corporation, which owns many of the sites, leased them to speculative developers. When complete, the development will bring 30,000 more people to work in central Croydon. They spend at present only about 35 minutes getting to work, on average; their employers pay about half the rent and rates they would pay in the City.[1]

Hammersmith is another portent for the planners. Here is a busy Victorian shopping centre, a focus of underground and bus routes, within twenty minutes of the West End; and bisected by London's new main road artery to the west. Office development has for some decades been moving west out of central London, first to the West End, then to Victoria, Knightsbridge, and Sloane Square, lastly more widely through west London; Hammersmith is the most natural extension of this trend for firms with foreign business arriving through the airport. Fourteen acres of Victorian property will be replaced by a comprehensive speculative development including offices, showrooms, shops, flats and public buildings.[2]

[1] 'Cranes over Croydon', *The Observer*, 19 March 1961; and 'City and Suburban', *The Economist*, 10 June 1961.
[2] *The Times*, 22 October 1960.

The Hammersmith plan is a *fait accompli* by a speculator; it had no part in the 1960 Review of the L.C.C. Development Plan, and indeed the L.C.C. have now decided to prevent similar developments by making planning conditions impossibly unattractive. We gather, then, that there is a serious general objection to such schemes on broad grounds of employment planning; but no; the L.C.C. are restricting further development so that a complete review of development in the County may be made. Yet, until the proposed Greater London Council makes its probable appearance in April 1965, there is no statutory authority for the review that should be made—throughout the Conurbation; and there can be no coherent policy on office development in the London Region. This is only one example, albeit one of the most serious, of the inadequacy of the present planning structure for London; an inadequacy which the imminent reform of local government will not by any means remove, for the new authority will control an area much too small for proper planning.

Planning London's Jobs

To conclude. What have we learned from the study of trends within the London Region in the last forty years, which will help us in planning for the next forty? I would suggest these things.

First: that we have gone about as far as we were able to, since 1945, in trying to divert employment out of London. We could go further only by extending control to the smallest factory and the most minor extension, and refusing permission, almost as a matter of course, to any application in South-east England; by instituting machinery to control office development and working it in the same way. The only likely effect would be to cripple some of the most dynamic sections of our economy, on which our deplorably slow economic growth in too large measure depends. Planners may talk readily—Barlow and Abercrombie so talked—of limiting employment here, encouraging it there, as if the economy were a series of taps, to be turned off and on. It could, of course, if we could but scrap our economic heritage, and start again; but, as the Federation of British Industries told the Barlow Commission, 'Like the eggs in an omelette, the elements of a fully formed economic system cannot be unscrambled.'[1]

Second: that on the basis of the post-1945 system of control London has continued to attract a very large part of the total national increase of employment: about one-third, compared with perhaps two-fifths in 1921–51. The proportion has been higher in manufacturing industry (two-fifths), where there has been control, than in service industry (one-quarter) where there has not. Evidently, then, the postwar trends are to be attributed in large measure to structural trends in the economy, and not to the operation of planning policies.

[1] *Royal Commission on the Distribution of the Industrial Population, Minutes*, Memorandum of F.B.I., para. 74.

Third: we can make an extremely rough extrapolation from post-1945 trends. It is virtually certain that up to 1980 national population will continue to grow at least as fast as in 1951–61; the proportion of the population of working age will increase;[1] we can assume that at least one-third of the extra national labour force will be in London Region. On these grounds we should expect at least another million workers in London Region by 1980. After that prediction is more hazardous, and there may arise a problem of lack of room (though I argue in the next chapter that this is fallacious): another million more would be a rough estimate to make for the additional workers between 1980 and 2000. There is no point in a more refined estimate; if the rate halved—an event which would require a quite unprecedented failure in momentum of the whole economic machine—the increase would still be of the order of one million in forty years.

Fourth, therefore: it behoves us to accept, wholeheartedly, this continued growth in London Region and indeed in South-east England as a whole; and to plan the location of employment, for maximum economic efficiency and social convenience, *within* the region.

Fifth: I would argue that the planner's job here is to intervene with the aim, so far as is possible, of *maximizing social benefits, minimizing social costs.* Planning now would work from quite different premises, and consequently with different techniques, from immediate post-1945 planning. In 1945, the sole yardstick of employment planning was to reduce unemployment: so great an evil was this, economically and socially, that consideration of cost seemed worthless and irrelevant. So a non-cost technique was adopted: control by licensing. Now, the job is subtler, the evils more insidious, and the techniques need to be more sophisticated. The imbalance between private costs and social costs needs to be corrected by private costs, socially imposed. Evidently, it will never be possible or practicable to distinguish every small piece of imbalance, and even if one could it would be administratively impossible to devise a system of charging to correct it. But we can make useful rough approximations. The main lines of attack, I would argue, are these:

1. The first and biggest problem is at the centre. Here, we are almost certain, the imbalance between social and private costs and benefits is greatest. There are various ways of correcting it according to source—for instance, charges on road users as a rationing device to ease traffic congestion—but the simplest, if crudest, means is the differential payroll tax, first suggested by Denys Munby as long ago as 1951.[2] The Treasury now have powers to impose such a tax, but paradoxically not to impose it differentially; this should be corrected. The most important question is the precise geographical weight of the tax. I would suggest a rate which would lie very heavily on firms in the present central area, and perhaps beyond; a much lighter rate in the rest of the L.C.C. area, and perhaps the rest of the Conurbation; and a lighter rate still, plus even financial inducements, in the Outer Ring. This would help achieve two

[1] From 55 per cent in 1960 to nearly 62 per cent in 1980.
[2] In 'The Cost of Industrial Dispersion from London', *Planning Outlook*, II, No. 3 (1951), 5–16.

objects: office firms, or parts of firms, which perform routine work and could safely decentralize into the Outer Ring would be encouraged to go there; those firms which must remain in the central area, for reasons of contact, would be persuaded to do so in a much wider, freer central London, perhaps as much as twenty miles across. Within this area planning policy would try to encourage the development of special-ized office 'quarters' for new sorts of office, like those which have already developed quite naturally in the West End,[1] separated by wide areas of residential development.

These two types of move would grapple with the principal evils resulting from the present concentration at the centre: long journeys to work and traffic congestion. The fully decentralized offices would attract workers from the town in which they were sited, or from neighbouring towns. The 'inner' offices would generate shorter radial journeys, either across the Green Belt or against the main traffic flow, both of which would even out flows on the long-distance commuter trains; as well as more cross-journeys, which may increasingly be made by private transport. The whole operation needs to be combined with the reshaping of London's transport and traffic system so as to achieve new nodes of accessibility, as attractive as the central one is today. To this I return in Chapter 5.

2. This measure would also take care of the inner zone. The small workshops in this zone would feel the incidence of a payroll tax very severely, since it would be coupled with a tax on obsolescent property which I advocate in Chapter 8. This severe stick should be accompanied by an especially succulent carrot. A large part of the proceeds of the payroll tax should therefore be diverted to once-for-all sub-sidies to encourage these firms to make long-distance moves into the Outer Ring. A smaller once-for-all subsidy would be paid for movement to the Suburban Ring. Factories at low rentals for the first lease period would be available in the reception areas. These would be grouped so as to provide, as far as possible, industrial quarters like those left behind.

3. In the suburban zone the problem is to encourage a very high rate of industrial mobility while keeping the employed population at roughly its present level. Small firms displaced from the Inner Ring, and offices from the centre, would enter; ex-panding factories would be encouraged to move out to the Outer Ring. The financial means to this end is through control of leases and rentals. Many factories in this zone are rented from the estate companies which built them in the twenties and thirties. A public development corporation[2] should gradually acquire controlling interest in these companies. It would then pursue a policy of letting small factory and office units; firms moving from the Inner Ring and the centre will receive subsidized rents for a limited term, the subsidies being met from the proceeds of payroll tax; rents for larger factories should be disproportionately expensive, so as to encourage the expanding firms to move further out.

[1] See W. T. W. Morgan, 'Office Regions in the West End of London', *Town and Country Plan-ning*, 19 (1961), 257–9.
[2] This idea is developed more fully in Chapter 6, pp. 133–4.

4. In the Outer Ring and beyond—a zone extending up to seventy miles from Charing Cross—the basic policy should be to welcome wholeheartedly the growth of new industry; and to plan for its further expansion in industrial towns, new and expanded, linked to new and improved transport routes. Much of the factory building should be done by a public development corporation or corporations. Firms moving from locations nearer the centre would get once-for-all help with their move, and subsidized rentals for a limited period; these costs to the community would again be met out of the proceeds of payroll tax. Within this outer zone, the planners should accept the implications of mobility of labour. For long-term mobility, they must find a way to provide homes that people can change easily. The British are badly behind the Americans in this respect. For mobility in the medium term, they need to provide new types of accommodation, such as simple flats and hostels for the worker who needs to commute from Monday to Friday. Both these demand a new type of development and building agency which operates on a large scale, either regionally or nationally, and which can dispose of houses by way of sale or rent. For the short-term commuter, the planners will have to accept that in this outer zone, people will increasingly get to and from their jobs by their own transport, in thousands of separate cross-movements; and that the average length of their journey may increase as the means of transport become faster or easier, or as their skills become more varied and specialized.

This chapter has set out to expound a conservative view of employment planning. It has been based on the fundamental thesis that economic forces cannot be halted or reversed, but only channelled to a limited extent. It follows that the resulting London of 2000 would not differ so strikingly, in its employment structure and distribution, from the London in which this book has been written. The total number of people working in the London Region in 2000, I have tried to argue, will not be so very different whatever the planners try to do. Nor will they find it possible to reverse internal trends. Almost certainly, many more people will work in the present central area than do now. But under effective planning, many less would work there than if the present drift continued without interference: of this difference, some would be diverted to work in expanded sub-centres, dispersed within the present Conurbation area up to about fifteen miles from the centre; others would be living and working in a vast outer zone between twenty and sixty miles from the centre, either living close to their work, or travelling in complex radial and cross-movements to it. This, in essence, is what I think employment planning is capable of.

Postscript, 1969

Jobs provide the starting point of any analysis, which is why they went at the front of *London 2000*. With one complication, which has proved embarrassingly evident since: the working population is by no means a constant proportion of the whole population. The British economy, and the London economy, got a big bonus during the 1950s by drawing more women, especially married ones, into the labour force; but that process cannot go on for ever. At the same time, more and more young adults are being taken out of the labour pool, because they are spending longer and longer at university or college. And the flukes of demographic change have provided that during the late 1960s and early 1970s, children and old people are increasing in numbers more rapidly than the working age groups who have to support them; this is a simple product of high birth rates in Edwardian England, and high birth rates again in the late 1950s and early 1960s. Within the South East Region, between 1964 and 1971, the working age groups are expected to increase only by 83,000; the dependent groups, that is the old and the young, by 781,000. In the 1970s things will get better again: the working groups will increase by 364,000, the dependent groups by 913,000. This still means, though, a continuing labour shortage; a shortage that is bound to bite more severely on the South Eastern economy than on the rest of the country's.

These estimates themselves depend, of course, on notions about migration; and in turn, those have to depend on a complex projection of the combined effects of labour shortages and government policies. The official regional population forecasts from the Government, published in November, 1966, show continuing net migration out of Britain's less favoured regions: a migration amounting over the period 1964–81 to 305,000 in the case of Scotland, 137,000 for Northern Ireland, 126,000 for Northern England, 128,000 for Yorkshire and Humberside and 134,000 for the North West. All in all, this is a loss of 830,000 people in seventeen years; the prosperous regions of the south and midlands would gain 899,000, the balance representing a modest net gain from abroad.[1] For the South East Planning Region, the estimates suppose a net loss to the rest of England and Wales (33,000 a year 1964–1971, 32,000 a year 1971–81) balanced by a net gain from outside the country (43,000 and 31,000 per year respectively) giving a fairly small net gain of 10,000 a year (1964–71) and a loss of 1000 a year (1971–81). There is thus a very large gain to other parts of the South and Midlands. Since these forecasts were made, two contradictory things have happened. On one hand, the economic base of the less prosperous areas has become shakier still, with the threatened rapid rundown of coal pits; on the other, the Government has set up a massive battery of financial inducements to firms to go to the Development Areas. 25 per cent grants on factory building, 45 per cent allowances on equipment (against 25 per cent elsewhere), an employment bonus amounting to £97 10s. a year for each man employed, with correspondingly lower rates for women and juniors, together make up a set of attractions which industrialists are bound to notice.

Therefore, the future may see a different pattern from the immediate past. *London 2000* estimated that in the 1950s, about one half the total increase of jobs in England and Wales (820,000 out of 1,630,000) was in the South East, of which 530,000 was in the London Region. The 1961 Census, in broad outline, gave a rather higher estimate: a smaller South East Planning Region, which excludes East Anglia, accounted for

[1] Revised projections of the regional distribution of the United Kingdom population in 1971 and 1981. *Economic Trends*, 157 (November 1966), pp. ii–xv.

TABLE 2

COMPONENTS OF POPULATION CHANGES, 1964–1981

(Thousand persons)

	Static population change 1964–1981 (i.e. excluding all effects of migration)	Effects of migration 1964–1981			Total projected change in population 1964–1981
		Total	Net population movement	Consequential net births minus deaths	
Northern England	+512	−167	−126	−41	+345
Yorkshire and Humberside	+628	−124	−128	+4	+504
North West England	+958	−133	−134	+1	+825
East Midlands	+451	+315	+233	+83	+766
West Midlands	+778	+97	+31	+66	+875
East Anglia	+153	+330	+267	+63	+483
South East England	+1,665	+477	+59	+418	+2,142
South West England	+295	+339	+309	+30	+634
England	+5,439	+1,134	+511	+624	+6,573
Wales	+313	−38	0	−38	+275
England and Wales	+5,752	+1,096	+511	+585	+6,848
Scotland	+842	−407	−305	−102	+435
Great Britain	+6,594	+689	+206	+483	+7,283
Northern Ireland	+394	−183	−137	−46	+211
United Kingdom	+6,988	+506	+69	+437	+7,494

Source: *Economic Trends*, November 1966, Table 5 (A)

591,000 of the net growth of employment of 1,007,000 in England and Wales between 1951 and 1961, or about 60 per cent. For the period since 1961, the figures in the *South East Strategy* can be compared with Ministry of Labour figures for the country as a whole: they show that during 1961–4 South East England added 223,000 workers or 28 per cent of the national total; from 1964 to 1966 the figure was 192,000 and the percentage 47. For the future, we have to reckon with a probable nil migration into the region, with a falling rate of natural increase, and with increasing labour shortages. Still in 1965, the *National Plan* was assuming a growth in demand for labour in the South East (including East Anglia) of 416,000 out of a total for England and Wales of 751,000—well over one half. These estimates almost certainly need refinement, but the Planning Council's Strategy of November 1967 did not attempt the exercise.

Therefore, one is left with an extremely rough and ready measure of the growth of the labour force: the growth of the population in the working age groups. The analysis by the Government Actuary's Department, which is based on the assumption that migration into the South East will dwindle to a trickle in the late 1960s and early 1970s, nevertheless assumes that a substantial part of the total growth in the working age groups will occur in the South East: 83,000 out of 268,000 (31·0 per cent) during 1964–71, and 364,000 out of 1,486,000 (24·5 per cent) during 1971–81.[1] But this in itself is based partly on assumptions about differential migration rates among different age groups.

The critical question then is where in the South East this growth is likely to be. Here, in one critical respect the historical analysis in *London 2000* was grievously wrong; though it was in good company, for every other analysis of that time, including the official South East Study, fell into the same error. Working from admittedly unreliable Ministry of Labour figures, *London 2000* concluded that the growth of jobs in the London Metropolitan Area in 1951–61 was about 500,000, broken down thus: Central London 150,000, Inner London (the rest of the old LCC area) minus 100,000, Suburban Greater London 150,000, the Outer Ring (Outer Metropolitan Area) 300,000. On this analysis, close on one-third of the total net employment growth of the London region had been at the very centre, and two-fifths had been in Greater London. Every other analysis of that time took on trust the figure of central London employment growth: 15,000 on average a year, 150,000 during the decade. Some analyses went further and assumed that the whole of this central growth was in office jobs; but for that, there was really no justification.

Finally, the belated publication of the 1961 Census Industry tables showed that the growth in employment was much less than this. In central London as defined in terms of six central areas (City, Westminster, St. Marylebone, Holborn, St. Pancras, Finsbury) the growth was 56,000.[2] Subtracting St. Pancras but adding Southwark, the growth was 88,000.[3] This central increase was dominated to an extraordinary degree by three industry groups—Insurance Banking and Finance, Professional and Scientific Services, and Miscellaneous services—which account for 76,000 out of the 88,000 increase in the second group. From this, it seems that the much-publicized growth of headquarters of offices of manufacturing firms was not a significant factor in the growth of central area jobs. During this same period, the rest of Inner London

[1] *Economic Trends, op. cit.*

[2] Standing Conference on London and South East Regional Planning, Technical Report LRP 721, 23 November 1966: *Population and Employment in the Conference Area: Report by the Technical Panel on recently available data.*

[3] Alan W. Evans, 'Myths about employment in Central London', *Journal of Transport Economics and Policy*, I (1967), pp. 214–25. Evans mentions several possible reasons for the discrepancy, chiefly the fact that many firms change all their employees' books centrally. He does not however mention the possibility that the Census figures are an underestimate, because the Census sample underestimated small households with several working members, which are particularly important sources of Central London employment.

(excluding St. Pancras but including Southwark) suffered a loss of 44,600 jobs; suburban Greater London gained 145,000. Thus the gain in Greater London was 157,000, out of a total gain in the South East Planning Region of 590,000. In other words, out of the total growth of jobs in the South East in the 1950s, Greater London gained only one quarter; central London only one tenth.

For the period since 1961, the evidence is summarized in the South East Planning Council's 1967 *Strategy*.[1] Because of changes in definitions, there is a split in the statistics in 1964; but both for the period before 1964 and the period after, trends are roughly the same as in the 1950s. Greater London accounted for about 30 per cent of the South East's net employment growth in the period up to 1964, for about 25 per cent afterwards. In both periods, about half the total extra jobs went to the Outer Metropolitan Area. Throughout, virtually the whole of the net growth was in service industry; in manufacturing, a loss in Greater London was compensated by gains outside, but the net effect over the region was virtually no increase. One has to be careful not to exaggerate the extent of the decentralization of jobs, above all through the rapid growth of service industry in the outer areas; for still, in the late 1960s, one half of the South East's jobs were in Greater London. But there is little doubt that overall, there is a steady and continuing trend: it is producing a new, polycentric region, in which London's former absolute dominance is becoming steadily more eroded.

There is a strange irony here; for, on the basis of quite misleading statistics, the Government took critical decisions about employment policies in the South East. Even before *London 2000* the Government had been gravely concerned at the apparent growth of office jobs in central London; and the 1963 Planning Act had sealed the notorious Third Schedule loophole, described in Chapter 3 of the book. Then in 1964, after publication of the *South East Study* and the arrival of a new Labour government, even more drastic measures were taken. The White Paper on Offices, issued on 4th November 1964, quoted an increase of nearly 200,000 office jobs in and adjoining central London since 1951, with the possibility of a quarter million more under existing planning permissions and use rights.[2] It therefore announced a control on all new development in the London Metropolitan Area (London Region) from midnight on 4th–5th November 1964. The position was formalized by an Act in the next year, which gave to the Board of Trade formal powers on the control of office growth, similar to those which had existed for two decades over factory development. In future, a developer seeking to build office space must seek an office development permit (ODP); such a permit would be given very sparingly, if at all, in the London area.

In the period of enthusiasm which followed the arrival of a new government in 1964, it was quite possible to believe that a virtual ban on new office development in

[1] South East Regional Economic Planning Council, *A Strategy for the South East* (H.M.S.O. 1967), Annex Tables C6–C10.
[2] *Offices: A Statement by Her Majesty's Government*, 4th November 1964 (H.M.S.O.), p. 2.

London was feasible. In practice, as with all such types of control, this has proved very far from the truth. All sorts of exceptions have had to be allowed for office developments which, for one reason or another, could not conceivably take place outside London. Developments like the new Stock Exchange, or the major Transportation Centre at Victoria, will either take place in London or not at all; if they do not take place, they will just mean inefficiency; and above all, in these two and other cases, that will seriously hinder the country's capacity to win invisible earnings.

What seems to be happening now in the service sector, and will probably happen on an increasing scale in the future, is a complex process of change resulting from a number of pressures. Continued restrictions on office building in London, coupled with enforcements of standards under the Offices, Shops and Railway Premises Act of 1965, will drive up rents—above all in central London, where rents have now rocketed to as much as £6 a square foot.[1] This in itself will inhibit the growth of office jobs, and there may well be a slight decline in central employment—as London Transport's

TABLE 3A

EMPLOYMENT, 1960 and 1964 (thousands)

	Great Britain		SE Region		Greater London		Outer Metropolitan Area		Rest of South East	
	1960	1964	1960	1964	1960	1964	1960	1964	1960	1964
Extractive	1387	1182	162	141	17	16	61	52	84	74
Manufacturing	8663	8704	2562	2592	1587	1507	628	705	347	380
Construction	1423	1614	488	551	274	302	110	127	104	122
Services	10541	11336	4216	4543	2704	2873	717	812	795	858
Total	22014	22836	7429	7827	4583	4697	1515	1696	1331	1434

TABLE 3B

EMPLOYMENT, 1964 and 1966 (thousands)

	Great Britain		SE Region		Greater London		Outer Metropolitan Area		Rest of South East	
	1964	1966	1964	1966	1964	1966	1964	1966	1964	1966
Extractive	1185	1043	142	128	12	13	55	49	74	67
Manufacturing	8731	8868	2596	2603	1478	1424	737	766	381	421
Construction	1617	1681	551	552	294	294	134	133	122	125
Services	11359	11709	4533	4731	2830	2936	843	917	860	878
Total	22892	23301	7821	8013	4614	4667	1769	1865	1438	1482

[1] *Location of Offices Bureau, Annual Report 1967–68* (London 1968), 10.

TABLE 4A

EMPLOYMENT CHANGES 1960–1964

	Great Britain	SE Region	Greater London	Outer Metropolitan Area	Rest of South East
Absolute Change, 000s					
Extractive	−205	−21	−1	−9	−10
Manufacturing	+41	+30	−80	+77	+33
Construction	+191	+63	+28	+17	+18
Services	+795	+327	+169	+95	+63
Total	+822	+398	+116	+181	+103
Percentage Change, per year					
Extractive	−3·9	−3·3	−2·4	−3·9	−3·1
Manufacturing	+0·1	+0·3	−1·3	+3·0	+2·3
Construction	+3·2	+3·1	+2·6	+3·6	+4·1
Services	+1·9	+1·9	+1·5	+3·2	+1·9
Total	+0·9	+1·3	+0·6	+2·9	+1·9

TABLE 4B

EMPLOYMENT CHANGES, 1964–1966

	Great Britain	SE Region	Greater London	Outer Metropolitan Area	Rest of South East
Absolute Change, 000s					
Extractive	−142	−14	+1	−6	−7
Manufacturing	+137	+7	−54	+29	+31
Construction	+64	+1	—	−1	+3
Services	+350	+198	+106	+74	+18
Total	+409	+192	+53	+96	+44
Percentage Change, per year					
Extractive	−5·8	−5·1	+0·8	−6·2	−5·4
Manufacturing	+0·7	+0·1	−1·8	+2·0	+4·0
Construction	+2·0	+0·1	−0·1	−0·4	+0·9
Services	+1·5	+2·2	+1·9	+4·2	+1·0
Total	+0·8	+1·2	+0·6	+2·7	+1·5

Source for Tables 3 and 4: DEA
(Totals may not add due to rounding.)

annual commuter census already indicates has been happening, since 1964. At the same time the Location of Offices Bureau, which moved 50,000 office jobs out of London between 1963 and 1968,[1] will find it increasingly easier to continue and accelerate the process—providing Government policies do not hinder them. But it will discover two limitations.

First, the decentralized jobs will not move very far: apart from some government offices, the effective limit for most firms seems to be thirty or forty miles out, that is about an hour's travelling distance from London.[2] Secondly, the jobs that are moving are on the whole the routine ones—and these are the jobs most likely to be affected by the rapid development of electronic data processing. The higher-level, decision-making jobs—what Jean Gottmann has called the quaternary, as distinct from the tertiary sector of production—seem still to be firmly established at the centre. Revolutionary devices, like the videophone, the conference phone and the instantaneous transmission and production of documents, may weaken the forces of centralization; but current indications are that some of these may not be fully commercially feasible for some decades. Meanwhile, there are certain forces in the organization of production, which may strengthen the concentration of the quaternary sector in the centres of the biggest metropolitan cities. This at any rate is the conclusion of the economist Folke Kristensson, in Stockholm, and of certain of his colleagues in other Swedish universities, who are engaged in an intensive study of the urbanization process.[3] If, as Kristensson calculates, as much as 18–28 per cent of total Metropolitan employment will continue to be concentrated at the centre, that indicates a continuous and fairly rapid resorting of the functions of the central area.

Here, there is a serious lack of any theoretical method for judging which functions should be in the centre, and which outside. In the case of commercial offices, competitive rents provide an answer—though even here, as LOB have recognized as a result of their research, long leases inject a serious time lag into the adjustment process. But in the case of big public institutions, the Government necessarily must make value judgements which are based on little more than hunches. In the case of the removal of Covent Garden market to Nine Elms, the evidence from cities all over the world was overwhelming: big wholesale markets no longer belong in the centre. In the case of the British Museum Reading Room, and of the other great national libraries of central London, no clear policy has emerged; in spring 1969, the com-

[1] *Ibid.*, 5.

[2] *Ibid.*, 17.

[3] Folke Kristensson, *People, Firms, and Regions: A Structural Economic Analysis* (1968). See also the use of this work in *The 1966 Outline Regional Plan for the Stockholm Area* (English Version), Stockholm 1968. Kristensson calculates that between 18 and 28 per cent of all metropolitan jobs will need to be located in the centre, and another 22–31 per cent in a 'band' close to the centre, with exceptionally good regional communications. Certain other work, notably that at the University of Gothenburg under Professor Sven Godlund, indicates that there may be a long term organizational trend towards the concentration of the highest levels of decision making in the biggest centres—even on a continent-wide scale.

mittee appointed to deal with the problem still had to report.[1] The question of the libraries is linked, in turn, to the whole future of the vast higher education complex of central London. Some academics will argue that central London is the last location to do work that involves reflection and scholarship; others, that the stimulus of many minds makes it the only place to do good academic work. Differing personal opinions like these are never going to be resolved. But they can be put against a background of the real costs of building and operating universities—or, indeed, anything else—in London. In research conducted during 1964–66 at Battersea College of Technology, now the University of Surrey, we tried to do this for one institution.[2] The work could and should be refined and extended to a much bigger range of institutions. Meanwhile, research is giving us some valuable information about the nature of linkages and networks in the centre of a modern metropolis.

If pieces of the central London economy can and should be detached and moved, where should they go? In *London 2000*, I argued for the creation of new nodes of employment in the suburban ring of Greater London, at places which would be served both by good radial rail lines and new motorways. This was the policy prescription of the Paris PADOG plan of 1960, and though the later 1965 Plan abandoned much of PADOG, it left the suburban nodes intact.[3] In London the redevelopment of Croydon provides an actual working model of such a suburban node, and it is not a model that has found much favour with Greater London planners. Croydon has deprived British Railways of the fares which commuters earlier paid to reach the centre, without any compensating advantage to the management, since the trains must still run on to the centre. But at the same time, because many commuters have switched to their cars, it has led to serious congestion problems in the centre of Croydon, which are being expensively met by road works and parking garages.

The moral planners draw from this is that the offices should be driven farther out. This may be the wrong moral. Croydon was probably a bad place for office development simply because though it was a major rail junction, it was far from arterial highways, either existing or planned. But there are, in London, several sites which combine equally good rail access, potentially good road access (via motorways, either under construction or actively planned) and potentially available space. Willesden Junction, Clapham Junction, and Lewisham–New Cross are cases. Providing there is the space, then the example of the new campus office complex in North Hamburg shows that the planners can contemplate even 60 per cent car usage with equanimity. Ironically, in London the government rejected the one type of site which would have rationalized travel to work by rail; the type presented by the Shell Building next to Waterloo, the big Stag Brewery office complex outside Victoria, or most dramatically the Pan Am Building above New York's Grand Central Station. When British Rail proposed a similar development in association with the rebuilding of

[1] Peter Hall, 'London's Akademigorsk', *New Society*, 2 May 1968.
[2] Roy Drewett, Peter Hall, John Oram, 'The Location of a University', mimeographed.
[3] Peter Hall, *The World Cities* (1966), Ch. 3.

Euston Station, the Government rejected it on the grounds that total office space in the centre of London should be restricted. That may be the case; it does not alter the fact that if there is to be any new office development for replacement in central London, then the most rational place for it is next to the main line termini. This suggests that the Greater London Council should aim at a double-barrelled office policy: on the one hand, a phasing-out of existing office permissions on converted housing in areas like Belgravia and Bloomsbury (which could be secured if the Planning Acts were amended to put a 'life' on all planning permissions, just as the Victorians did when they licensed noxious industry in London); on the other, a selective policy of permissions to develop around railway stations on the periphery of the central area. Such a policy might just be achieved without a change in the Planning Acts, if developers were told that they could trade in permissions on less profitable old offices for permissions on more profitable new ones.

The argument that has been used against this is that development at the centre, at a time when the residential population is growing fastest at distances up to forty miles away, can only lead to a big extension of very long-distance commuting. This was the fear expressed in 1963 by the Standing Conference, who thought that between 1961 and 1971 there might be as many as 375,000 extra long-distance travellers into central London from outside the Greater London conurbation. Given the stagnation of central London employment since 1964, it is doubtful whether anything like this figure will be recorded. Between 1951 and 1961, according to the Censuses, the net increase in long-distance commuting to the centre was only 60,000. In addition, the net increase of 100,000 workers in the rest of London probably meant a net increase of 100,000 commuters into Greater London from outside, but most of these were not travelling very long distances. In so far as the evidence permits, then, long-distance commuting has not increased as fast as the pessimists thought. And as already noted, since 1964 the number of commuters into central London seems actually to have declined. Notably, the mainly long-distance British Rail commuters share in the general decline.

Two separate pieces of research, in fact, now indicate that over a long period central London's commuting influence has extended much less spectacularly than many observers have believed.[1] Between 1921 and 1961, in terms of the percentages of resident employed workers who commuted to the major area of employment of Greater London, the commuting field extended quite markedly, but only within about 25 miles of the centre. Beyond 25 miles, even in 1961, London's commuting influence diminished very rapidly save along one or two exceptionally fast lines, like those to Southend and Brighton. The explanation may lie in the really significant

[1] Roger Leigh, 'Regression Analysis of the Journey to Work to Central London, 1951', *London School of Economics Graduate Geography Discussion Paper No. 2* (1967); Patricia Ellman, *Report of the Socio-Geographic Enquiry*, in: Royal Commission on Local Government in England, Research Papers No. 1, *Local Government in South-East England* (Greater London Group, London School of Economics and Political Science) (H.M.S.O. 1967).

phenomenon of the intervening forty years: the growth of about a dozen independent centres of employment in the outer metropolitan area, between twenty and forty miles from central London. None of them had a very significant commuting field in 1921; by 1961 their catchment areas had the clear effect of preventing the extension of the London commuting area, especially west and north west of London. The most important single trend in the economy of South East England is this gradual transition from a region dominated by a single metropolitan centre, to the poly-centric urban region of the future.

It is the future of these outer centres, therefore, that really provides the clue to the development of the London region up to A.D. 2000. And here, the late 1960s provide a rather melancholy record of contradictory policies. If development were not subject to controls, there seems little doubt about what would be happening in this outer metropolitan area. There would be a substantial decentralization of factory employ-ment out of Greater London, and an increasing amount of decentralized routine office employment. This basic employment would generate incomes which, together with the relatively high incomes of many London commuters, would in turn support a very heavy superstructure of service employment. The most useful rules of thumb for government policy might be to try to decentralize factory employment as far as possible, and even out of the region, wherever this was feasible; but to allow offices to locate in the new towns, where they could perform a valuable role in helping to balance the notorious over-reliance on factory industry there. But the Government, bent on diverting growth out of the region altogether, continues to restrict permission to develop offices anywhere in the South East. This is coupled with an equally severe limitation on the granting of IDCs for factory development.

Almost certainly, this policy is misconceived because it cannot do anyone any good and may do a lot of people harm. Even for factory employment, the careful calcu-lations of the economist A. E. Holmans have shown that controls have severe limitations. In this sector the controls have operated, though with varying degrees of severity, since 1945. Yet Holmans concludes that of the total growth of factory employment in the South East from 1951 to 1961, amounting to 590,000, less than one quarter could have been affected by Industrial Development Certificates. The rest took place mainly through small-scale increases in employment, year by year, which passed through the meshes of the control net. To try to control increases like these, Holmans rightly argues, would have meant an impossibly large and complex bureau-cratic apparatus.[1] The Government did all it could; but it could not stem the natural tendency of thousands of plants to extend *in situ*. If this is true of factories, it is undoubtedly even truer of offices. Repeatedly, the Location of Offices Bureau has observed the willingness of many firms to move, but not more than a critical 'contact distance' from central London. If they are not allowed to move here, they will stay where they are—often in unsuitable premises, until the inspectors catch up with them.

[1] A. E. Holmans, 'Industrial Development Certificates and Control of the Growth of employment in South-East England', *Urban Studies*, 1 (1964), pp. 138–152.

Since location in London is undoubtedly accompanied by some congestion and journey to work effects, and location in new towns normally will not be so accompanied, the case for the present policy seems to be non-existent.

Both in manufacturing and services, the fact is that employment growth in the South East is still associated with the simple fact, first noted by Professor J. Harry Jones in the Barlow Report, of the regional structural effect: the South East grows because the structure of its economy is better geared to growth than that of other regions. True, a much publicized article in the *National Institute Economic Review*, in 1963,[1] appeared to contradict this thesis; its analysis showed that a differential growth effect, the effect whereby one industry grows faster in a given region than in another given region, was more important in many regional cases. But this largely arose because the analysis was based in the very large and heterogeneous industrial categories formed by the many orders of the Standard Industrial Classification: the engineering industry appears to grow much faster in London than in Lancashire, because it is a different sort of engineering industry. A similar analysis of manufacturing industry in the 1964 *South East Study*, based on the much finer minimum headings, shows the structural effect very decisively.[2] Thus in 1962, the South East had 54·7 per cent of employment in those industries that had shown the best growth record over the previous three years; the northern part of England had only 22·7 per cent. In the 1965 *National Plan*, a revised version of the National Institute analysis, which was apparently based on a much finer industrial subdivision, showed that in every region the structural effect was decisive.[3] Though the Government may do its utmost to rectify this imbalance, all the evidence is that it will continue to tell. This is why the official forward projections of population have to assume continuing migration out of the unfortunate regions, and why the South East is assumed to have such a large proportion of the additions to the working age labour force during the 1970s.

[1] 'The Regional Problem', *National Institute Economic Review*, 25 (August 1963), Table 3, p. 41.

[2] *The South East Study* (H.M.S.O. 1964), Appendix Table 23.

[3] *The National Plan* (Cmnd. 2764, H.M.S.O. 1965), Table 8.7 and Appendix A, paras. 13–15. No indication was given of the actual industrial breakdown used.

CHAPTER 4

People and Homes 2000

I ended the last chapter by suggesting in broad terms how the expansion of jobs might be planned within the London Region so as to minimize the burden, both human and economic, of commuting and traffic congestion at the centre. We need now to see how this is to be combined with the job of building houses and flats and all the necessary social facilities that make up civilized urban life in the twentieth century. In this chapter I am chiefly concerned to estimate future *numbers* of people, household groups, and homes. I look first at the estimates made in the plans of the later wartime and early postwar periods, to see how far events have justified them. I conclude that they have not been very reliable pointers and that it is necessary to do the social sums again. Then I make broad estimates of the future population of the London Region up to 2000. I look in more detail at the way people are likely to group themselves into households during the same period, and use these facts to make estimates of total demands for homes. Then I turn to look at the supply of existing homes, and estimate the likely demand on the building industry for new homes. Lastly I consider where, in broad terms, we should build the homes within the Region. I am not however concerned in this chapter with detailed siting; that I take up in Chapter 6.

The section on population estimates is highly technical and some general readers may prefer to avoid it, looking only at the table which summarizes the conclusions on page 110.

The Abercrombie Plans and After

The Barlow Report appeared in 1940. In 1943 and 1944 Professor Patrick Abercrombie took its basic recommendations and applied them to the detailed planning of the London Region. His scheme for a new pattern of life and work for ten million people is contained in the two great advisory plans—the County of London Plan, which he produced jointly with J. H. Forshaw for the London County Council in 1943; and the Greater London[1] Plan, for the Coalition Government in 1944.

For this region, Abercrombie made the following population plan.

(1) The total population of the region would remain static, at just over ten million people. (This would mean a virtually static population for the wider London Region also, at eleven and a quarter million; according to the detailed proposals a decline of 100,000 would take place.) This was a fundamental assumption based on the Barlow recommendations. It presupposed that there would be no natural increase within the Region, and no net immigration.

(2) Within the Region the County of London Plan proposed first that the L.C.C. area should be replanned at a standard net residential density of 136 persons per acre (with variations at the centre and the edges). This would mean that three-quarters of a million people would need to go elsewhere: 618,000 of them in schemes of planned decentralization.

(3) Then there were older built-up areas, just outside the L.C.C. area, like West Ham, Leyton and Willesden. These were also overcrowded and should be redeveloped at 100 or 75 persons per acre, which would mean that they would lose half a million people: 415,000 of them in planned decentralization schemes. Thus in all, the congested inner districts of the London Region would lose 1,033,000 people by planned movement and another quarter of a million by spontaneous movement; new homes must therefore be found for over a million and a quarter people.

(4) But these homes could not be found in the suburban zone, which stretched as far as the inner boundary of the Green Belt (approximately the outer edge of the Conurbation); the planned density there was the existing density of 50 per residential acre, and population would remain static. So the new homes must be found outside the Conurbation altogether.

(5) The Green Belt would accommodate 325,000 people in planned 'quasi-satellite' estates and extensions of existing towns. Some of this expansion was regarded as an unfortunate necessity; plans had been made and could not be altered.

(6) The Outer Country Ring—the zone beyond the Green Belt, stretching to the borders of the Abercrombie Region—must therefore provide most of the new homes for the expatriate Londoners. 677,000 of them would go here—402,000 into New Towns and 275,000 into expansions of existing towns.

(7) Another 168,000 would go outside the 'Abercrombie Region' altogether, but within a radius of 50 miles of London: that is mainly within the boundaries of the London Region as defined in this book.

(8) This would leave 100,000 people to be accommodated outside this zone, up to 100 miles from London. Like the 168,000 in the 50-mile ring, these would go into expansion of existing towns.

The net effect of these changes on the main Rings of the Region is set out in Table 5.

[1] On the definition of 'Greater London' here, see the footnote on page 48.

TABLE 5

THE ABERCROMBIE PROPOSALS

Sources: P. Abercrombie, *Greater London Plan 1944*; Ministry of Housing and Local Government, *Annual Report 1956*.
All populations in thousands

Area	1938 mid-year estimate	Proposed changes in population							Total proposed change	Ultimate population
		OUT		IN						
		planned	un-planned	Quasi-satellites planned	Expanding towns planned	Expanding towns un-planned	New towns planned	New towns un-planned		
L.C.C. Area	4063	−618	−119						−737	3326
Inner areas outside L.C.C.	1911	−415	−114						−529	1382
Suburbs	2366		−4						−4	2362
Conurbation	**8340**	**−1033**	**−237**						**−1270**	**7070**
Green Belt	977			+125	+200				+325	1302
Outer Country Ring*	1007				+261	+214	+383	+19	+677	1684
Abercrombie Region	**10324**	**−1033**	**−237**	**+125**	**+261**	**+214**	**+383**	**+19**	**−268**	**10056**
50-mile Ring	1074				+164	+4			+168	1242
London Region	**11398**	**−1033**	**−237**	**+125**	**+425**	**+218**	**+383**	**+19**	**−100**	**11298**
100-mile Ring					+100				+100	

(Brackets in the "Total proposed change" column: −737 and −529 grouped as −1266; +325 and +677 grouped as +1002. In the "Expanding towns planned" column: +261 and +275 bracketed.)

* Figures for the Outer Country Ring are residuals obtained by subtracting other proposals from the totals for the 'Abercrombie Region'.

In 1947 the Abercrombie proposals, somewhat modified by events, became accepted Government policy. A Ministry of Town and Country Planning memorandum accepted a population for the 'Abercrombie Region' of 10,053,000—only 3,000 less than the original Abercrombie proposal. It followed that the figure for ultimate decentralization—over a million and a quarter—was also accepted, though the detailed proposals in the memorandum provided for only 1,069,000; the balance of 198,000 would be housed under further proposals then being considered, one of which bore fruit in Basildon New Town in south Essex.

Plan and Reality

Thus amended, the Abercrombie Plan became the basis for the policies of the various planning authorities within the London Region. Under the Town and Country Planning Act of 1947, basic responsibility for planning passed from the hundreds of Borough, Urban and Rural District councils within the Region, to eighteen County and County Borough authorities. In the years following 1947 these planning authorities were required by the Act to prepare Development Plans covering the twenty years 1951–71, which were to be submitted for approval to the Minister. In Table 6 the population proposals in these Development Plans have been aggregated for the main concentric Rings of the London Region and have been compared with the Abercrombie Plans taken from Table 2. The result is curious. These plans, which were mainly approved by the Minister between 1954 and 1958, already provided for a population for the London Region much larger than Abercrombie had envisaged in 1944 or the Ministry had accepted in 1947. For the Abercrombie Region they planned for 10,891,000 (against Abercrombie's 10,056,000); for the wider London Region, for 12,508,000 (against 11,298,000). Partly this is the acceptance of a *fait accompli*; for the 1951 Census returns showed that the population of both Abercrombie and London Regions was already running above ultimate Abercrombie levels, though the population of the congested inner area had by then sunk nearly to the planned figure.

Thus was established a game of leapfrog between plan and reality, which between 1951 and 1961 continued with accelerated force. For the entire London Region, the Development Plans provided for population to grow by 842,000 from 1951 to 1971; the 1961 Census showed that 93 per cent of this increase had already occurred in the first decade of this period. For the Outer Ring alone, of the projected increase of 1,011,000 to 1971, 964,000 had arrived by 1961.

Planned and Unplanned Growth

But the plans were falsified in another way. Abercrombie foresaw growth in the outer part of the Region mainly as a matter of planned decentralization. Altogether, 1,033,000 Londoners would move by plan, 237,000 spontaneously. The latter minority would almost all be accommodated in town expansions within the 'Outer Country Ring' of the Abercrombie Region.

In fact the story has been very different. Nearly two-fifths of Abercrombie's planned moves—383,000—were to go to New Towns. By 1961 the eight London New Towns had added some 235,000 to the 1946 populations of their areas,[1] but

TABLE 6

TARGETS AND REALITY, 1944-71

Sources: *Greater London Plan 1944*; *Memorandum of Ministry of Town and Country Planning on the Greater London Plan* (1947); Development Plans; *Censuses*, 1951 and 1961. (Figures for Outer Ring include some subsequent to original Development Plan, plus arbitrary estimates where no exact forecasts existed.)

| | all populations in thousands | | | | | | |
	1938 mid-year estimate	1944 Aber-crombie 'Ultimate' popula-tion	1951 Census	1971 Target in Develop-ment Plans	1961 Census	1951-71 Projected Change	1951-61 Actual Change
London Region	**11398**	**11298**	**11665**	**12508**	**12453**	**+843**	**+788**
Abercrombie Region	**10324**	**10056**	**10343**	**10891**	**10842**	**+548**	**+499**
Conurbation	**8340**	**7070**	**8348**	**8180**	**8172**	**−168**	**−176**
Outer Ring	3058	4224	3317	4328	4281	+1011	+964
Suburban Ring:	4277	3744	5000	5030	4977	+30	−23
Suburbs Proper	1911	2362	3274	3380	3359	+106	+85
Inner areas out-side L.C.C. Area	2366	1382	1726	1650	1618	−76	−108
L.C.C. Area	4063	3326	3348	3150	3195	−198	−153

not all these by any means were immigrants: the natural increase in these towns has been very high. The eight towns had achieved by 1961 over half their Abercrombie targets.[2] But beyond this almost exactly half Abercrombie's planned moves—525,000 —were to go into expansions of existing towns; and here the record is one of very

[1] Estimate from *1961 Census, Preliminary Report*, Table J, and *Report of the Ministry of Housing and Local Government for 1960*, 82.

[2] Present agreed plans are for the New Towns to take about 70,000 more people (over their 1946 populations) than Abercrombie postulated. In summer 1962 the Minister of Housing and Local Government proposed that the target size of Harlow and Stevenage be increased by another 60,000 apiece; agreement has not yet been reached, though the Stevenage Development Corporation have welcomed the proposal (February 1963).

slow progress. The instrument finally chosen for the purpose was the Town Development Act, drafted in the dying days of Labour rule and enacted by the Conservatives in 1952. It aims to promote the expansion by an extremely cumbersome procedure of agreement between the overcrowded 'exporting' district and the 'receiving' district council; the Government has to approve, and then pays half the capital cost of new water and sewerage schemes, while the 'exporting' authority pays a housing grant. Since 1952 the L.C.C., after endless frustrations and delays, has made agreements with seventeen authorities between forty and eighty miles from London; about half a dozen further agreements were on the way at the end of 1962. In addition the overcrowded authorities of inner Essex have made an agreement with Canvey Island and those of inner Surrey with Frimley and Camberley. But the schemes agreed by Greater London authorities up to end-1962 provide for only about 180,000 people; other schemes, in various stages of negotiation, may provide for another 55,000. The L.C.C. admit that the actual transfers may take a long time; in fact up to the end of 1962 only about 28,000 people had moved from Greater London under expansion schemes, 24,000 of them from the L.C.C. area.[1]

So the great explosion of population in the Outer Ring between 1951 and 1961 was also housed by the private builder. Table 7 shows that between 1952 and

TABLE 7

PUBLIC AND PRIVATE BUILDING, 1952–9

Source: Ministry of Housing and Local Government Returns, reclassified by London Transport

| | New Dwellings, June 1952–June 1959 | | | | |
	TOTAL	Public	per cent	Private	per cent
ENGLAND AND WALES	1,878,605	1,168,274	62·2	710,331	37·8
LONDON REGION	485,011	279,267	57·6	205,744	42·4
Outer Ring	290,040	151,463	52·2	138,577	47·8
Outer Part	109,062	42,850	39·3	66,212	60·7
Inner Part	180,978	108,613	60·0	72,365	40·0
Suburban Ring	119,120	59,872	50·2	59,248	49·8
L.C.C. Area	75,851	67,932	89·6	7,919	10·4

1959 about half the new dwellings built in this ring were privately built. But within the Outer Ring there was an important distinction between the inner part and the outer part. In the inner part Abercrombie made specific proposals, involving a

[1] This paragraph is based on 'Expansion of Country Towns', *Town and Country Planning*, 30 (1962), 439–44; and L.C.C. Press Notice of 12 December 1962.

public : private building ratio of 3 : 1. The actual ratio in 1952–9 was exactly 3 : 2; 108,000 dwellings were built by public enterprise, about half of them by the New Town Corporations. In the outer part, where the Abercrombie proposals were less explicit and no New Towns were planned, public enterprise built only 43,000 dwellings in 1952–9; the public : private ratio was 2 : 3.

The central feature of decentralization policy in the fifties, therefore, was the failure to meet the rapid expansion of population in the outermost part of the London Region (the thirty-fifty mile ring) by the designation of more New Towns, which should have been provided on a scale at least equal to the plans for the original eight towns in the twenty-thirty mile ring. The result is only too woefully evident in any ride across the face of the Home Counties. Admitted, the average postwar effort of the speculative builder is a vast improvement on the horrific suburban sprawl of the thirties. Partly this reflects higher standards of popular taste; mainly it is attributable to the system of national land use planning set up under the 1947 Act. The speculative builder is no longer free—as, with rare exceptions, he was in the thirties—to put his houses where he likes; he must submit his plans to the local planning authority for approval. The County Planning Authorities of the Outer Ring have pursued the general policy of establishing large areas as extensions of the Metropolitan Green Belt; they have permitted development only in clearly defined areas within the existing towns, plus very isolated infillings of the villages. They also have exercised some influence over detailed layout. Ribbon development and sporadic infilling, such as disfigured the main roads of the Suburban Ring in the twenties and thirties, are no more. But whatever may have been the ideals of the 1947 Act, in effect it established a completely negative system of planning; initiative remained with the private developers, and planning officers were often too overworked to give every plan the detailed criticism and improvement it needed. The result is a very widespread failure of planning at the most local, intimate level, where its impact on people is most direct and immediate—immediately around their own homes. Given the economic facts of life which I described in the last chapter, it was inevitable, and foreseeable, that people would demand new houses in large numbers in this outer zone. That they should have been fobbed off with something second-rate, both technically and visually, was by no means inevitable; it means that there was something seriously wrong with the whole machinery of planning.

The Need for a New Policy

In the London Region during the fifties, then, the plans have been overwhelmed by events: something which should never have happened. Wherein lies the failure?

The root cause was the inadequacy of the projections of population in the plans of 1943–4. Here two misconceptions were at fault. In the first place, as I tried to show in the last chapter, Barlow was mistaken in lightly assuming that the growth of employment of all sorts could be limited in the London Region; though in

Abercrombie's hands the Barlow recommendation was turned into a crude absolute limitation on all further jobs, which was economic nonsense. Neither Barlow nor Abercrombie, in fact, showed any proper sense of the working of the forces of economic history. Table 8 shows that the population of the London Region rose much faster in the Victorian period than after 1918 (as did the country's); and that the share of London Region in the national increase during 1931–51, or 1951–61, was not substantially different from its share in the nineteenth century.[1] The only difference is that since 1900, higher living standards and better transport have allowed the diffusion of homes at lower densities over much wider areas; that is all.

TABLE 8

POPULATION: LONDON REGION AND ENGLAND WALES, 1861–1961

Source: Censuses

	1861	1921	1931	1951	1961
London Region					
population, thousands	4235·0	9577·0	10627·1	11665·4	12453·4
increase, thousands		5342·0	1050·1	1038·3	788·0
increase per cent per annum		1·4	1·0	0·5	0·7
England and Wales					
population, thousands	20066·2	37886·7	39952·4	43757·9	46071·6
increase, thousands		17820·5	2065·7	3805·5	2313·7
increase per cent per annum		1·0	0·5	0·5	0·5
London Region increase as per cent England and Wales increase		30·0	50·8	27·3	34·1

To Barlow's misconceptions about the growth of employment, Abercrombie added misconceptions of his own about demography, borrowed from the population experts of the thirties. All the expectations of the time were that the birth rate would continue to fall as it had done throughout the interwar period, while death rates would fall less fast, so that population would first only just reproduce itself, and then decline. Consequently no specific provision was made at all in the Greater London Plan for natural increase; its estimates assume a static population. Not until 1949 did the Royal Commission on Population publicize the radical change resulting from the 'baby boom' of the late war and immediate postwar years. This boom has continued—to the experts' surprise—and the Registrar-General has had to revise upwards his estimates of future population regularly throughout the fifties. Table 9 shows the result of this changed situation in the London Region during

[1] Cf. the historical analysis of employment growth, page 47.

the decade 1951–61. The figures for natural increase are estimates only, because they have had to be produced by extrapolation; but the general point is evident. Of the increase of 788,000, two-thirds was due to natural increase. To keep the population of the London Region static, it would have been necessary not only to have prevented any net immigration, but to have deported 531,000 Londoners to compensate for this natural increase. A task of this order might deter even the most enthusiastic supporter of provincial industry or culture.

TABLE 9

LONDON REGION: POPULATION INCREASES, BY RINGS, 1951–61

Source: Census 1961, Preliminary Report; Extrapolation from Registrar-General's Annual Reviews, 1951–59

all figures in thousands	Population, 1961	Change, 1951–61 (plus unless indicated)		
		total	natural	migration
England and Wales	46071·6	2313·7	1961·7	352·0
London Region	12453·4	788·0	530·9	257·1
Outer Ring	4281·5	964·1	221·3	742·8
Suburban Ring	4976·8	−23·3	164·7	188·0
L.C.C. Area	3195·1	−152·8	145·0	−297·8

So Abercrombie was very wrong; and no one corrected him in time. Perhaps the statisticians were too slow in recording what had happened; the researchers in analysing the statistics; the administrators in accepting the conclusions of the researchers; the politicians in accepting the implications. Whatever the cause, the Outer Ring of the London Region—the most dynamic major area of Britain in the nineteen-fifties—has grown half-planned, if that. This fact has important implications for the near future. For the amount of land allocated for development in the plans of the various authorities depended directly on their population estimates; and these depended somewhat less directly on Abercrombie. The result became one of Britain's worst-kept public secrets: though the Ministry of Housing and Local Government did not reveal the precise amount of building land left in the Region, it was acknowledged that there was very little left. J. R. James, chief planner at the Ministry, admitted in October 1961 that there had been a grave under-estimate of the forces that had piled people up in the 'growth areas' of South-east England and the Midlands, and forecast that at least two million more people would have to be accommodated in the zone at the edge of the London Region, forty to seventy miles from central London, by 1980.[1] Successive Ministers of Housing and Local Government have reiterated that more land must be found for building in the rural areas around the country towns of this zone.

[1] Town and Country Planning Association Annual Conference, October 1961.

The Future Population of London Region

The critical need, then, is for new demographic forecasts. The Ministry have their own estimates for the period up to 1980. In the sections that follow, I have made separate estimates both for 1960–80 and 1980–2000. Inevitably, the estimates for the second twenty-year period are more hazardous. They depend to a large extent on the behaviour of people still unborn; when they marry, how many children they have. Still I think it is right to make them. Once made, they can be remade to fit changed circumstances. The real need is to keep the estimates under continuous review; which was precisely what the planning machine failed to do during the early fifties.

TABLE 10

PROJECTED POPULATION OF LONDON REGION, 1961–1980–2000, ON VARIOUS ASSUMPTIONS

Source: Registrar-General's estimates of future population of England and Wales

all figures in thousands	1961 actual	1980	2000
(1) 30 per cent national increase		**+1305**	**+1567**
London Region	**12453**	**13758**	**15325**
Outer Ring	4281	5587	7154
Suburban Ring	4977	4977	4977
L.C.C. Area	3195	3195	3195
(2) 33·3 per cent national increase		**+1449**	**+1740**
London Region	**12453**	**13902**	**15642**
Outer Ring	4281	5731	7471
Suburban Ring	4977	4977	4977
L.C.C. Area	3195	3195	3195
(3) 35 per cent national increase		**+1523**	**+1828**
London Region	**12453**	**13976**	**15804**
Outer Ring	4281	5805	7633
Suburban Ring	4977	4977	4977
L.C.C. Area	3195	3195	3195

It is fair to assume from Table 5 that there is no present reasonable likelihood that the share of the London Region in the net national increase will be less than 30 per cent, while it may approach 35 per cent, as it has during 1951–61. The Registrar-General's current estimate is that the population of England and Wales will rise by 4,350,000 to 50,422,000 between 1961 and 1980, and then by 5,224,000 to 55,646,000 between 1980 and 2000. On this basis Table 10 makes various estimates of the population of London Region on different assumptions about the share of national growth. In the rest of this chapter the highest assumption—35 per cent—will be used as a close approximation to the actual rate during 1951–61. This gives a population for

94

London Region rising from 12,453,000 in 1961 by 1,523,000 to 13,976,000 in 1980 and then by 1,828,000 to 15,804,000 in 2000. This last figure is nearly half a million more than the estimate based on the lowest, or 30 per cent assumption.

In Table 11, and in the rest of this chapter, I assume that the future growth of population in London Region must all be accommodated in the Outer Ring; that there will be no net increase in the L.C.C. Area or the Suburban Ring. This is not to deny that the net figures may conceal very large counterflows of population, in and out. Continued natural increase of population in the inner areas will cause continued net emigration; the net emigration figures themselves will conceal even bigger in- and out-flows. The real significance of these flows is that they may change the demographic and social composition of the population at large. Observers believe—though it cannot be proved precisely until publication of the 1961 Census Migration Report —that there is a continuing and growing immigration of young professional people, relatively highly educated and highly paid, into certain parts of inner London; that though many of them move out again when they marry or have children, there is yet a significant and growing *net* immigration of such people into the inner area, which may be a powerful contributory cause of the housing problem in London since 1950.[1] I shall have cause to notice this tendency when I turn to the household patterns of the London population.

But at this stage only absolute numbers count. The objection that may be made is that the extra people cannot be accommodated in the Outer Ring of the London Region. This is fallacious. To house three and a half million extra people there within forty years, would mean raising the 1961 population of the Outer Ring by about two-thirds. The present gross density of the Ring is only 2 persons per acre, compared with 14 for the Suburban Ring, which was developed in ways notoriously wasteful of land. It is clear that properly planned development of the Outer Ring would not notably disturb the present balance of built-up and open land; and few people who know this Ring well would argue that by and large, the present balance was unsatisfactory.

The Significance of Household Patterns

For the planning of homes, though, the important statistics are not those of individuals, but those of individuals grouped into households; that is, according to the Census, 'single persons living alone or groups of individuals voluntarily living together under a single menage in the sense of sharing the same living room or eating at the same table.'[2]

Perhaps the most striking single social characteristic of the London Region is its low average household size: 3·08 people in 1951, against 3·19 for England and Wales

[1] Cf. Christine Cockburn, 'Rented Housing in Central London', *The Guardian*, 21 February 1963.

[2] *Census 1951, Housing Report*, xvi.

as a whole. But while the Outer Ring recorded the national average—3·19—and the Suburban Ring just below—3·17—in the County of London the average fell to 2·82 and in certain Boroughs to even lower figures: 2·45 in the City, Chelsea and Hampstead, 2·44 in Kensington and Paddington, and 2·30 in Westminster.[1] Table 11 shows that these averages reflect important local differences in the proportions of households in different sizes. Big households (6 people and over) are everywhere rare, and two-person households do not show much variation. But while the inner zone has a very high proportion of one-person households and a low proportion of three-to-five person households, in the outer rings the proportions approach near the national average.

TABLE 11

SIZE OF HOUSEHOLD, 1951

Source: Census 1951, Housing and County Tables

	Number of persons in Household percentages of all Households				Average number in Household
	1	2	3–5	6 and over	
ENGLAND AND WALES	10·7	27·6	53·8	7·8	3·19
LONDON REGION	12·4	28·3	52·9	6·5	3·08
Outer Ring	9·5	28·3	54·8	7·4	3·19
Suburban Ring	9·2	27·8	56·5	6·5	3·17
L.C.C. Area	19·7	29·3	45·5	5·5	2·82
Westminster City and Met. B.	34·9	31·0	30·9	3·2	2·30

What is the explanation of these differences? One important reason for them is differences in demographic structure. Table 12 shows for the London Region in 1951 the relationship between demographic structure and household formation. In this table the 'Headship Rate' is the proportion of members of the demographic group who are heads of households, expressed as a percentage. Married males naturally have a very high headship rate, but the over-sixties form smaller average households than do the younger ones, because their children have grown up and formed separate households. Non-married people of both sexes have lower headship rates because they are either still living in households with married heads (the bulk of the age 15–40 group) or with each other (the older age-groups, who tend to have headship rates of about 50 and average households of about 2 persons). Table 12 shows that household formation in London Region *as a whole* does not diverge strikingly from

[1] 1961 figures: 2·66 in L.C.C. area, 2·27 in Hampstead, 2·24 in Paddington, 2·22 in City, 2·21 in Kensington, 2·12 in Chelsea, 2·09 in Marylebone, 2·05 in Westminster. Thus certain boroughs have become *more* divergent in their household size since 1951. *Census* 1961, County Report, *London*, Table 3.

TABLE 12

DEMOGRAPHIC GROUPS AND HOUSEHOLD STRUCTURES, ENGLAND AND WALES, LONDON REGION AND RINGS, 1951[1]

Source: Census 1951, General, County and Conurbation Tables

Demographic Group	England and Wales			London Region		
	Per cent population	Head-ship Rate	Average House-hold	Per cent population	Head-ship Rate	Average House-hold
Large Household Formers*	**20·3**	**89·0**	**3·6**	**20·7**	**91·5**	**3·5**
Married Males, under 40	9·1	80·2	3·6	9·2	84·2	3·5
Married Males, 40–60	11·2	96·2	3·7	11·5	97·4	3·6
Small Household Formers†	**17·2**	**65·9**	**2·5**	**17·5**	**64·7**	**2·4**
Married Males, 60 plus	4·8	96·6	2·9	4·8	96·7	2·9
Non-married Males, 40–60	1·6	37·2	2·5	1·6	38·2	2·2
Non-married Males, 60 plus	1·9	56·5	2·4	1·7	54·8	2·2
Non-married Females, 40–60	3·5	48·1	2·3	3·8	47·7	2·2
Non-married Females, 60 plus	5·4	62·1	2·1	5·6	59·7	1·9
Non-household Formers‡	**62·4**	—	—	**61·8**	—	—
Non-married, 15–40 ⎱ both	15·0	3·7	2·4	15·1	5·4	2·0
Children under 15 ⎰ sexes	22·1	—	—	21·1	—	—
Married females	25·3	—	—	25·6	—	—
Average size of Household			3·2			3·1

Demographic Group	Outer Ring			Suburban Ring			L.C.C. Area		
	P'cent popu-lation	Head-ship Rate	Aver. house-hold	P'cent popu-lation	Head-ship Rate	Aver. house-hold	P'cent popu-lation	Head-ship Rate	Aver. house-hold
Large Household Formers*	**20·1**	**89·5**	**3·7**	**21·5**	**92·3**	**3·5**	**20·0**	**92·6**	**3·4**
Married Males, under 40	8·9	81·5	3·6	9·0	84·1	3·5	9·7	87·4	3·3
Married Males, 40–60	11·2	95·9	3·8	12·5	98·3	3·5	10·3	97·6	3·5
Small Household Formers†	**17·5**	**62·8**	**2·5**	**16·2**	**63·6**	**2·5**	**19·6**	**68·2**	**2·2**
Married Males, 60 plus	5·2	95·6	2·9	4·6	96·7	2·9	4·5	98·3	2·8
Non-married Males, 40–60	1·5	31·7	2·0	1·4	37·3	2·7	2·2	44·9	1·9
Non-married Males, 60 plus	1·9	52·9	2·3	1·4	52·9	2·4	1·9	59·3	1·8
Non-married Females, 40–60	3·3	41·7	2·5	3·6	46·7	2·4	4·7	54·2	2·0
Non-married Females, 60 plus	5·6	56·9	2·0	5·2	55·7	2·0	6·3	67·9	1·8
Non-household Formers‡	**62·4**	—	—	**62·2**	—	—	**60·6**	—	—
Non-married, 15–40 ⎱ both	14·7	2·9	2·6	14·5	4·0	2·2	16·5	10·1	1·8
Children under 15 ⎰ sexes	22·2	—	—	21·2	—	—	19·5	—	—
Married Females	25·5	—	—	26·5	—	—	24·5	—	—
Average Size of Household			3·2			3·2			2·8

* **Large formers:** Average household 3 or over.

† **Small formers:** Average household under 3.   ‡ **Non-formers:** Headship Rate under 15·0.

[1] Figures for London Region (and consequently for Outer Ring) are based on aggregate figures for London and eight Home Counties, which are found to correspond demographically to London Region. In calculating average household size of different groups, certain arbitrary values have had to be assumed: thus 8–9 person households as average 8·5, and 10 person and over households as 11. No further breakdown of single persons (into unmarried, widowed, divorced) is possible, because London County tables do not make the analysis.

the national pattern. (The only significant difference is the higher headship rate and lower average household size of unmarried persons between 15 and 40; and the lower headship rates, coupled with lower average household size, among the older non-married people.) But within the Region there are very important differences. As percentages of total population, the large-household-formers (married males under 60) remain relatively constant from one Ring to another; but the proportion of the small-household-forming groups rises towards the centre of the Region and the proportion of non-household-forming groups falls. Headship rates rise for every group towards the centre for every group but especially sharply for the non-married, while the average household size falls. (There is of course a close and necessary relationship between headship rate and average household size; for the entire population, indeed, the relation is a simple inverse one.)

In his book *Housing Needs and Planning Policy*,[1] J. B. Cullingworth concluded that nationally, variations in household formation were explicable almost entirely in terms of the demographic structure, headship rates of various groups remaining constant. Cullingworth was not concerned with regional trends, though for many regions his conclusions would probably apply. But the inner part of London is highly anomalous. Thus if we apply the national headship rates to the actual numbers in the chief demographic groups in the inner (L.C.C.) area in 1951, the result is a shortfall of 95,000 households, and an increase in average household size from 2·82 to 3·08—the same as the London Region as a whole. The anomaly represents variations in social habit as between the L.C.C. area and the country as a whole. Again, Cullingworth concluded that in the whole country the increase of households between 1931 and 1951 could be explained almost entirely by changes in demographic structure; this holds good for the Outer and Suburban Rings of the London Region, but the L.C.C. area is once more anomalous. Here the population in households fell by 18·3 per cent but the number of households fell by only 0·8 per cent; projection by the Cullingworth method gives a figure 73,000, or 6 per cent too great. Of this anomaly rather less than half is the result of a change in the classification of households between 1931 and 1951, which exceptionally affected the County of London.[2] The other half, some 40,000 households, represents additional formation due to *increased headship rates* among certain groups. These cannot be identified because in 1931 there were no data for the calculation of headship rates. But to take an example, the half-million unmarried people between 15 and 40 in the L.C.C. area in 1951: an increase in headship rate of this group from 5 to 10 per cent would give 25,000 extra households. The most superficially likely explanation—though it is extremely speculative—is first an increase in the proportion of young adults who are heads of households (a result of the increasing migration of young professional,

[1] 1960.
[2] A change in the treatment of residents in boarding houses, affecting some 32,360 people in the L.C.C. area, who presumably almost all became 'one-person household heads'. (*Census* 1951, *London*, viii and footnote to Table 16.)

managerial and skilled people into inner London from all over the country); and secondly the increasing desertion of old people by their married offspring, due to the decentralization of working-class families out of traditional areas into distant housing estates and New Towns.

These are social changes which are likely to have a continuing and profound effect on household formation within inner London. Until the publication of the migration data of the 1961 Census—the first complete study of the subject ever undertaken by the Census authorities—all our interpretations of the changing social pattern of London have to be based on *net* changes, which are a very inadequate guide. Many observers believe that a certain pattern of migration is being established on a large scale in certain parts of inner London. Young unmarried people move in to complete their education in London, or while they begin their careers. As they marry and have families, most of them move out to the suburbs. These areas of inner London have therefore a very mobile young population—in Chelsea it is estimated that 25 per cent of the adult population move every year[1]—living in relatively small households. If this tendency continues, we should expect the number of households to fall much less fast than population, or to increase while population remains static.

Forecasting Household Formation

Because the inner L.C.C. area presents special problems, the job of forecasting the future household pattern of the London Region has to be split into two parts.

For the Suburban and Outer Rings, the 1931–51 trends showed that the demographic structure was approaching closer and closer to the national average; and that changes in household formation could be explained almost entirely by differences in demographic structure. Unfortunately the 1961 preliminary returns show that though this rule continued to prove satisfactory in the Outer Ring,[2] in the Suburban Ring it produced a serious shortfall in estimation compared with the actual figure of households. So in Table 13 the projected demographic structure has been based on the national pattern only in the Outer Ring; in the Suburban Ring it is assumed that the structure will remain as divergent as in 1951. Even then projection gives a shortfall of households for 1961, indicating that headship rates may have been rising between 1951 and 1961 in the Suburban Ring as they did between 1931 and 1951 in the Inner or L.C.C. area. However Table 14, which combines the demographic projections with alternative assumptions about headship rates, represents the best estimate of the likely numbers of different sorts of households in the Suburban and Outer Rings for 1980 and 2000 that we can make on the basis of the information at present available.[3]

[1] *L.C.C. Development Plan, First Review 1960*; County Planning Report, Vol. 1, para. 81.
[2] And for the whole country: see L. Needleman, 'A Long Term View of Housing', *National Institute Economic Review*, 18 (1961), 20.
[3] Early 1963.

TABLE 13

PROJECTED DEMOGRAPHIC STRUCTURE OF SUBURBAN AND OUTER RINGS
1961, 1980 AND 2000

Source: Registrar-General's Quarterly Report, 4th Quarter 1960, Appendix D; Report by
the Government Actuary on the Second Quarterly Review of the National Insurance Acts
(H.M.S.O. 1960), Table C; an assumed 35 per cent of national population increase in London
Region; demographic structure of Outer Ring same as England and Wales; demographic
structure of Suburban Ring same divergence as 1951.

All figures in thousands	1961			1980			2000		
	Suburban Ring	Outer Ring	Both Rings	Suburban Ring	Outer Ring	Both Rings	Suburban Ring	Outer Ring	Both Rings
Married Males:									
under 40	433	377	810	473	556	1029	513	791	1304
40–59	637	492	1129	577	596	1173	607	835	1442
60 plus	204	184	388	269	325	594	264	424	688
Non-married Males:									
40–59	70	69	139	45	65	110	30	63	93
60 plus	105	111	216	110	157	267	80	159	239
Non-married Females:									
40–59	159	133	292	90	96	186	55	76	131
60 plus	338	300	638	353	422	775	289	458	747
Non-married, both sexes:									
15–39	662	591	1253	627	762	1389	597	956	1553
Total Population	4977*	4281*	9259*	4977	5805	10784	4977	7633	12610

* Actual 1961 figures.

Projection for the L.C.C. area is confused by many imponderables. The demographic structure, already markedly divergent from national structure in 1931, became more so by 1951;[1] and headship rates rose during the same period. Between 1951 and 1961, either demographic structure has further diverged, or headship rates have further increased, or both; for projection on the basis of 1951 divergence and 1951 headship rates gives a shortfall of 32,000 households. So in making the projections in Table 15 I have included an alternative, more sophisticated hypothesis, which projects the increasing divergence of demographic structure between 1931 and 1951 forward, on a straight-line basis, to 1961, 1980 and 2000. For 1961, at any rate, this produces a projected figure close to the actual total of households. In both assumptions the population of the L.C.C. area is assumed static at the 1961 figure

[1] Coefficient of divergence (maximum 1.00): 1931 ·042, 1951 ·048. Cf. Outer and Suburban Rings combined: 1931 ·015, 1951 ·014

100

TABLE 14

HOUSEHOLD STRUCTURE, SUBURBAN AND OUTER RINGS, 1961, 1980 AND 2000,
ON TWO ALTERNATIVE ASSUMPTIONS

Based on Table 17

Assumption (A): 1951 Headship Rate for Ring.
Assumption (B): 1951 Headship Rate for England and Wales.

Heads of Households, thousands	1951 actual	1961 actual	1961 (A)	1961 (B)	1980 (A)	1980 (B)	2000 (A)	2000 (B)
Outer Ring								
Large Household Formers*	**590**		**779**	**776**	**1025**	**1019**	**1446**	**1437**
Married Males, under 40	238		307	302	453	446	645	634
Married Males, 40–60	351		472	474	572	573	801	803
Small Household Formers†	**361**		**483**	**517**	**695**	**735**	**802**	**844**
Married Males, 60 plus	162		176	178	311	314	405	410
Non-married Males, 40–60	16		22	26	21	24	20	23
Non-married Males, 60 plus	32		59	63	83	89	84	90
Non-married Females, 40–60	46		55	64	40	46	32	37
Non-married Females, 60 plus	105		171	186	240	262	261	284
Non-household Formers ‡	**14**		**17**	**22**	**22**	**28**	**28**	**35**
Non-married, 15–40, both sexes	14		17	22	22	28	28	35
Total Households	**965**	**1318**	**1279**	**1314**	**1742**	**1782**	**2276**	**2316**
Suburban Ring								
Large Household Formers*	**993**		**990**	**960**	**965**	**934**	**1028**	**995**
Married Males, under 40	380		364	347	397	379	431	411
Married Males, 40–60	613		626	613	568	555	597	584
Small Household Formers†	**517**		**540**	**569**	**574**	**602**	**495**	**516**
Married Males, 60 plus	224		197	197	260	260	255	255
Non-married Males, 40–60	26		26	26	17	17	11	11
Non-married Males, 60 plus	38		55	59	58	62	42	45
Non-married Females, 40–60	85		74	77	42	43	26	26
Non-married Females, 60 plus	144		188	210	197	220	161	179
Non-household Formers‡	**29**		**27**	**25**	**25**	**23**	**24**	**22**
Non-married, 15–40, both sexes	29		27	25	25	23	24	22
Total Households	**1539**	**1611**	**1558**	**1553**	**1563**	**1559**	**1547**	**1534**
Total Households, Outer and Suburban Rings	**2504**	**2929**	**2837**	**2867**	**3305**	**3341**	**3823**	**3850**

*†‡ For definitions see footnote to Table 9.

of 3,195,000,[1] and 1951 headship rates are assumed to prevail. If these estimates prove valid, then demographic changes should not greatly alter the number of households in inner London up to 2000; though about 1980 they will increase the

[1] The L.C.C.'s current estimate is that total population of the County of London will fall to 2,900,000 in 1972 and rise thereafter to an 'ultimate' figure of 3,330,000. L.C.C. Plan 1960, *op. cit.*, paras. 129 and 132.

numbers of small households by perhaps 20–40,000 and reduce the numbers of large households by a corresponding amount. Later the balance should be tipped the other way, and by 2000 there may be a larger proportion of large households than in 1951.

TABLE 15

HOUSEHOLD STRUCTURE, L.C.C. AREA, 1961, 1980 AND 2000,
ON TWO ALTERNATIVE ASSUMPTIONS

Assumed throughout: static population; 1951 Headship Rates.
    Assumption (A): 1951 divergence of demographic structure from England and Wales.
    Assumption (B): Increasing divergence from England and Wales demographic structure, observed 1931–51, projected on a straight line basis.

Heads of Households, thousands	1951	1961				1980		2000	
	actual	actual	(A)	(B)		(A)	(B)	(A)	(B)
Large Household Formers*	**621**		**585**	**590**		**578**	**592**	**619**	**643**
Married Males, under 40	283		276	289		285	323	307	370
Married Males, 40–60	338		309	301		293	270	312	273
Small Household Formers†	**444**		**440**	**453**		**470**	**488**	**408**	**452**
Married Males, 60 plus	147		151	151		166	166	163	163
Non-married Males, 40–60	33		29	32		24	35	17	38
Non-married Males, 60 plus	38		40	41		51	54	40	45
Non-married Females, 40–60	85		69	73		50	61	38	55
Non-married Females, 60 plus	142		152	156		178	171	150	152
Non-household Formers‡	**56**		**52**	**50**		**47**	**41**	**36**	**35**
Non-married, 15–40, both sexes	56		52	50		47	41	36	35
Total Households	**1121**	**1110**	**1077**	**1092**		**1095**	**1121**	**1063**	**1131**

*†‡ For definitions see footnote to Table 12.

Households and Housing Needs

Together Tables 14 and 15 give estimates of the likely numbers of households in London Region in 1980 and 2000. But how do they relate to the need for housing? The answer is that first, not all households necessarily need a separate dwelling; but second, there may be potential households which have never formed due to lack of accommodation. Corrections for both must be made from the 1951 Census figures.

For the first, Cullingworth has argued that a simple arbitrary criterion is not necessarily less realistic than a complicated one. Tests indeed show that for large areas like England and Wales, the London Region or the L.C.C. area, simple and complicated formulae give approximately similar results. In Table 16 I have therefore used Cullingworth's assumption for those households who will not want a separate dwelling: 25 per cent of all sharing households in 1951. This would give separate

102

accommodation to 30 per cent of one-person sharing households; 75 per cent of two-person sharing households; and 100 per cent of larger sharing households. But I have introduced also a higher standard: 20 per cent of all sharing households in 1951, which would give separate dwellings to 50 per cent of the one-person sharing households.

TABLE 16

CORRECTIONS FOR 'HOUSEHOLD NEED', 1951

	thousands of households							
	Total House-holds	Estimated Households not needing separate Dwellings		Esti-mated Poten-tial House-holds	Estimated Net Correction		Estimated Net Correction as per cent of total Households	
		(A)	(B)		(A)	(B)	(A)	(B)
London Region	3625	200	250	176	− 24	− 74	−0·7	−2·1
Outer Ring	965	18	23	47	29	24	3·0	2·5
Suburban Ring	1539	75	94	86	11	− 8	0·7	−0·5
L.C.C. Area	1121	107	134	43	− 64	− 91	− 5·7	−8·1

Assumption (A): 20 per cent of sharing Households do not need a separate Dwelling.
Assumption (B): 25 per cent of sharing Households do not need a separate Dwelling.

The other element—the 'potential' households—is very difficult to estimate. They have to be obtained from the detailed analysis of household composition in the sample tables of the 1951 Census for larger areas such as England and Wales, the Greater London Conurbation and the L.C.C. area.[1] These show that in addition to 'primary family units' some households contain separate 'family nuclei' —a married couple with children, a lone parent with children. Cullingworth assumes that many, if not all, of these nuclei would form separate households if opportunity offered. The sum is complicated on the one hand by 'family nuclei' who may not want to go, and on the other by close relatives within the 'primary family unit' who may want to move. It is simplest to assume these cancel each other out and to take the number of family nuclei as the number of potential households.

Table 16 sets out estimates both for the 'satisfied sharing households' and for 'potential households', and expresses the net correction as a percentage of total 1951 households. These percentages have been applied to the estimates of total future households in Tables 14 and 15 to obtain this final estimate of likely housing needs in 1961, 1980, and 2000:

[1] *Census 1951, One Per Cent Sample Tables*, Part II, Table VI.8. There are no details for London Region, so estimation is necessary.

HOUSEHOLDS NEEDING SEPARATE ACCOMMODATION
(thousands)

	1951		1961		1980		2000	
	max.	min.	max.	min.	max.	min.	max.	min.
LONDON REGION	3601	3550	4027	3974	4466	4337	5010	4836
Outer Ring	994	989	1358	1351	1835	1786	2385	2333
Suburban Ring	1550	1531	1622	1603	1574	1545	1558	1526
L.C.C. Area	1057	1030	1047	1020	1057	1006	1067	977

Thus the different assumptions made at various stages about demographic structure, headship rates and need for separate accommodation have produced very different maximum and minimum estimates. I think the maximum estimates are to be preferred, if only because they are based on assumptions that give a closer fit to 1961 actuality.

On these grounds, we shall need to find separate accommodation in the London Region for 440,000 extra households between 1961 and 1980, and for 544,000 more between 1980 and 2000. In all rings, demographic changes should inflate the proportion of small households about 1980 but should restore the balance roughly to 1951 levels by 2000.

The Supply of Housing

To see what demands these needs will place on the building industry, it is first necessary to discover how far the supply of dwellings falls short of demand at the present time. Table 17 does this for 1951 and 1961. It is based on the Census figures of all dwellings, occupied and vacant.[1] An arbitrary proportion—three per cent—has been deducted as a suitable vacancy rate. This is the figure suggested by Cullingworth as necessary to secure necessary elasticity in the housing market; it is considerably higher than actual average vacancy rates in 1951. The 1951 figures also contain a correction, suggested by Cullingworth, for what might be called 'quasi-dwellings': households which in 1951 were sharing dwellings, but which had reasonably separate essential facilities. I have used a narrower definition than Cullingworth: households with exclusive possession of all five listed facilities in the 1951 Census.[2]

Table 17 shows a serious and continuing shortage of housing in the London Region. It is heavily concentrated in the Suburban and Inner (L.C.C.) Rings of the Region; it has been reduced considerably in the decade 1951–61, especially in the L.C.C. area. This last fact is due to the quite remarkable increase in separate dwellings in the L.C.C. area in that decade: 135,000, or 16·6 per cent, in an area where new building on hitherto undeveloped land is negligible. Here, though not in the Outer or Suburban Rings or in the country as a whole, Table 18 shows considerable divergence between this figure and the Ministry returns for new housing and slum clearance. This could be explained by a change in the working definition of a dwelling

---

[1] 1961 figures are best possible estimate based on figures in *Census 1961, Preliminary Report*, which relate to *occupied* dwellings.

[2] Piped Water. Cooking Stove, Kitchen Sink, Water Closet, Fixed Bath.

104

between the 1951 and 1961 Censuses, which has artificially inflated the number of dwellings in 1961;[1] or by actual conversions of houses into separate dwellings, which do not figure in Ministry lists.[2] The most probable explanation is that many of the 1951 'quasi-dwellings' had by 1961 become real dwellings, either through change of definition or through actual conversion.

TABLE 17

HOUSING DEMAND AND SUPPLY, 1951 AND 1961

Sources: Censuses, 1951 and 1961

All figures in thousands	'Maximum' Corrected Demand	Total Dwellings Occupied and Vacant	'Quasi-Dwellings' (1951 only)	Total Dwellings and 'Quasi-Dwellings'	Less 3 per cent for Vacancies	Excess of Demand
1951:						
London Region	**3601**	**3124**	**90**	**3214**	**3118**	**483†**
Outer Ring	994	944	10	954	925	69
Suburban Ring	1550	1360	38	1398	1356	194
L.C.C. Area	1057	821	42	863	837	220
1961:						
London Region	**4027**	**3851***		**3851**	**3735**	**292†**
Outer Ring	1358	1353*		1353	1312	46
Suburban Ring	1622	1544*		1544	1498	124
L.C.C. Area	1047	955*		955	926	121

* The 1961 Census, Preliminary Report, shows occupied Dwellings plus an unknown number of unoccupied Dwellings. The estimate here is based on the 1961 figures and on the difference between occupied and total Dwellings in 1951.
† The Ministry estimate the deficiency for the Conurbation alone at 350,000 in 1951 and at 150,000 in 1961, as compared with 414,000 and 225,000 shown here. *London* (Cmnd. 1952, H.M.S.O. 1963), para. 38.

The figures for unsatisfied demand in Table 17, it must be emphasized, are based on what we ought ideally to provide: they are not statements of the actual shortage. For one thing, actual vacancy rates tend to be much lower than the three per cent postulated. In 1951 they were under two per cent, and if this still holds good the shortage in London Region may well be reduced by 80,000. For another thing, they include the estimated demands of all sorts of people who might never have thought consciously of having a separate dwelling, because it has never seemed in question. Nevertheless, the planner is interested in this ideal world, which people might

[1] 1951: '. . . a structurally separate dwelling . . . generally comprises any room or suite of rooms intended or used for habitation, having separate access to the street or to a common landing or staircase to which the public has access'. 1961: 'A building or part of a building which provides separate living quarters.' [2] Save for a small number which were grant-aided.

105

decently expect to live in; and Table 17 is an estimate of that. It shows that in addition to the demands from new households in the forty years up to 2000, we need nearly 300,000 extra dwellings in London Region *now*. A reasonable demand would be that these should be provided over a ten-year period.

TABLE 18

UNSATISFACTORY DWELLING UNITS, 1951

Source: Census 1951, County Reports

All figures in thousands	Total Dwelling Units (including 'Quasi-Dwellings'	Satis-factory Units (all facilities)	Semi-Satisfac-tory Units (no bath or share bath)	Unsatisfactory Dwelling Units	
				Low Standard	High Standard
All Dwellings:					
London Region	**3214**	**1932**	**600**	**682**	**1281**
Outer Ring	954	588	172	194	366
Suburban Ring	1398	969	205	224	428
L.C.C. Area	863	375	223	265	488
Shared Dwellings:					
London Region	**524**	**90**	**152**	**282**	**434**
Outer Ring	54	10	6	38	44
Suburban Ring	213	38	55	120	175
L.C.C. Area	256	42	91	123	214
Unshared Dwellings:					
London Region	**2621**	**1843**	**448**	**330**	**778**
Outer Ring	873	578	166	129	295
Suburban Ring	1164	931	150	83	233
L.C.C. Area	585	333	132	120	252
Unoccupied Dwellings:					
London Region	**69**				
Outer Ring	27				
Suburban Ring	20				
L.C.C. Area	22				

The final estimate in calculation of housing needs, and the most difficult of all to estimate, is the need to replace obsolescent housing. All observers have noticed the quite extraordinary paucity of information available in this country on the age of housing. But even were this information available, it would give no necessary indication of the degree of obsolescence. Some observers have insisted on a quite arbitrary requirement, such as the replacement of all houses over a century old.[1] In London

[1] Cf. L. Needleman, *op. cit.*, 24–5.

this would mean the complete destruction of huge areas of great architectural merit: Bloomsbury, South Kensington, Chelsea, Bayswater, Belgravia, Pimlico; Hampstead, Highgate, Dulwich and Blackheath villages. The 100-year target, useful as it may be for the rows of labourers' cottages in northern textile towns and mining villages, is quite misleading for inner London.

Neither do slum clearance targets provide a guide. The estimates made of unfit houses in 1955 were based on widely different standards of survey and even on different criteria.[1] For what they were worth, they showed that London Region had, relatively, a much smaller problem than other big industrial areas; and so did the inner (L.C.C.) area. The Region contained 65,000 'houses declared unfit' and the L.C.C. area 21,000, compared with Liverpool's 88,000 or Manchester's 68,000. Within the region, 71 per cent of these houses had been demolished by mid-1962; within the L.C.C. area, 83 per cent.[2]

Almost certainly, in inner London the definitions used by local medical officers of health were too narrow to include the real problem houses, as the Ministry now recognize. These are the big Victorian houses in multi-occupation, which represent London's most unfortunate inheritance from the nineteenth century. Speculatively built on the fringes of fashionable London, in North Kensington, Camden Town and Islington, they often remained half-built for years—a process which can hardly have done much good for their structure—and rapidly degenerated into multi-occupation by working-class families. The only satisfactory criterion here is lack of adequate facilities. As in defining 'quasi-dwellings', it seems reasonable to take as criterion the exclusive possession of all five listed criteria in the 1951 Census.[3] For comparison I have also used a 'lower' or Cullingworth criterion—exclusive possession of four, no bath or shared. Table 18 shows that on the high criterion 1,281,000 dwellings in London Region were obsolescent in 1951; on the low criterion 681,000. Eighty-three per cent of all dwellings in multi-occupation were obsolescent on the high standard compared with 40 per cent of all dwellings and 30 per cent of unshared dwellings. In the L.C.C. area 57 per cent of all dwellings and 84 per cent of shared dwellings were obsolescent. Comparable 1961 proportions for the L.C.C. area were 52 and 84 per cent; obsolescent units (high standard) totalled 465,000.[4]

Not only is obsolescence very difficult to define; it is very difficult to say what it means in terms of housing need. How far can obsolescent housing be renovated to

[1] *Slum Clearance* (Cmd. 9593, H.M.S.O. 1955), iii.

[2] Ministry of Housing and Local Government, *Housing Return, 30th Sept. 1962, Appendix* (Cmnd. 1853, H.M.S.O. 1962). The Ministry said another 16–20,000 would be declared unfit in the L.C.C. area by 1960: *Royal Commission on Local Government in Greater London, Memorandum of M.H.L.G.* (H.M.S.O. 1958), paras. 8–9.

[3] Since this was written F. T. Burnett and Sheila F. Scott have analysed provincial areas of unsatisfactory housing, using criteria of small dwellings and low rateable values as well as the criterion of household facilities. See 'A Survey of Housing Conditions in the Urban Areas of England and Wales', *Sociological Review*, N.S., 10 (1962), 40. It is not certain that these criteria would apply in the rather special circumstances of inner London.   [4] *Census 1961, London.*

provide satisfactory housing conditions? How much will have to be demolished and replaced completely? These are questions which must await a more complete survey of living conditions in the six and two-thirds million houses in England and Wales built before 1915. It is only possible to say here that these dwellings need some form of renewal.

Demand and Supply: The Final Sum

It is now possible to bring together the separate estimates of this chapter so as to provide a final figure of the likely demand for housing in the forty years 1961–2000. This is done in the table below.

	Excess of Demand 1961	Obsolescent Dwelling Units 1951		Increase of Households due to Demographic changes				Total Demand 1961–2000.	
				1961–80		1980–2000			
		high std.	low std.	max.	min.	max.	min.	max.	min.
				all figures in thousands					
London Region	292	1281	681	439	363	544	499	2556	1835
Outer Ring	46	366	419	477	435	550	547	1439	1222
Suburban Ring	124	428	223	–48	–58	–16	–19	488	270
L.C.C. Area	121	488	265	10	–14	10	–29	629	343

The final maximum estimate would mean the construction or conversion of 66,000 dwellings a year in London Region over forty years; the minimum estimate, 47,000 a year. Society might of course decide during these years to alter its standards: to decide, for example, that even a well-converted old building was no longer tolerable, so that a higher rate of renewal of building set in. But against this the estimates take no account of the undoubted decline in the numbers of obsolescent units since 1951. The significant fact is that in the decade 1951–61, housing construction in London has been running at about the maximum levels. Table 19 shows that the net increase of new buildings over slum clearance has been some 65,000 a year. But in the Outer Ring the rate was slightly above, in the Suburban Ring much above the maximum rate, while in the Inner Ring it only just reached the minimum rate: which provides a measure of the problem of renewal in this ring in the next forty years.

The estimate appears a very conservative one. But this is because it is an average estimate over a long period—forty years. The fact is that most of the effort should be spread not over the next forty years, but concentrated in the first twenty—or even the first ten. A twenty-year attack on the 1961 shortage and the obsolescent houses of 1951 would demand a maximum rate of construction of 106,000 units a year, a minimum rate of 70,000. This would mean a major remobilization of the economic resources of London Region and indeed of the country as a whole, since the problem of obsolescence is relatively much larger in provincial Britain than in London.

TABLE 19

INCREASE IN DWELLINGS, 1951–61

Source: Ministry of Housing and Local Government Returns; Censuses, 1951 and 1961

All figures in thousands	Ministry of Housing and Local Government Returns			Census returns Net increase
	New construction*	Slum clearance†	Net increase	
London Region	**693·0**	**39·7**	**653·3**	**726·7**
Outer Ring	414·5	14·1	400·4	408·6
Suburban Ring	170·1	8·6	161·5	183·6
L.C.C. Area	108·4	17·0	91·4	134·5

* Extrapolated from 1952–9 figures, as amended by London Transport Executive.
† Since 1955 when present slum clearance programme began.

It is one of the major political challenges of the next two decades, and it is a challenge which can almost certainly be met only by a massive shift of investment from the private to the public sector. The evident fact is that private enterprise, brilliantly capable though it may be of providing a great variety of consumer goods at prices people can afford, cannot economically produce the most essential consumer good of all. L. Needleman's study showed that two-thirds of households in the country still cannot afford the economic rent of a new house, and something like 90 per cent cannot afford to buy one out of income; on optimistic assumptions these proportions might fall to 40 per cent and 73 per cent by 1980.[1] In fact, most people who buy houses must do so by using capital in one form or another; in 1958 39 per cent of households in England (not Wales), and 36 per cent in the Greater London Conurbation, were owner-occupiers; by 1962 the figure for England (not Wales) had risen to 43 per cent.[2] Very roughly, therefore, another 30 per cent of households can buy if they use capital; if this proportion remains fixed, by 1980 three out of five households might be able to afford to buy their own dwelling. For at any rate part of the remainder, it seems clear that some form of subsidy, or building control, or both, will therefore be inevitable if we commit ourselves as a nation to decent housing standards for everyone within the foreseeable future. If this is done, by a crash programme, the demands on the building industry will fall greatly after 1980, because household changes will not continue to throw up extra demands at the same rate as in the recent past; this was the conclusion which Needleman drew from his study of national

[1] L. Needleman, op. cit., 27–9.
[2] D. V. Donnison, Christine Cockburn, T. Corlett, *Housing since the Rent Act* (Occasional Papers on Social Administration No. 3, Welwyn 1961), 13; D. V. Donnison, 'The Changing Pattern of Housing', *The Guardian*, 5 October 1962.

trends.[1] If by then the nation had accustomed itself to a high rate of investment in building—which would be a good thing both economically and socially—it could then afford the luxury of a faster rate of renewal than in the past; it could for instance begin to renew the Edwardian and early Georgian suburbs—Edmonton, Willesden, Wimbledon—in 1985 instead of, conceivably, 2015.

The Geography of Housing: The Density Argument

The estimates of the preceding pages have been based on one critical assumption, which I must now defend: that there will be no room for significant numbers of extra people in the Inner or Suburban Rings of the Conurbation, so that redevelopment there will be limited to replacement of obsolescent housing; the extra households will have to be housed in the Outer Ring of the Region, or possibly farther out.[2]

One school of architects and planners would attack this assumption. They would say that it is possible, and on planning grounds desirable, to rehouse many extra people within the Conurbation, by increasing the densities at present permitted in Development Plans. They argue on three grounds: economic (the most important), social and aesthetic. I will examine each in turn.

The economic argument is the necessity to save scarce land in a densely populated country such as ours, and especially in the highly urbanized parts such as the London Region. I think this argument fallacious, for four main reasons.

The first is the simple point, long recognized, that by increasing the net density of population on residential land, we do not increase by anything like the same proportion the number of people who can be accommodated within a given area, because of the necessary provision for community services: main roads, shops, schools, open space. Take as example the density which Abercrombie and Forshaw fixed as standard for the County of London: 136 people per net residential acre. This gives a gross density (taking into account 'community' land) of 71 persons per acre. Had they fixed instead a net density of 200 persons per acre, they would have increased the gross density only to 87 persons per acre.[3] This means, for instance, that had the whole vast Stepney-Poplar Comprehensive Redevelopment Area been developed at 200 instead of 136 persons per acre, the increase in accommodation would have been only 7,520 people: a negligible gain in view of the loss of amenity involved. True, as J. R. James has pointed out, the net saving in land is greater if the increase takes place at relatively low densities: at an open space and community service standard of

[1] L. Needleman, *op. cit.*, 21.

[2] Since this was written the Ministry of Housing and Local Government have stated their belief that room for 100,000 extra dwellings can be provided within the Conurbation between 1963 and 1973 by using new sites (as at Croydon Airport and Erith Marshes), by reallocation of land now used for non-residential purposes, by increased densities and by conversions. *London* (Cmnd. 1952, H.M.S.O. 1963), paras. 55–6. This however would make a very small impression on the total housing need up to 2000 as I have calculated it.

[3] *County of London Plan* (1943), 81–2.

8 acres per thousand people,[1] an increase in net density from 24 to 40 per acre saves 17 gross acres per thousand people, while an increase from 159 to 222 per acre would save only 1·8 acres per thousand.[2] So there is a strong case for developing the undeveloped parts of the London Region at a higher density than for increasing the already higher density in the Inner Ring. There is also an *a priori* case for re-developing the low-density Suburban Ring at a higher density: an argument which I examine later.

The second point is that the need to save land is not so axiomatic as is sometimes asserted. Even in the highly urbanized London Region only about 30 per cent of the total area is developed; and in the Outer Ring—the area really in question, where as we have already noticed the gross density of population is only about 2 per acre— some 80–85 per cent of the total area is still under agriculture or woodland.[3] (Nor is all the remaining 15–20 per cent 'urbanized': for Best's calculations indicate that in 1960, out of 5·1 million acres in England and Wales not under agriculture or wood-land, only 4·0 million acres represented 'urban development', though for southern English counties the relative discrepancy would almost undoubtedly be smaller.[4]) Here the 'high-density' planners ally with the farmers in claiming that we cannot afford to lose valuable farmland. But Wibberley has calculated that to replace the produce of *all* the land in the country (5–700,000 acres) likely to be lost to urban development in 1950–70, would require merely an increase of net output on the remaining land of some £1 per acre; while a scheme of planned intensification would alone yield £3·5 per acre within five years.[5] In fact Wyllie in 1954 estimated that over the decade 1940–50 farm output per acre in terms of calories increased on average by nearly 2·5 per cent per year, enough to offset in one year the expected loss of land over the next twenty years without any more ambitious additional form of improve-ment.[6]

Third, and most important, the value of farm produce is only one element—a very minor one—in the complex balance sheet of urban development. Since 1955 the technique of calculating this social balance sheet has been developed and sophisti-

[1] Abercrombie and Forshaw (above) assumed only 4.

[2] *The Guardian*, 29 September 1961. Cf. Ministry of Housing and Local Government, *Residential Areas: Higher Densities* (Planning Bulletin, No. 2, H.M.S.O. 1962), 5.

[3] These very approximate calculations are based on the total area under crops, grass and rough grazing in the counties concerned in 1959 (*Agricultural Statistics 1959*, H.M.S.O. 1961), plus an allowance for woodland based on the Forestry Commission *Census of Woodlands* 1947–9 (H.M.S.O 1952–3).

[4] Robin H. Best and J. T. Coppock, *The Changing Use of Land in Britain* (1962), 229. Compari-son between Best's 'urban' figure for Middlesex in 1950 (*ibid.*, 157) with agricultural returns for that date shows virtually no discrepancy unaccounted for.

[5] G. P. Wibberley, *Agriculture and Urban Growth* (1959), 117, 199–200.

[6] Quoted by P. A. Stone, 'The Economics of Housing and Urban Development', *Journal of the Royal Statistical Society*, Series A, 122 (1959), 460. Fertile Agricultural land is worth £5 per acre per annum. Cf. the same author's 'The Impact of Urban Development on the Use of Land and other Resources', *Journal of the Town Planning Institute*, 47 (1961), 128–34.

cated by economists, notably by P. A. Stone,[1] who calculated the costs of rehousing 154 people from a one-acre slum clearance site in a central urban area, all costs expressed on a comparable annual basis. At one extreme, they could all be rehoused on the site, in 12-storey blocks; at the other, only 70 of them could be rehoused on the site, in 2-storey blocks, the other 84 being decentralized into 2-storey houses on a peripheral site. The comparative costs are set out in Table 20, to which has been added an estimate (based on Stone's figures) for rehousing the decentralized 84 people in a *re*development of a low-density suburban area to a higher density. The least dense redevelopment at the centre, it is seen, is the cheapest. Most people would doubt this because of the fixed belief that high land costs compel dense development near the centre. But Stone shows that land costs are a negligible part of real annual costs. The savings in site and public utility costs with increases in density are less than the rise in maintenance and servicing costs which arise from use of high buildings. Another important conclusion is that redevelopment of suburban sites is extremely uneconomic. It can be justified only where the expected life of the existing development is short and its density low—as in the case of the L.C.C.'s Roehampton scheme and the private developments by Span and others in the Victorian mansion suburbs of London.

The calculations in Table 20 take no account of transport costs. Because of the savings in these, Stone estimates that the comparative advantage of putting population in new or expanding towns should probably be increased by £10–£15 per person as compared with central London. Table 20 is also based on provincial construction costs. In London Stone concludes that overspill development would prove, relatively, even more favourable.

Why, then, does redevelopment ever take place in the central areas at high densities? Stone shows that this is because for public authorities the balance of advantage lies the other way, because of the distorted structure of public finance. On one side, the grant of subsidies for high buildings represents a high proportion of total construction costs; on the other, the local authority which exports population may suffer through loss of marginal rate payments and of rate deficiency payments.

This argument leads to the fourth economic point, which is the simplest and perhaps the most striking: that higher densities mean higher costs, not merely to the community at large, but to the public purse. Sir F. Osborn in 1955[2] calculated the capitalized cost of central government subsidies on various sorts of local authority housing; some of his calculations are set out in Table 21. They show that while a 2-bedroom, 4-person house built at 15 dwellings per acre cost £698 in capitalized subsidies, a flat of the same size at 35 dwellings per acre cost £2,572 and at 60 per acre £2,700. £10,000 of capitalized subsidies would house 57 people in the houses, 15–16 people in the flats. Recalculation of the sum on the basis of the new 1961

[1] Stone, 1959, *ibid.*, Table 12, 448.
[2] F. J. Osborn, 'How Subsidies distort Housing Development', *Lloyds Bank Review*, N.S. 36 (April 1955), 25–38.

TABLE 20

COMPARATIVE ANNUAL COSTS OF HOUSING 154 PEOPLE IN CENTRAL AND
PERIPHERAL ESTATES

Source: P. A. Stone

			Type of central redevelopment				
			2-Storey Flats	3-Storey Flats	4-Storey Flats	5-Storey Flats	
						With Lifts	Without Lifts
Density of central redevelopment, persons per acre			70	91	108·5	122·5	122·5
Persons remaining to be rehoused elsewhere			84	63	45·5	31·5	31·5
Reduced costs* of construction in centre (*housing only*)			£9·0	£10·8	£12·8	£17·5	£14·1
Type of overspill development	Costs of housing overspill population in 2-Storey Houses, per person		£	£	£	£	£
(a) Town extension	Industrial move	£14·8	1850	1900	2050	2600	2200
(b) New Town	voluntary	£22·3	2500	2400	2400	2850	2400
(c) Town extension	Industrial move in-	£19·0	2250	2200	2250	2750	2300
(d) New Town	voluntary	£26·5	2850	2650	2600	3000	2550
(e) Suburban Redevelopment† (in 4-Storey Flats), 14 dwellings per acre. Costs per person		£67·2	6275	5217	4447	4261	3844

* Based on the fact that replacement of old buildings by newer ones, with longer life, creates 'improvement values'.

† Based on a 40 per cent 'improvement value' on existing buildings, which would be approximately correct for the average interwar suburb. 4-Storey Flats are the most economical type of suburban redevelopment under these conditions. My calculation, based on Stone's data.

Housing Act subsidies shows that £10,000 would house 109 people in the houses, 21–22 in the flats. Osborn concludes:

'On the face of things, we have drifted into a practice of encouraging financially, out of taxes collected from the whole nation, the maintenance of over-grown and over-concentrated urban fabrics and, in the case of large cities still growing, the continuance of a fundamentally uneconomic growth.'[1]

TABLE 21

THE COST OF HOUSING SUBSIDIES

Based on F. J. Osborn

	1955 Subsidy Rates			1961 Subsidy Rates		
	2-Bedroom 4-Person House	2-Bedroom 4-Person Flat		2-Bedroom 4-Person House	2-Bedroom 4-Person Flat	
		Case 1	Case 2		Case 1	Case 2
Floor area, square feet	800	750	750	800	750	750
Building Cost	£1440	£2500	£2500	£1600	£2750	£2750
Site cost per acre*	£3000	£29000	£60000	£3000	£30000	£70000
Density per acre, dwellings	15	35	60	15	35	60
Site cost per dwelling	£200	£829	£1000	£200	£860	£1020
Capitalized subsidy, per dwelling	£698	£2572	£2700	£368	£1809	£1928
Subsidy/Site Cost	2·3	3·1	2·7	1·8	2·1	1·9
Subsidy/Total Cost	43%	74%	77%	20%	50%	51%
Site Cost/Total Cost	12%	25%	29%	11%	24%	27%

* Including development costs (roads and dwellings).

The truth of this last assertion depends on a much more sophisticated social sum of the total costs of a big city than we now have; but we can agree with Osborn that it is not the State's business to be confusing the sum in this way. The argument remains the same as when Marshall made it in 1884, and Ebenezer Howard quoted him in 1898:

'. . . there are large classes of the population of London whose removal into the country would be in the long run economically advantageous . . . (when they) are very poorly paid, and do work which it is against all economic reason to have done where ground rent is high.'[2]

Faced with such economic arguments, the 'high-density' school have latterly showed sign of retreating to sociology. They have appealed to the work of the English school of sociology which has studied the patterns of 'traditional' working-class areas. A classic study in this genre, Young and Willmott on Bethnal Green, brought out the extraordinary wealth and complexity of community ties in such an area, arising from kinship ties and long residence:

[1] *Ibid.*, 35–6.
[2] A. Marshall, 'The Housing of the London Poor', *Contemporary Review*, 45 (1884), 224–7, quoted in E. Howard, *Garden Cities of Tomorrow* (1946 edition), 66.

'. . . when they are combined, as they are in Bethnal Green, they constitute a much more powerful force than when one exists without the other. Then people have a number of links, or ways of orienting themselves, to the same person: he was at school, he is a relative by marriage, he lives in a well-known neighbourhood.'[1]

But in Greenleigh, the L.C.C. estate where overspilled Bethnal Greeners were housed, everyone was a stranger, there was a sense of isolation. Most Bethnal Greeners—Young and Willmott argued—wanted to avoid this fate; they wanted to stay in their old neighbourhood, within the net of community, at any price; and the price would be high density redevelopment.

All this is true—within its frame of reference. But how wide is this? How typical is the 'traditional' working-class area of inner London? Clearly there is a contrasting working-class neighbourhood, characterized by rapid change of residence, many recent immigrants, relatively few old-established family links, and shallow communal roots; a pattern represented by London's great problem belt, the twilight zone which stretches through West London from Paddington to North Hammersmith.[2] Is it worth preserving this sort of community? On available indices of social malaise, we would beg leave to doubt. And again, how permanent is the traditional pattern likely to prove? Certainly, after a twenty-year period of conscription, it is no longer true to say (as Young and Willmott do) that working-class children haven't time to grow away from their families in adolescence.[3] The expatriate Bethnal Greeners managed, on Young and Willmott's evidence, to forge a new pattern of life for themselves readily enough: they had already got seven times as many telephones per head as Bethnal Green.[4] And when J. B. Cullingworth visited overspill families, from London and elsewhere, in Swindon in 1959, he found that though 98 per cent had left relatives behind and 70 per cent had relatives only in the place they had left, only 32 per cent said they disliked the separation and a mere 20 per cent thought it caused hardship either to their relatives or themselves. The complaints of exiled Londoners were not sociological, but severely economic: there was too limited a choice of jobs, too few neighbourhood shops, not enough variety of shops or entertainment in the town centre.[5]

At last, the sociological argument comes back to economics: how much are we willing to pay for social ties? Willing to pay, that is, in competition with all the other

[1] M. Young and P. Willmott, *Family and Kinship in East London* (1957), 92.

[2] On problem belts see the early Chicago sociologists, especially E. W. Burgess in R. E. Park, etc., *The City* (Chicago 1925), 54–9. Charles Booth mapped 'criminal streets' for London in the eighties (*Life and Labour*, Map Volume). Within London Terence Morris has studied *The Criminal Area* (1958) in Croydon, but there is no wider study of social malaise.

[3] Young and Willmott, *op. cit.*, 156. Cf. the perceptive account of a modern working-class adolescence in Alan Sillitoe's *Key to the Door* (1961).

[4] Young and Willmott, *op. cit.*, 131.

[5] J. B. Cullingworth, 'The Swindon Social Survey: A Second Report on the Social Implications of Overspill', *Sociological Review*, N.S., 9 (1961), 151–66. Proportions are of those with relatives alive.

good things that we might, as a society, be doing with our money instead? Would Bethnal Greeners like a high density flat, or a motor-car? The only way to find out is to give them an open-ended choice; which rules out any form of indirect subsidy to the sociologist-planners.

There is, however, a third argument for high density: the simplest, the least pretentious and the best. It says that we need a few high expensive buildings in London, for strictly aesthetic reasons. Wren and Gibbs and Hawkesmore, the argument runs, were subsidized by the authorities of the day to give London one of the finest skylines in the world; why should not the architects of today have the same advantage? The answer to this must be subjective. Mine is that here as elsewhere, the argument for a subsidy ought to be fought on the merits of the individual case, or on groups of cases; we ought to say we will pay so much extra for a given effect. This demands only that we give the decisions about spending money to people with sense and discrimination; and this is essential anyway for good public architecture, be it horizontal or vertical. Height has no merit of itself, as the South Bank proves.

The logical conclusion of the arguments in the preceding paragraphs would be that in inner London, we should stop redeveloping at the Abercrombie-Forshaw density of 136 (or more) people per net residential acre and go down to 60 or 70, at which level we could accommodate most people in houses. This would reduce average gross density from about 70 to about 40 people per acre. As a large part of the County has been redeveloped since 1945 at 136 per acre, the effect would probably be a final reduction of the population of the L.C.C. area from 3,195,000 (1961) to between 2 and $2\frac{1}{4}$ million people. The net rate of migration out of the County is already so high—300,000 in the decade 1951–61—that any Government might well think the forced emigration of another million people was impolitic. But there is a pragmatic answer: to make the 136-person-per-acre standard a permissive one, while abolishing differential subsidies on high flats and expensive sites. Local authorities would then be moved to charge economic rents for their flats, and should be subsidized from central funds to meet special defined cases—for instance, old people who had always lived in the area and should not be asked to go now. If then local authorities still thought they should subsidize their expensive flats, this would be a proper matter for local democracy to decide.

Conclusion

This chapter has chiefly consisted of sums to forecast the future—the basic art of the planner, albeit the least dramatic. They show, for what they are worth, that we should expect the population of London Region to rise quite sharply, by a million and a half people and by about half a million effective households between 1961 and 1980; and by another million and three quarter people and half a million effective households between 1980 and 2000. These extra households will need to be accommodated in the Outer Ring of the Region—or possibly, depending on convenience, a little way beyond. In addition, we have seen that there is a very large problem of obsolescence, chiefly concentrated in the Inner Ring and the inner parts of the Suburban Ring. And there may be further overspill from these same areas if the density of redevelopment in them is reduced in the future: anything up to one million more people in the years up to 2000.

The job of the local planners thus divides itself into two parts: new building in the Outer Ring; and renewal in the inner part of the London Region. They share some problems, and some common answers. But they are basically separate jobs; and the problems of renewal of the Inner Ring are much more closely related to those of reconstruction in the Central Area. So I shall discuss them separately: new building in Chapter 6, and renewal in Chapter 7.

But before this is done, another problem arises. In this and the last chapter I have done two quite separate jobs of statistical projection. I ended Chapter 3 with a very tentative and loose prediction that by 2000 there might be another two million jobs in the London Region; and although I suggested techniques for diverting some of the growth out of the central area, I specifically discounted hope that all of it could be so diverted. In this chapter I have concluded that there may be perhaps three and a quarter million extra people—including the workers reckoned above—by 2000 and that homes for these people, and possibly a million more, would have to be found on previously undeveloped land in the Outer Ring. So the two independent predictions contain a clear implication. The transport problem in the London Region, already severe, will increase. There will be more strain on the street system at the centre; and commuting into the central district will increase to some extent. It is necessary therefore to consider immediately the third side of the triangle: working, living—and moving.

Postscript, 1969

The forecasts of population growth in *London 2000* were much attacked for accepting, in too facile a fashion, the fact of continued growth. But in the event, they proved a spectacular underestimate. The simple reason, which *London 2000* failed sufficiently to stress, was that the main reason for the explosive increase of population was not the much publicized drift south; it was the fact of natural increase of population in the South East. The South East had roughly one-third of the country's population, and therefore if its natural rate of increase were close to the national average (which it was), then it could expect one-third of the country's natural increase: an increase which was everywhere accelerating, as the birth rate rose continuously from 1955 to 1964. In the London Metropolitan Region, of the total growth of population between 1951 and 1961 of 796,000, natural increase contributed 575,000 and returning servicemen 87,000; civilian migration contributed only 134,000. The corresponding proportions for the South East Region were more balanced however: of a total gain of

1,218,000, natural increase represented 663,000, returning servicemen 112,000, and net migration gain only 443,000.[1]

In the years since 1962, when most of *London 2000* was written, the trend in population has changed; and in two ways. In 1962, the birth rate was still rising; and belatedly, the Registrar General's projections of future population growth were rising too. The national birth rate, expressed both in absolute terms and in the rate per thousand, reached a maximum (18·5 per 000) in 1964, and in that year the official forward projection also reached a maximum: 54·3 million in England and Wales by the year 1981, 66·4 million by the year 2000. At the same time this was a period of very heavy net immigration into the South East, not so much from the rest of the country, as from abroad: the immigration rate reached flood proportions in early 1962, just before the gates went up in the form of the Commonwealth Immigration Act. As a result, any projection of the future growth of London and the South East, made just after *London 2000* was published (say in 1964), would have been exceptionally high— much higher than the estimate in the book. Thus in March 1964, the official *South East Study* assumed that even when net immigration into the South East Region was cut to half the unrestricted rate, the result between 1961 and 1981 would still be a net increase of 1,708,000 in the London Metropolitan Area, and 2,955,000 people in the South East Region.[2]

The Labour government came into office in October 1964, pledged to a vigorous programme of regional development in the unfortunate regions of the north, Scotland and Northern Ireland. It was logical and natural that they should start by reviewing the hotly debated figures in the *Study*. But in the event, the *Review* came up with almost precisely the same answer. Only the composition of the increase was different; and this is significant, for the tide was already beginning to turn. This was the year when the future projections of natural increase were at the highest; but already, the net immigration into the South East was much reduced, chiefly because of the 1962 Immigration Act. Therefore, though the net result was the same, the *Study* assumed that two sevenths of the increase would be migration; the *Review* assumed that almost all the growth would represent natural increase within the Region.

By 1967, the picture of future growth had completely altered. For three successive years, since 1964, the national birth rate had shown steady decline: the rate per thousand was 18·5 in 1964, 18·1 in 1965, 17·7 in 1966, and 17·3 in 1967. Additionally, and even more remarkably, net migration into the region had dropped almost to zero. For one thing, in the event the Labour government restricted Commonwealth

[1] London Region from *South East Study* (H.M.S.O. 1964), Appendix Table 7: South East from *East Midlands Study* (H.M.S.O. 1966), Appendix Tables 4b and 4c. The figures for South East England in the *South East Study* are misleading because they include East Anglia.

[2] The often quoted figure in the *Study*, 3·5 million between 1961 and 1981, applied to South East England, including East Anglia. The figures quoted here have been reduced for the sake of comparability with figures in later Studies, which exclude East Anglia. This lack of comparability between the *Study* figures and later figures has led to much elementary confusion, even among experts.

118

immigration even more severely than a Conservative one had; for another, the over-spill programme was already having its effect in decanting Londoners out of the London region, and indeed out of the South East, altogether. For the future, the proposals of the *South East Study* could only accelerate this process; for of the big planned counter-magnets there suggested, four (Swindon, Northampton, Peterborough and Ipswich) were outside the region altogether, while three more sites within the region (Newbury, Stansted and Ashford) were either certain, or likely, to be abandoned. Therefore, the South East Planning Council's *Strategy for the South East*, in November 1967, could posit realistically that over the coming twenty years there would be no significant net migration, either into or out of the region. Of course, it could be argued that this represents a convenient statistical fluke; Swindon, Northampton and Peterborough are all only a few miles beyond the regional boundary. But it can hardly be denied that these cities are far enough from London to constitute effective counter-magnets, and thus fulfil their specified objective of reducing pressure in the capital.

TABLE 22

COMPOSITION OF POPULATION INCREASE

South East plus East Anglia, 1961–81

*South East Study 1964:**

Total increase 1961/81	3500
By Natural Increase	2400
By Net Migration	1100

South East Review 1965/6†

Total increase 1961/81	3450
By natural increase	2500
By Net Migration	950

South East Strategy/East Anglia Study 1967/8‡

Total increase 1961/81	3110
By Natural Increase	2565
By Net Migration	545

* *South East Study* (H.M.S.O. 1964), p. 24. This figure is not precisely comparable with later totals because of subsequent area changes. It includes Dorset (later excluded from the South East region) and excludes the Soke of Peterborough (later combined with Huntingdonshire and transferred into the new East Anglia region).

† From Standing Conference LRP 600, 9 March 1966, which gives a 1964/81 estimate (2,900,000) plus an estimated 550,000 actual increase in 1961/4. The comparable figure for 1964/81 in the 1965 *National Plan* was 3,061,000 (*The National Plan*, Cmnd. 2764, H.M.S.O. 1965, Table A2, p. APP-11).

‡ *A Strategy for the South East* (H.M.S.O. 1967), Tables A7, A8 (p. 75); *East Anglia: A Study* (H.M.S.O. 1968), Table 4, p. 41, and Appendix Table 6, p. 126.

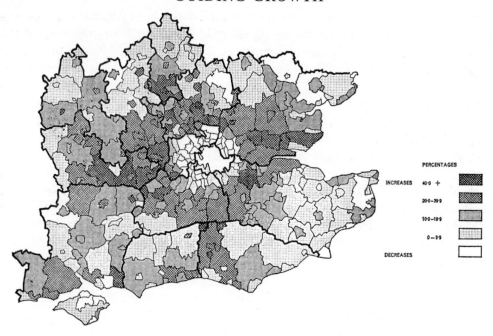

Fig. 3. POPULATION GROWTH, 1951–61 AND 1961–66. The pattern of population growth in 1951–61 was dominated by a ring of heavy increases about 20–35 miles from central London (above). By 1961–66 this had dissolved, to be replaced by separate areas of growth around major growth centres such as Solent, Reading, Luton and Southend (below).

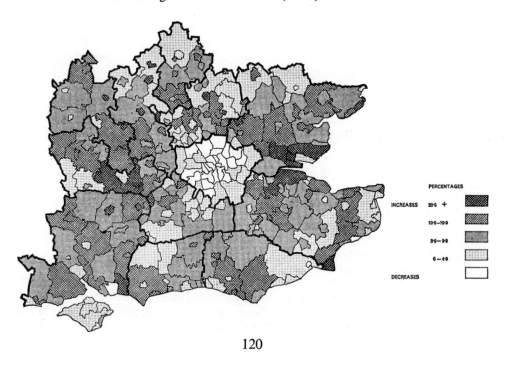

The overall result, in the *Strategy* projection of December 1967, is that both for the London region, and for the South East as a whole, the expected rate of growth is reduced well below the estimates either of the 1964 *Study*, or the 1965 *Review*. The population growth between 1964 and 1981, 2·14 million, is made up of 2·08 million by natural increase, and of only 60,000 net migration.[1] The overall rate of growth, of 7–8 per cent per decade, is above that of certain decades between 1921 and 1951, but well below the rates of growth obtaining throughout the nineteenth century.[2] Since the different estimates in the *Study*, the *Review* and the *Strategy* are so difficult to compare because of boundary changes and different time horizons, Table 23 has been specifically prepared to allow easy comparison. In it, all figures relate to the same time span, 1961–1981, and to the same area, the South East Planning Region. The result, in only three and a half years, is that the expected population growth has been reduced from 2,955,000 (*Study*, March 1964) to 2,620,000 (*Strategy*, November 1967). And these estimates, be it noted, are less in the nature of planners' goals, than of what is realistically likely to happen.

TABLE 23

THE POPULATION FORECASTS: 1964–67

All figures in thousands	Actual Growth 1951–61	Actual Population 1961
Total South East	**+1140**	**16350**
Greater London	− 220	7990
Outer Metropolitan Area	+1010	4520
Rest of South East	+350	3850

	South East Study 1964		South East Review 1965/6		South East Strategy 1967	
	Forecast Growth 1961–81	Forecast Population 1981	Forecast Growth 1961–81	Forecast Population 1981	Forecast Growth 1961–81	Forecast Population 1981
Total South East	**+2955**	**19305**	**+2910**	**19260**	**+2620**	**18970**
Greater London	Nil	7990	Nil	7990	+30	8010
Outer Met. Area	+1708	6228	+1561	6081	+1380	5900
Rest of South East	+1247	5097	+1349	5199	+1210	5060

Totals may not agree due to rounding.

One final point emerges from this table; it refers to the distribution of the population growth within the South East. *London 2000* dealt almost wholly with the

[1] South East Regional Economic Planning Council, *A Strategy for the South East* (H.M.S.O. 1967), Table A8, p. 75.

[2] *Ibid.*, Table A6, p. 74.

situation in the Metropolitan Area (or, as it was known in the book and generally at that time, the London Planning Region). Though some of the new towns proposed in the book were outside the limits of this region, which broadly formed a circle of radius 40 miles from central London, the assumption was that these limits, in a rough and ready way, represented the limits of the outer growth of London then and for the foreseeable planning future. And this was yet another respect, in which *London 2000* soon proved far too conservative. In the first place, while it was being written the pattern of population growth was changing. The map of growth between 1951 and 1961 (Fig. 3) shows a fairly solid ring of maximum increase in the belt 20–35 miles from central London, fingering out along the main railway lines towards places like Southend or Brighton; the map of growth between 1961 and 1965 shows quite a different pattern, with rings of growth around a number of towns at considerable distances from London. By this time, places like Reading (40 miles), Southend (35 miles), Southampton and Portsmouth (75 miles) already had quite well-marked suburban rings of population growth. This powerfully reinforces the thesis already put forward; that by the early 1960s, the so-called London Region was exploding into a series of separate areas of growth, distributed widely across the South East Region. and focussed on the bigger towns in the area beyond the metropolitan Green Belt, In the second place, this existing trend could only be fortified by the basic policy assumption of the *South East Study*: that the maximum possible growth should be steered into the parts of the South East outside the Metropolitan Area, by the location of the big new counter-magnets there. In the decade 1951–61, 70 per cent of the net growth of population in the Region had taken place in the Metropolitan Area. The *South East Study* proposed that this proportion should be cut to less than 60 per cent for the period 1961–1981; the *Review* cut the proportion to near half. Finally, the 1967 *Strategy* assumes that of the total growth between 1961 and 1981, this proportion be maintained: 1,380,000 increase in the Outer Metropolitan Area, 1,210,000 in the Rest of the South East, with a negligible increase of 20,000 in Greater London.

This is a perfectly reasonable policy; for it is now clear that the Metropolitan Area was a statistical convenience, arbitrarily defined. It still leaves open, though, some critical questions about the future grouping and massing of people within the whole South East Region, which have not adequately been answered by the summer of 1968. Some informed critics, particularly Peter Self and his colleagues of the Town and Country Planning Association, have deplored the tendency to disperse London overspill into separate towns which are too small to provide an adequate choice of job opportunities and social opportunities. Most people would probably now agree that (save for a small minority) the overspill schemes started under the Town Development Act, in areas like West Suffolk, were too small and were located in towns that were too small. The TCPA go further, and question whether a town like Swindon or Peterborough is big enough, even if it is expanded to take a total of 150,000 or 200,000 people. The reasoning is that these towns are too isolated, set as they are in relatively thinly peopled countryside. This question is related only in an indirect way to the question of location. A new town in the Metropolitan Area at (say) Stansted would have relatively limited accessibility to jobs, whereas a new city joining Southampton and Portsmouth would offer the largest concentration of job opportunities anywhere in the South East outside Greater London. Nevertheless, it does remain true in general that developments in the Outer Metropolitan Area are more likely to command a wide range of jobs and social opportunities than towns further out; this is a matter of overall population densities. The TCPA draw the conclusion that it would be better to concentrate more new developments into the Outer Metropolitan Area, and to concentrate investment outside this area into those limited areas where existing concentrations of people and jobs justified it. Southampton-Portsmouth would presumably be justified on these grounds; Northampton-Milton Keynes could make a strong case; Swindon and Peterborough are much more doubtful starters. But ironically, both these last two are going ahead.

The Housing Problem

Chapter 4 of *London 2000* is an elaborate exercise—some would say over-elaborate, given the shaky nature of the statistical base—to try to calculate the true extent of London's housing shortage. Shortly after it was published, the official *South East Study* tried the same exercise, starting from the same point: the crude net deficiency, represented by the excess of households over dwellings. Taking a rather lower standard for the number of households not needing separate dwellings, the Ministry naturally emerged with a lower estimate of shortage: 150,000 against 225,000.[1] Significantly, the Ministry have since revised this estimate, culminating in an estimated shortage of 230,000 dwellings in 1964. The *South East Study* estimates took no account of obsolescent housing: a rather extraordinary omission, in view of the extensive knowledge about the deficiencies of London housing that had emerged from the Rachman scandals some years earlier. They did however estimate that in addition to 150,000 houses needed to cope with shortage, 400,000 more would be needed to cope with growth in households arising from population growth and fissioning of the population into more and more households. As there was room only for about 200,000 homes within London, the calculations of the *Study* culminated in an estimate of 350,000 households, or upwards of one million people, who would have to be found overspill housing outside Greater London.[2]

Both *London 2000*, and the official *Study*, therefore have their deficiencies. The Milner Holland report on London housing, published in March 1965, represents a massive attempt to repair this deficiency by a close examination of 1961 Census data —much of it not available for the earlier pieces of analysis. After examining the

[1] *Report of the Committee on Housing in Greater London* (Chairman: Sir Milner Holland Q.C.), (H.M.S.O. 1965), p. 99.
[2] *Ibid.*, pp. 105–6.

TABLE 24

THE HOUSING SHORTAGE:

Households by density of occupation, size and quality of accommodation:
Greater London Conurbation, 1961

Density of occupation and size of household	Households living in multi-occupied dwellings		Households living in separate dwellings (i.e. not shared)	Households in all dwellings
	without own stove and sink	with own stove and sink		
Severely overcrowded (more than 1½ persons per room)	(1)	(2)	(3)	(4)
(1) 3 or more persons	13,130	24,000	51,930	89,060
(2) 2 persons	13,050	10,070	7,200	30,320
Less severely overcrowded (more than 1 but not more than 1½ persons per room				
(3) 3 or more persons	8,310	39,440	174,010	221,760
Not overcrowded (1 person per room or less)				
(4) 3 or more persons	8,980	87,310	1,031,480	1,127,770
(5) 2 persons	21,180	134,570	644,610	800,360
(6) 1 person	61,110	111,710	271,400	444,220
(7) TOTAL ALL DENSITIES OF OCCUPATION	125,760	407,100	2,180,630	2,713,490
(8) Total in heavy type (most urgent need)	64,650	73,510	51,930	190,090
(9) Total number of households without a bath*	40,490	151,720	340,180	532,390

Source: *Milner Holland Report*, Table 4.27, p. 103.
* No breakdown available by density of occupation or size of household combined with type of dwelling.

London 2000 estimates, as well as those of the Centre for Urban Studies, the Milner Holland committee made the best estimates they could, on a slightly different basis. First, they estimated the extent of physical homelessness—a phenomenon that had excited dramatic attention in 1963 and 1964. This they estimated was the plight of 1500 households, involving in all 7000 people. Then they estimated the number of 'concealed' households, or 'quasi-households' in the terminology of *London 2000*: households that had never come into formal existence, because of the extent of housing shortages. They estimated that betweeen 45,000 and 80,000 of such households existed.[1]

Lastly, Milner Holland tried to measure the extent of overcrowding and poor housing conditions. The trouble is that there are so many alternative ways of measuring these phenomena: there is a scale of overcrowding, measured by the numbers of households living at more than specified densities per room, there is a scale of multi-occupation, measured by the number of households sharing a dwelling, and there are various scales of poor housing conditions, as measured in the Census by lack of basic amenities like baths. All these can be combined in various ways. The Milner Holland way was to relate them, on the assumption that lack of amenities was more serious, the larger or more overcrowded the household; their calculations are set out in Table 24. From this it is seen that there are 190,000 households in most extreme need, with an additional number (estimated at between 366,000 and 532,000) with no access to a bath.[2] It was actually impossible to fix the total more firmly than this, because there is an unknown amount of double counting involved.

Milner Holland found that the problem of bad housing was concentrated to a high degree into certain parts of inner London. Basically, as *London 2000* tried to stress, London has two quite different sorts of inadequate housing. First, there are the houses which are occupied each by a single family, but which are basically inadequate in that they lack basic facilities like baths. These are traditionally concentrated in the East End and in certain inner boroughs south of the Thames, like Southwark. In Stepney and Southwark, more than half the single family dwellings had no bath in 1961. Secondly, there are areas where the housing stock is better, but is overcrowded and ill adapted to the needs of its present occupants; these are the areas of multi-occupied big houses, which are chiefly in west and north London. While in the east the housing problem is getting better, Milner Holland found in the west it is all too often getting worse. Ranking the old metropolitan boroughs of London on a number of indices of housing stress, and then comparing the number of appearances in the table, the Milner Holland committee were able to produce an index of the intensity of the housing problem (Table 25). Finsbury ranks worst, followed successively by Islington, Paddington, St. Pancras, Hammersmith, Willesden, Kensington, Lambeth and Stoke Newington. It is highly significant that these boroughs form a solid arc surrounding central London, but only (save for Lambeth) on its north and west sides.[3] The real weight of the London housing problem, as *London 2000* indicated, is no longer concentrated in the East End; it is in London's West Side.

To summarize the Milner Holland estimates: there are 1500 homeless families, 45,000–80,000 'concealed' households, 190,000 households in urgent need of better housing, plus 366,000–532,000 in less urgently deficient housing. In all this there is an unknown element of double counting, particularly with the 'concealed' households. The best estimate, therefore, is that the extra housing need amounts to homes for

[1] *Ibid.*, p. 101.   [2] *Ibid.*, p. 104.
[3] *Ibid.*, Fig. 6 (following p. 90).

TABLE 25

SEVEN INDICES OF HOUSING STRESS, 1961

(The local authority districts in each case are ranked in descending order)

Rank	I. MULTIPLE OCCUPATION		II. OVERCROWDING			III. DOMESTIC FACILITIES	
	Households (all sizes) living in multi-occupied dwellings	Households of 3 or more persons in multi-occupied dwellings	Households (all sizes) living at more than 1½ persons per room	Households of 3 or more persons living at more than 1½ persons per room	Households in multi-occupied dwellings without own sink and stove	Households without access to a fixed bath	Households lacking or sharing at least one of the four domestic facilities*
	%	%	%	%	%	%	%
1	*Islington* 59	*Islington* 24	*Paddington* 14	*Islington* 8	*Paddington* 12	Southwark 59	*Islington* 77
2	Hornsey 54	Hackney 20	*Kensington* 13	*Stepney* 8	*Islington* 12	Stepney 57	Deptford 70
3	*Paddington* 48	Hornsey 19	*Islington* 11	*Paddington* 8	*Kensington* 11	*Finsbury* 56	Southwark 68
4	Hackney 48	*Willesden* 17	*Hammersmith* 10	*Finsbury* 7	Hampstead 9	Bethnal Green 55	*Finsbury* 67
5	*Willesden* 42	*Battersea* 15	*Willesden* 10	*Hammersmith* 7	*Hammersmith* 9	Poplar 51	*Battersea* 67
6	*Kensington* 39	*Finsbury* 14	*Stepney* 10	*Willesden* 7	*St. Pancras* 9	West Ham 51	*St. Pancras* 65
7	*Battersea* 38	*Hammersmith* 13	*St. Pancras* 8	Shoreditch 7	*Willesden* 9	Bermondsey 49	*Paddington* 65
8	*Hammersmith* 37	Tottenham 13	*Stoke Newington* 8	Southwark 7	Shoreditch 8	*Islington* 45	Hackney 65
9	*St. Pancras* 34	*Paddington* 12	Hampstead 8	*St. Pancras* 7	*Stepney* 8	Deptford 44	West Ham 65
10	*Finsbury* 33	*St. Pancras* 12	*Finsbury* 8	*Kensington* 6	*Finsbury* 8	Hackney 42	Stepney 64
11	Fulham 32	Lambeth 12	Lambeth 7	Bermondsey 6	Lambeth 8	Shoreditch 42	*Stoke Newington* 63
12	Tottenham 32	*Stoke Newington* 11	Southwark 7	Poplar 6	Hornsey 7	Battersea 41	Bethnal Green 62
County of London	30	10	7	5	7	31	55
Greater London Conurbation	20	7	4	3	5	20	38
England and Wales excluding Greater London conurbation	3	1	2	2	1	22	29

Source: *Milner Holland Report*, Table 4. 24, p. 89

* Hot and cold water, bath and W.C.

All figures are percentage of the total number of households in the district.

The italicized districts are those which appear three or more times in the table and least once in each of the major groups I, II and III.

between 600,000 and 800,000 familes—probably, between 1,800,000 and 2,400,000 people.[1] This is much more than anything estimated earlier. Added to the *South East Study* estimates, it could mean a total overspill problem of between two and three million extra people by 1981. But this is unrealistic; it ignores the possibility of modernization, or even rebuilding, *in situ*.

On this critical question, there has been little apparent advance in thinking since *London 2000* was written. *London 2000* suggested that it would be economically rational to reduce net densities in inner London from 136 per acre, the figure enshrined in the Abercrombie-Forshaw London Plan of 1943 and subsequently in the Development Plan, to 60 or 70, at which point (as in a new town like Cumbernauld) it would be perfectly feasible to accommodate almost everyone in houses with gardens. I do not know of any evidence since which finally controverts this argument. The most important piece of counter-evidence comes from the *Fulham Study*, commissioned by the Ministry of Housing from Taylor Woodrow, and published in 1964. This came to the conclusion, then still fairly revolutionary, that a large area of twilight housing in West London could be redeveloped at an average net density of 250 per acre, all in low-rise four or five-storey structures, round enclosed open spaces, with 76 per cent of the land preserved as open space, and with one garage to each household.[2] Since complex servicing arrangements and lifts would be unnecessary, the costs would be more closely comparable to those of single family housing than to the high-density high-rise structures previously analysed in studies like that of Dr. Stone. This is an important discovery, and it has led to a profound modification in Ministry of Housing subsidy policies: in the 1967 Housing Act, the subsidies have been recast so as to make it virtually uneconomic for local authorities to build the very tall industrialized blocks which had been so popular in certain London boroughs. The growing evidence of the unpopularity of these structures with their tenants, and the admittedly fortuitous collapse of one of them in a gas explosion in early 1968, can only underline the point. It seems certain that for the future, low rise-high density solutions will be the order of the day in inner London.

Few will doubt that this is a better solution than the tall blocks. The question still is whether it is the best solution; whether, in fact, it is still not more economic to redevelop at lower densities and export the families to new towns and expanded towns. We have to remember that we are talking here about public money and public subsidies. This is not a matter of cheeseparing; it is a matter of the most effective use of public funds in relieving the housing problem in London. If, for a given amount of resources, it is possible to provide more houses in new towns than flats in London, public policy seems to dictate a new towns solution—unless there is some overwhelming reason for rehousing families within London, as sometimes there may be. In the *Fulham Study*, Taylor Woodrow have shown that the balance of advantage can be closer than we earlier thought. They have not shown that it is closed.

All this has to do with the use of public funds. If on the other hand we are dealing

[1] *Ibid.*, p. 104.   [2] Taylor Woodrow Ltd., *Fulham Study* (London 1964), *passim*.

with unsubsidized housing—whether built by local authorities, housing associations, or private enterprise—there is no reason why high-density housing should not be built in London, providing that this does not give rise to social costs which are borne by the community at large. Some of the arguments against high-density schemes are frankly invalid. For instance, it has been argued against the *Fulham Study* that it ignores the problem of public open space, because the projected density of 250 per acre assumes that this space will be provided outside the limits of the area. But this assumes that conventional open space is necessary. In many areas of West London, differential migration has produced a very distorted population structure with very large numbers of young adults. These people are more likely to seek recreation in the King's Road Drugstore than on football fields. The open space standards, which Abercrombie developed for the population of the East End in 1938, should not be applied blindly to situations and locations where they are no longer apposite. On the other hand, if all these young people owned cars which caused traffic congestion, that might well be an argument against a density of 250 per acre in inner West London.[1]

[1] However, this argument is exceedingly complex. For one thing, as the Ministry of Transport have recently argued, congestion costs strictly speaking are imposed by road users on other road users, and are not a general 'community cost' in the strict sense. *Road Track Costs* (H.M.S.O. 1968), 5–6. For another, if this is the case, a road pricing solution seems more appropriate than a regulatory-planning solution to the problem.

Regent St.

Oxford St.

Haphazard renewal with shops on main street

1   *Aerofilms*

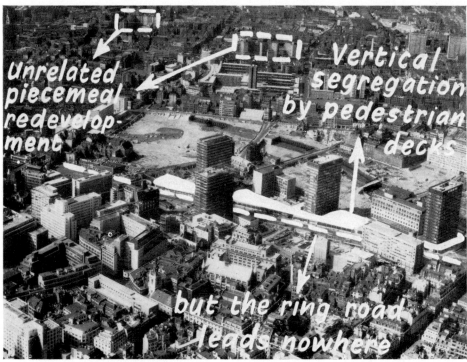

Unrelated piecemeal redevelop- ment

Vertical segregation by pedestrian decks

but the ring road leads nowhere

2   *Aerofilms*

1   OXFORD STREET

2   BARBICAN, CITY OF LONDON

Contrasted styles of urban renewal in the centre of London. (1) shows the piecemeal reconstruction which is the general rule; it freezes the existing street system and can only hinder comprehensive replanning in years to come. (2) shows fully comprehensive redevelopment of a war-devastated area on a basis of 'vertical segregation': pedestrians on high-level decks, moving vehicles at ground level, parked cars underground. But all around is unrelated piecemeal redevelopment.

3

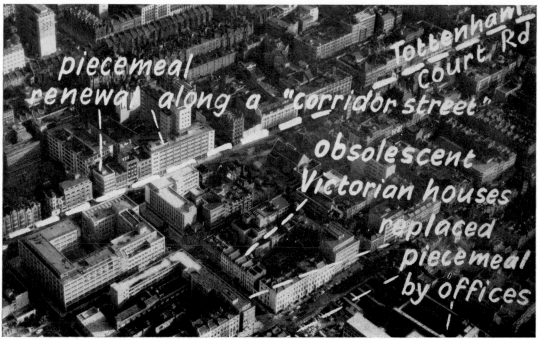

4

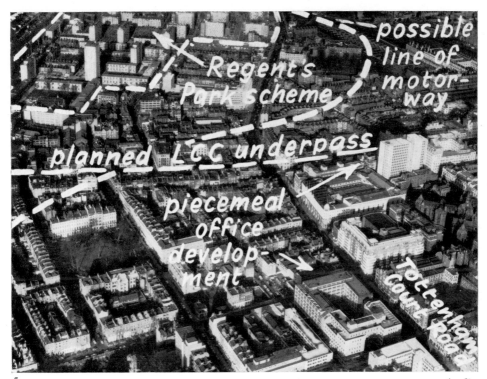

5

3, 4, 5 FITZROVIA

Fitzrovia lies immediately west of Tottenham Court Road. In 1935 (3) it consisted of almost uniform nineteenth-century houses, broken only by the rebuilt Middlesex Hospital (1928). But by the mid-1950s the houses, then about a century old, were ripe for renewal. Only permissive planning powers existed; so the area has been rebuilt piecemeal, on the old street plan, with no attempt to adapt pedestrian and vehicle circulation to the age of the motor vehicle (4). Northwards (5) in the Regent's Park redevelopment by the Borough of St Pancras, the internal replanning shows better understanding of the pedestrian-vehicle conflict. But the bounding main roads are still being redeveloped with shops facing traffic, and the £2$\frac{1}{3}$ million underpass (centre) threatens merely to transfer the existing bottleneck elsewhere. The real solution for traffic is an urban motorway, for which a line still exists (1963) through obsolescent property.

Aerofilms

6 KING'S CROSS

7, 8 CAMDEN TOWN

King's Cross (6) is an area of mainly obsolescent property ripe for early redevelopment. It is a major traffic junction and it lies astride the most obvious line for a north-south motorway through central London. Though the motorway may be a long-term project, the area should be comprehensively redeveloped in such a way that it can be incorporated later.

Camden High Street (7, bottom) mixes through traffic, local traffic and pedestrian shoppers, to their mutual frustration and danger; to avoid jams, through traffic turns off through a residential area, intensifying the problem (8). The Ministry of Transport have proposed to make Camden High Street one-way for fast-moving traffic, and the street shown in (8) the main through traffic street in the opposite direction. This solution sacrifices everything to traffic flow, and is contrary to the proposed redevelopment of the area which would make the High Street a pedestrian precinct and would establish a one-way ring road round it. This ultimate solution should be combined with the diversion of through traffic on to urban motorways through the railway and canal areas to the east (7, top).

lines of motorway avoiding residential "precincts"

"by-pass" through residential area

Camden High St. area —

7

Aerofilms

SCHOOL

Camden St.—

Speed track for filtering rush-hour cars

KEEP LEFT

8

Built 1957

now to be 6-lane speedway

9

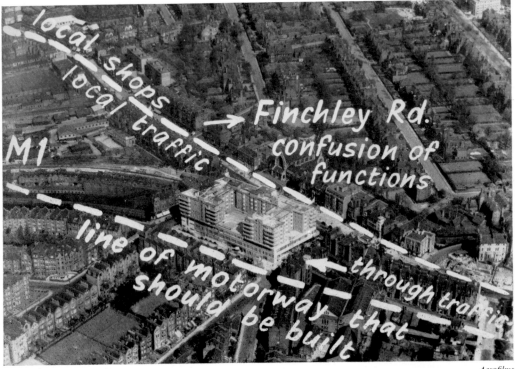

local shops

local traffic

M1

Finchley Rd.
confusion of functions

line of motorway that should be built

through traffic

10

Aerofilms

M1

Finchley Road

line of motorway plan

Area of major postwar reconstruction

11

Aerofilms

9, 10, 11 FINCHLEY ROAD

An extreme example of a radial road which performs three irreconcilable functions: through arterial road (West End to M1), intermediate-distance main road, and local shopping street. The solution currently proposed is to widen the road, which will merely intensify the problem (9). A better ultimate solution, demonstrated in Map 5, would provide a radial motorway for through traffic and a relief-road for medium-range traffic, allowing the shopping area to be sealed off for pedestrians and short-term parking. But to the south (11) post-1950 developments have almost blocked the most suitable line for a motorway, because long-term road projects were not shown in the County Development Plan.

12

12 KENSAL NEW TOWN, NORTH KENSINGTON

13 PADDINGTON

14 WARWICK CRESCENT REDEVELOPMENT,
PADDINGTON

As the East End slums are progressively cleared, attention focusses
on the problem of London's 'West Side': the big 'houses in
multi-occupation', built in the Victorian age for single families
with servants, which have degenerated into overcrowded apartments with inadequate sanitary facilities. In some of these areas
of Paddington and North Kensington, overcrowding actually
increased between the 1951 and 1961 Censuses. In the area shown
in (12) and in (14) large-scale redevelopment was taking place in
1963; but these individual areas represent only a small part of
the total problem.

13

14

15

London County Council

16

17

London County Council

15 ALTON STREET, POPLAR

16 MUNSTER SQUARE, REGENT'S PARK, ST PANCRAS

17 WARWICK CRESCENT REDEVELOPMENT, PADDINGTON

'Precinctual planning' in two schemes by the London County Council Architect's Department (15, 17) and in a design by Armstrong and McManus for the Borough of St Pancras (16). These schemes protect residents from intrusion by the motor vehicle; as far as possible, main roads are sealed off from direct frontage development, so that they can effectively carry fast-moving traffic. At Warwick Crescent (17) the motorway has subsequently been replanned along the Harrow Road; a viaduct over the existing road will probably be necessary, with considerable loss of amenity to residents. This need not have occurred if the line for the motorway had been surveyed and defined in earlier Development Plans.

18

Aerofilms

18 NORTH CIRCULAR ROAD

19 WEST BERLIN

20 COBO HALL ROOF PARKING DECK, DETROIT

In (18) the legacy of inadequate road planning in the interwar period: arterial road carrying fast traffic, direct frontage development of houses and factory; none of it obsolescent for decades, and so quite uneconomic to rebuild properly. This scene represents one of London's least tractable planning problems.

Modern road planning is based on the fully-segregated urban motorway. The example of West Berlin (19) shows that the motorway can be completely and imaginatively integrated into the city. But this demands comprehensive planning of more than the motorway alone.

The Detroit example (20) should provide a model for a 'first-stage' programme of motorways for London: a motorway terminates at the edge of the central business district in direct ramps to a car park, without need to enter the ordinary street network.

19

Roads Campaign Council

20

City of Detroit

21

22

23

21 ESSEX

22 CAMBERLEY

23 ST ALBANS

Representative examples of 'spec' building in what is now London's 'Commuter Country'—the ring twenty to forty miles from central London. Complete insensitivity to the surrounding landscape, maladroit layouts and rigid planning requirements on road widths combine to multiply brick and asphalt deserts over the face of the Home Counties. New types of development agency may be needed to improve the standards of future schemes of this type.

24

Aerofilms

24 CRAWLEY, SUSSEX

25, 26 HOOK NEW TOWN PROJECT, HAMPSHIRE

Contrasted New Town styles. Crawley (24) represents the traditional planning of the post-1945 crop of New Towns: houses are grouped in neighbourhoods around schools and shops; neighbourhoods are separated from each other by main roads and green wedges of open space. The London County Council's Hook plan (25, 26) would have provided much more compact housing than the older New Towns; neighbourhoods would have disappeared from most of the town, but instead two-thirds of the town's 100,000 people would have been able to walk to a central shopping area within ten minutes. Cumbernauld New Town, near Glasgow, is being planned on similar principles. These plans will probably provide the model for a second generation of London New Towns.

25

26

27

Aerofilms

27 VALE OF AYLESBURY, FROM THE CHILTERN SCARP

28 BICESTER, OXFORDSHIRE

29 PRINCES RISBOROUGH, BUCKINGHAMSHIRE

1961 average population density in the 'Outer Ring' of London Region was only 2 per acre. Making all allowance for areas of high landscape value like the Chilterns (27, right), it is clear that there is plenty of room in areas like the Vale of Aylesbury (27, left) to accommodate the large numbers of extra Londoners who will need to be housed here by 2000.

Between fifteen and twenty New Towns should probably be built in the 'Outer Ring' by the year 2000 to help house the extra population. Bicester (28) and Princes Risborough (29) are two out of twenty-five possible sites suggested in Chapter 6. Bicester is 57 miles from London, with good access to the West Midlands industrial area; Princes Risborough is only 40 miles from London with good road and rail access to London and the Midlands.

Site of New Town

← North

A41 to London
(by-pass
needed)

railway
to London
and
Birmingham

A41 to
Birmingham

28

Aerofilms

← North

Site of
New Town

A4010
to Midlands

A4010 to
Wycombe and
London

to
Midlands
↑
railway →   to London

29

Aerofilms

Site of New Town   new roads needed
                    to   to
                    A20   Channel link

← North

railway to
Ashford

30   *Aerofilms*

A33 4 miles   railway to Reading and Basingstoke

← North

A30
(and M3)
7 miles

Site of New Town extends to west   *Aerofilms*

31

30 HAMSTREET, KENT

31 SILCHESTER, HAMPSHIRE

Two more of the suggested twenty-five New Town sites. Hamstreet has
an exceptionally favourable position in relation to a future Channel link;
Silchester offers a unique opportunity for an imaginative town design
based on the remains of the Roman town.

CHAPTER 5

Travel 2000

The transport problem, in any city as big as London, is the one that strikes more of us more immediately, more of the time, than any other. But it is not a primary problem: it only arises from the patterns of living, working and playing within the region. To reach an adequate solution, we need to go beyond transport, to the causes that bring it about.

Traffic Generation

Through the uses people make of London's land, they generate journeys. The first essential in traffic planning is to study this relation. In the course of a normal day, the average Londoner makes a number of journeys. Some are *random*: journeys to weddings, funerals, banquets. No traffic analysis can generalize about these. Others are *scatter trips*, regular in nature but complex in pattern: to shops, cinemas, bowling alleys, libraries, friends' houses. Yet others are regular, Monday–Friday *home-to-work trips*; with complex patterns of *cross-trips* to suburban service centres and industrial zones, superimposed on the great radial flows into the centre. Lastly there are *work trips*, classifiable under the main economic activities of London: wholesale trips focused on the docks and warehouses, the rail goods termini and the road transport depots; the retail trips in the central business area and suburban shopping centres; the manufacturing trips between factory and factory, within London or between a London and a provincial factory.

As yet, London lacks adequate material for analysis of traffic generation. The deficiency will be remedied about 1964, when a London Traffic Survey, based on a sample study of 50,000 households and a sample of commercial firms, will be ready. Until then, we have only the vaguest notions. The London Transport Travel Surveys of 1949 and 1954 tell us something of personal traffic habits: for instance, in 1954 71 per cent of all 'work journeys' were by public transport and only 8 per cent by

car, compared with 66 per cent and 23 per cent for the category 'other journeys'.[1]
We know from the periodic surveys of traffic volumes by the Metropolitan Police
that at junctions in east and south-east London traffic was dominated by heavy
commercial vehicles, while in west London it was dominated by private cars. But
about the precise relation between traffic flows and land use, we know virtually
nothing; and until we do we cannot begin to plan either land use, or the circulation
system to accompany it.

Basic Facts and Trends

We do know these facts.

First, the commonplace: that the basic problem of London traffic today is the
increased use of the motor vehicle. The best estimate we can make is that the total
number of vehicles in the London Region increased from 1,137,000 in 1951 to
2,679,000 in 1961; that private cars increased from 595,000 (0·16 per household) to
1,701,150 (0·42 per household, slightly above national average).[2] In this period in
England and Wales, the total number of vehicles increased by 8 per cent per annum
compound; in London Region by 9 per cent per annum compound. The current
estimate is that in the whole country the number of vehicles will rise from 9 million
in 1960 to 17 million by 1970, 25 million by 1980, 30 million by 1990, and 34
million by 2000.[3] On past trends we should expect about a quarter of these to be in
the London Region.

Within London, however, there are considerable differences in motorization. The
ratio of cars per household, or all vehicles per head of population, within the inner
or L.C.C. area is much below that for the outer rings or the national average. This
is extraordinary, for so much economic activity is concentrated in the L.C.C. zone.
Part of the explanation may be the social composition of the population, with a
bigger proportion of the classes who still buy cars less. But the main reason must
be that vehicle ownership is choked off at the centre by congestion.

This is reinforced when we look—secondly—at vehicle *use*, or traffic. Despite the
continued increase of employment in central London—perhaps 150,000 between
1951 and 1961—road traffic in the central area rose by only $3\frac{1}{2}$ per cent per annum
between 1951 and 1955, and by 5 per cent per annum between 1955 and 1960, compared with 7–8 per cent per annum in the country as a whole.[4]

This increase at the centre—limited as it may be—has two critical effects.

The first is direct: the mounting congestion and increasing paralysis on the streets.
In 1905 congestion in central London was already so serious as to justify a major
Royal Commission report. Between then and 1962, no major improvement scheme

---

[1] *London Travel Survey* 1954, 13.
[2] Estimates based on the annual Census of Road Vehicles (Ministry of Transport).
[3] Department of Scientific and Industrial Research, *Road Research 1960* (H.M.S.O. 1961), 14.
[4] *Ibid.*, 11. These figures are based on 24-hour continuous counts.

was finished in central London; there was some increase in the efficiency of existing streets through traffic lights, one way streets and waiting restrictions; but traffic at typical Census points increased two or three-fold. As a result, the average speed of central London traffic has fallen steadily, by 1·9 per cent per annum during the fifties; by 1960 in normal working hours it was down to exactly 10 miles per hour.[1] This process should continue, with temporary relief from traffic engineering techniques; the very limited American experience indicates that average speeds in central Manhattan are down to 4–6 miles per hour,[2] at which level they somewhat mercifully tend to stick.[3]

In this vicious circle, the private vehicle plays a part out of all proportion to its actual numbers. In the morning rush period (7–10), out of 1,238,000 people entering central London on an average day in 1962, less than 10 per cent (123,000) used private transport, of whom some 94,000 were travelling in 64,000 cars. But whereas a person travelling one mile by train in this period uses less than 1 square foot, and the traveller by bus in an average street uses 6 square feet, the traveller in a car carrying 1½ people (the average) uses 42 square feet. Only one extra car travelling one mile on a road where the average speed is 10 miles per hour (as in central London) causes a total loss of 0·105 vehicle hours to other vehicles. R. J. Smeed, who made these calculations, allows that 'the economic value of the time gained (by the motorist) may be greater than the economic value of the time lost to other road users.'[4] But, as things are at present, there is no way of telling.

The second, indirect effect is as serious: the growing crisis in the public transport sector. The growth of private motoring, and of the home-based life, increasingly deprive the public carrier of his off-peak and weekend returns, which helped to make his whole system pay; he is left with the highly uneconomic job of shuttling huge numbers of commuters to work within two hours in the morning and back home at night. Sunday traffic on London Transport has fallen from 70 per cent of Monday–Friday traffic in 1938, to just over 50 per cent in 1960; in Boston the figure is down to 35 per cent, in Toronto 32 per cent.[5] There is an even more uneconomic peak within a peak: one-sixth of peak-period (4.30–7.0) traffic out of central London leaves between 5.30 and 5.45.[6] For long periods at midday and at weekends, then, equipment lies idle, maintenance has to go on, wages must still be paid. As a result, working

[1] R. J. Smeed, *The Traffic Problem in Towns* (Manchester Statistical Society, 1961), 9.

[2] L. C. Hawkins, 'Urban Passenger Transport and the Private Car', *British Transport Review*, 3 (1954–5), 299.

[3] P. H. Bendtsen, *Town and Traffic in the Motor Age* (Copenhagen, 1961), 61.

[4] R. J. Smeed, *op. cit.*, 21–3.

[5] L. C. Hawkins, 'Mass Transportation in the Future', *Journal of the Institute of Transport*, 29 (1961–3), 107; W. Owen, *The Metropolitan Transportation Problem* (Washington 1956), 85.

[6] Ministry of Transport and Civil Aviation, *'Crush Hour' Travel in Central London.* (Report of the First Year's Work of the Committee for Staggering of Working Hours in Central London.) (H.M.S.O. 1958), 4. One in three central London workers stops work at 5.30; one in two in the West End. *Ibid.*, 10.

expenses per passenger mile are higher for London Transport than for provincial undertakings (where the problem may be less serious);[1] and the differential appears to be growing.

This is the central dilemma of London and of cities like it. Here the vision of the future presented by the American nightmare—Los Angeles—is grossly misleading. There, as in other western American cities, commercial concentration at the centre was always relatively weak, land values relatively low, suburban sprawl relatively great; to build freeways and parking lots presented no real difficulty. But London, like the cities of eastern North America, has always had a high concentration of people, jobs, economic activity at the centre. In New York, Boston, Chicago, efficient public transport once existed, but upon the rapid growth of private motoring (from about 1930) it degenerated or went into partial disuse.[2] Now, congestion has so increased that the city centres have in some cases actually begun to decay; in Boston the centre was saved by the construction of a central freeway, which, at £15 million a mile, is surely the most expensive piece of urban surgery ever carried out;[3] in central New York, four department stores closed Manhattan branches between 1948 and 1959, and total retail trade stagnated.[4] This is the lesson for London: if the city centre once chokes itself, decay sets in, and is cumulative.

New York offers the closest American parallel to London. In London, the proportion of rush-period travellers (7–10 a.m.) using private transport rose from 7 per cent in 1954 to 10 per cent in 1960; in New York, the proportions entering by car or taxi in the same period were 8 per cent in 1948, 11 per cent in 1954, and 12·5 per cent in 1960. It appears then that London is almost precisely eight years behind New York. Continuation of these trends, even if the total numbers of commuters were pegged, might mean 80,000 commuters' cars trying to enter London's central area every morning by 1968, compared with 65,000 on average in 1961 and perhaps 100,000 on 29 January 1962, the day of chaos arising from the Underground Strike. If the American trends apply, these people will not be deterred from driving their cars till average traffic speeds fall to about half the 1961 level. The slightly larger central business district of New York took in no less than 116,500 private cars in an average morning rush period in 1960.[5]

Los Angeles experience may well be relevant, though, for the fast-growing Outer Ring of the London Region, where there are many small centres of concentration and densities are low. Here the London travel survey found even in 1954 that car ownership and use—even for work journeys—were much higher than in the Great London

[1] e.g. in Glasgow, where many workers go home to lunch and provide extra 'peaks'.

[2] W. Owen, op. cit., 79.

[3] Ibid., 49. Valuations in central Boston fell 35 per cent, 1926–50: J. A. Volpe in British Road Federation, Urban Motorways (1957), 177.

[4] R. J. Smeed, 'Visit to the United States', Traffic Engineering and Control, 2 (1960), 96–7; P. H. Bendtsen, op. cit., 45, 110.

[5] Hub-bound Travel in the Tri-State New York Metropolitan Region (Regional Plan Association), Bulletin No. 91 (1959), Table 9, and No. 99 (1961), Tables 4 and 5; London Transport Census 1960.

Conurbation. In extreme cases like Hemel Hempstead and St. Albans, only one-third of work journeys were by public transport in 1954 (against 71 per cent in the Conurbation) and 15–16 per cent were by car (against 8 per cent).[1] In this zone traffic planning has the delicate job of encouraging reasonable mobility—especially between home and work—while avoiding the creation of a motorized slum. To this end, we need to continue and strengthen the post-1945 policy of housing the population in well-defined, medium-sized communities where most of the population need travel only a short distance to work, and connected by a fairly dense network of all-purpose roads to allow flexible routing of journeys between one town and another. On only a few major radial roads will traffic flows justify motorway construction, though the towns themselves will need to segregate different sorts of traffic, as in the plans for Cumbernauld in Scotland or the abortive New Town at Hook.

Paying the Cost

The key to the problem at the centre is clearly regulation: first of the numbers of vehicles on the streets, secondly of the peak flows in both the public and private sectors of transport. Unless there is regulation, any improvements, however dramatic or costly, will be swamped after a short period by extra traffic: for urban traffic if not for population, it has truly been pointed out, Malthusian rules apply.[2]

In this, as in most problems of rationing, two alternatives exist: some form of licensing, where society or its representatives decide on what is permissible and then issue permissions to that end; or the use of the price mechanism. I want to argue that the price mechanism is the subtler and therefore the more effective regulator; and that it is quite technically feasible to apply it to most city transport problems.

By charging a price for a thing, we perform at least two important functions: we repay part of the cost of production—in the case of an investment, we repay part of the invested capital and a share of the interest; and we bring demand and supply into reasonable equivalence. The second function is often hard to find in modern life, and this is especially true of transport. Since railways have commonly been regarded as a public service, at least in part, they charge not what the market will bear, but a price related to the cost of production of trains. But even this is true only in a very general way, because of the wide use of cross-subsidization, and even because of diversion of resources into other fields. Thus the users of M1 do not pay directly for it, but indirectly through road licences and petrol tax; a great deal of which money is diverted to building roads in Wester Ross, or into building rockets or schools. The classical link between demand and supply, through price, is simply not present in large sectors of transport. As Denys Munby says: 'At the moment the transport system is run neither entirely on business principles nor entirely as a public service, as

[1] *London Travel Survey*, 1954, 34.
[2] P. A. White, 'The Problem of the Peak', *Journal of the Institute of Transport*, 28 (1958–60), 270–1.

with the Health Service or Education. It is an extraordinary mixture of the two systems . . .'[1]

The results for urban traffic are hardly short of pernicious. Though road users, generally, pay much more to use the roads than they cost to build and maintain, in urban areas the reverse obtains. The cost of supplying reasonably uncongested road space in central London is many times that in rural areas. But we may use both for nothing. Consequently, the only regulator of urban congestion is the fact of existing congestion. But this is ineffective, because of the paradox that in deciding whether to put his car on the road, the motorist considers only the extra cost of congestion to him; not the social cost of the extra congestion he causes to all the existing road users. It has been estimated that even on a very narrow definition of the costs of congestion, they amounted to £140 million on urban roads in 1958: 7 per cent of the real cost of all road users' transport, and 0·7 per cent of net national income.[2]

Instead of correcting this, the present structure of public finance worsens it, by ensuring that for many urban motorists the fixed cost of buying a car does not exist, or is only part of true cost. At least two-fifths of all new cars, at a very conservative estimate, are bought by firms (for their representatives or for car pools), or by fleet operators, or by professional people;[3] all of whom enjoy tax relief on their purchases.

The solution, economists have recognized, is to make road users pay a share—calculated as accurately as possible—of the 'individual costs' of supplying the road space they use. In other words, to try to relate the cost of using any piece of road to its direct costs, including the costs of congestion it brings about.[4] This presents many difficulties. For instance, we do not know, for enough representative situations, how much extra people are willing to pay to travel faster. We deal with this only by introducing a charging system, and then finding in practice the points at which it 'clears the market'.

But here arises the central difficulty. How to find a system which is localized enough in application to regulate traffic efficiently, without being administratively impracticable? You could regulate London's traffic very subtly by placing a toll gate on every street corner; but it would not work. The practical alternatives are three: specially expensive licences to use certain streets or areas; a comprehensive system of parking charges; and a new solution, whose implications are revolutionary: electronic charging.

The most popular suggestion for licensing has been a special licence to enter the

---

[1] D. L. Munby, 'Future Developments of the Internal System of Transport', *Journal of the Royal Society of Arts*, 108 (1960), 801.

[2] D. J. Reynolds and J. G. Wardrop, 'Economic Losses due to Traffic Congestion', *Fifth International Study Week in Traffic Engineering*, Nice, 1960.

[3] *The Economist*, 197 (1960), 365.

[4] D. L. Munby, 'The Roads as Economic Assets', *Bulletin of the Oxford Institute of Statistics*, 22 (1960), 274.

central area of London on workdays.[1] This seems a blunt economic instrument; its aims could better be met by graded parking charges. One exception, which parking fees do not meet, is the extra congestion in the very short morning and evening rush periods. Here a special licence fee would have salutary effects. If it applied generally, to public as to private transport, it would help spread the peak. It would discourage commercial firms from using their vehicles, often in situations where they contribute abnormally to congestion, in the rush periods.

In only one other situation does a licensing solution seem applicable to moving traffic: the provision of urban motorways. American experience proves conclusively that if only one freeway is provided without an attempt to regulate demand, the result will be irresistible political pressure to build six more freeways to relieve the resulting congestion.[2] Freeways in London would be expensive to build; they should be first-class roads, reserved for those who are willing to pay for first-class travel. It is often argued that it is administratively impossible to charge tolls on urban freeways. But they are charged, successfully, on several: for instance the Greater New York end of the New Jersey turnpike. Interestingly, though Gilbert Walker concludes that American turnpikes have not been a success generally, those that have, seem to be the urban ones, such as the New Jersey and the bridges and tunnels built by the Port of New York authority.[3]

The second alternative—parking fees—is the one already most widely adopted in London. But this is extraordinarily recent. As late as 1954, Alan Day and Ralph Turvey were arguing *as an academic exercise*[4] that the price mechanism should be used to limit parking space where its social cost was high; that this cost could be defined as the value of traffic flow, or the value of another person's parking; and that in the case of off-street parking, this could be defined as the cost in competition with alternative uses for the site. These revolutionary concepts of 1954 are now accepted Government orthodoxy, following the reports of the Parking Survey of Inner London in 1956–7. In the central area, short-term street parking on weekdays should be completely regulated by charging by 1964 at the latest.

There is still, however, a long way to go before we have a completely satisfactory system. First, the pricing system for metered on-street space needs to be made more flexible: the present system, by which space in Mayfair is charged the same rate as space in the remoter parts of Bloomsbury, is absurd, as may be seen by comparing the state of the streets in the two areas on any weekday afternoon. Secondly, the system needs extension to each and every area where parking contributes to congestion.

---

[1] See G. J. Roth, 'A Pricing Policy for Road Space in Town Centres', *Journal of the Town Planning Institute*, 47 (1961), 287–9.

[2] Cf. W. Owen, *op. cit.*, 109, 136, 188.

[3] G. Walker, 'Toll Roads in the United States', *Traffic Engineering and Control*, 2 (1960–1), 712–17.

[4] A. C. L. Day and R. Turvey, 'The Parking Problem in Central London—an Economic Appraisal', *Journal of the Institute of Transport*, 25 (1952–4), 406–11.

The reports of 1956–7, which recommended metering in inner London, were not competent to consider other areas: since then, only a few major suburban centres such as Woolwich and Croydon have taken steps to meter their shopping and business areas. Yet in these inner areas the results of the age of pre-planning are often most serious—as witness any of the Victorian shopping centres which sprawl along and off the main radial roads. Thirdly, in the central area a state of imbalance has occurred, in which parked cars are being displaced from the streets without finding off-street accommodation at the economic price. The market mechanism should correct this, but only when kerbside parking is completely and effectively regulated.[1] At that point, of course, the economic price will be much higher than motorists in the past have been willing to pay; so that they will tend to turn back to public transport. Estimates of the cost of off-street parking are £210 per car (Birmingham), £315 (Cardiff),[2] £400 (the Woolwich 'autostacker'),[3] £600 (the American average)[4] and £870 (estimate by the director of Lex Garages for an open-sided multi-storey car park in central London).[5] At this last figure, the commercial rate would be about £1 10s. per car for Monday–Friday peak parking; since the estimate was made costs have probably risen, and Lex Garages themselves now charge more than this.

An effective system of parking charges must be comprehensive but flexible. It must provide a wide variety of types of parking at a wide variety of (economic) rates. The short-term 'errand' parker would get metered space near his object of call. The medium-term visitor or shopper would get space adjacent to the building, provided by the owners of that building, either directly, or through use of rented space. The long-term commuter would get relatively expensive parking in garages directly accessible from freeways, without any need to enter the ordinary street system.[6] The commercial firm needing space for loading or unloading would pay rent for it, as part of the rent of the building; replanned areas would of course contain no facilities for street loading. This itself would encourage the more economical use of private goods transport than at present; it should be accompanied by the development of a cheap and rapid 'goods taxi service' within central London.

Until recently, carefully graduated parking charges were the best traffic regulators available. But since 1955, advances in electronics have made it possible to 'meter' the movements of all vehicles and to charge them an economic rate for the use of a

---

[1] The Road Traffic Act 1956 provided that surplus proceeds from parking meters must go to the provision of off-street parking space.

[2] E. W. Parkinson, 'Prospects for Parking', *Journal of the Institution of Municipal Engineers*, 86, (1959), 122–3.

[3] Note in *Traffic Engineering and Control*, 2 (1960–1), 179.

[4] H. Manzoni, 'Urban Traffic Congestion', *Journal of the Institution of Municipal Engineers*, 86 (1959), 200.

[5] B. R. Davies, 'Urban Congestion and the Parking Problem', *British Transport Review*, 5 (1958–60), 408–9.

[6] This is being done in Detroit: J. D. McGillis, 'Parking Problem solved in Detroit', *Traffic Engineering and Control*, 3 (1961–2), 490–2.

section of the street system. The principle is that a fully automatic record is made of the identity of cars passing a series of checkpoints. The records are then transferred to magnetic tape and are sorted electronically to provide records relating to particular cars. The computer then automatically calculates the charges relating to the car and provides an itemized monthly bill for posting to its owner. In Washington (D.C.) it has been estimated that the future maximum traffic needs can be met by a system costing less than £25 million, of which two-thirds would be the cost of the response blocks on cars (about £8 each) which would presumably be the responsibility of individual car owners.[1] Evidently, this technique would provide a complete system of traffic control. It could be applied to the ordinary street system (by areas), to parking, and to each stretch of an urban motorway system, all charges being aggregated into a single monthly bill. Since the fixed costs may prove high in relation to total costs, the economies of installing the system may well depend on future estimated traffic volumes at the expected rates of charging. These should be a subject for immediate investigation in any future traffic plan for London.[2]

The technique of charging to 'clear the market' has considerable application in public transportation also. Some of these applications follow automatically. For instance, the system of electronic charging should theoretically be applied to public service vehicles; and if the rates were varied according to degree of congestion in certain areas and at certain times of day, this might lead to more sharply differentiated charges to passengers also. The present system of public service charges, in London and elsewhere, is of course based heavily on the principle of cross-subsidization: profitable parts of the service subsidize unprofitable parts. If public transport operators found their 'indivisible' costs divided, they would either have to extend the principle of cross-subsidization, or relate their charges more directly to costs. They might be encouraged, for instance, to introduce more sharply differential fares to deal with their main problem—that of the peak. Season ticket concessions, for instance, might be suspended altogether during the peak periods. Politically, the idea of differential peak fares has always been regarded as anathema. (So, once, were parking meters.) Presumably for this reason, it was ignored by the Committee of Inquiry into London Transport in 1955, and rejected cursorily by the Committee for Staggering Working Hours in Central London in 1958.[3] This difficulty would be met if some way were found of passing the responsibility for travel costs on to central London employers. The introduction by British Railways and London Transport of 'travel vouchers', on the lines of luncheon vouchers, would achieve this; but at the cost of increased tax avoidance and of encouraging long-distance commuting. On

---

[1] Statement of William Vickrey to the Joint Committee on Washington Metropolitan Problems, 11 November 1959.

[2] An alternative and much cheaper scheme has now been evolved, in which activators on the road surface convey impulses to meters on vehicles, where they are recorded and aggregated. The estimated cost for all the congested areas of this country is as low as £50 million.

[3] Committee for Staggering Hours, *op. cit.*, 24.

political grounds, it may well be necessary to exempt public transport from the full rigour of economic charges for roadspace.

This would not be so serious, because one of the main objects of the new charging system would be to shift custom from relatively uneconomic types of road use (like private cars) to more economic types (like public buses). Indeed, the most important short-term effect of economic charging would be to encourage, in general, the efficient users of urban roadspace: thus taxis at the expense of cars, the common carrier's van instead of the firm's own under-used one.[1] A new system of charging should be accompanied by new systems of urban transport, designed to use road-space economically. Two which should be urgently considered are the provision of very small self-drive minicabs, which could be parked in suitable compounds on the streets; and a new rapid-frequency city goods service for loads of all types up to, say, a ton in weight.

Pricing: A Yardstick for Investment

Price, I said earlier, performs two essential functions. I have considered that of rationing. But there is another. The return which is expected on an investment will determine whether or not it is made. If the expected return cannot be expressed as a price, investment decisions will be more difficult to make, and there is more likeli-hood that they will be wrong. This is precisely what seems to have happened in the history of road investment in this country between 1950 and 1960. The Select Com-mittee on Estimates which considered trunk road investment came to the conclusion that 'no adequate scheme (of priorities) exists . . . the Sub-Committee formed the impression that one result of the lack of a national plan has been an over-emphasis on motorways through fields to the neglect of the problem of urban bottlenecks.'[2] Thus research on the returns to be expected from the M1 started three months after its construction. Since then the Road Research Laboratory have started to devise social cost-benefit accounts for road investment, expressed as rates of return. From the early results, fragmentary and inconclusive as they are, P.E.P. have argued that there is a much higher return on urban than on rural road improvements.[3]

Within urban areas, investment problems are complicated. First, it is necessary to express the expected returns on rail improvements on the same social basis as the Road Research economists have used; at present, British Railways consider only the private returns—the normal commercial basis of accounting—so that they would

---

[1] The average load in central London in spring 1960 was found to be only 0·4 tons, compared with 0·8 tons over the whole of Greater London: *Road Research 1961* (H.M.S.O. 1962), Table 9, page 18. In his Philadelphia study, E. M. Horwood found very serious under-use of trucks: 'City Center Goods Movement', *Highway Research Board Bulletin*, 203 (Washington, D.C., 1958), 85.

[2] *First Report from the Select Committee on Estimates*, 1958-9: Trunk Roads, paras. 11–13. H.M.S.O. 1959.)

[3] Political and Economic Planning. *The Cost of Roads* (May 1961), 133–5.

not consider (for instance) the saving in congestion on the roads that a new tube line would bring. Christopher Foster has argued that the railways should use social cost-benefit accounting, even though this would put them on a different basis from other nationalized industries.[1] It is chastening to realize here that only very recently have the railways begun to consider accurately the basis of calculation of *private* returns on existing sections of the system or on specific projected improvements.[2] Second, within urban areas the job of social cost-benefiting accounting may involve costing some rather imponderable elements. It is however perhaps possible to isolate four main points.[3] First, the time costs of all travel: this is in itself difficult to calculate because it means valuing the time we save. Second, the cost of improvement. Third, the value people put on quality of travel, especially upon the convenience of private motoring. Fourth, aesthetic and human aspects, upon which we can never hope to put an accurate price: the Road Research economists value accidents, but society might decide to value them higher; how do we consider the value of St Paul's as against the car park we might put on its site? These difficulties are challenges, to which ingenuity may well find answers. Albeit imperfect, such techniques can alone allow us to make rational investment decisions, especially on the matter most relevant to city transport planning: how much to invest on providing for the private motor car.

The Future of Mass Transportation

In other words: only through price, can we discover the sort of transport system people really want. Therefore, any attempt to sketch the transport system of London 2000 is hazardous speculation. But it is possible to make some informed guesses, by looking at the American example. There, one basic error was made, which now needs costly correction. This consisted in insulating one sector of transport—the private sector—from the influence of the price mechanism, while allowing the public sector to bear the full economic consequences.

This process has gone on for a long time. Right at the start of the American automobile revolution—in 1923—their ratio of cars to population stood where ours stood in 1962.[4] Within these forty years, while the Americans built roads regardless of cost and allowed efficient mass transport systems to decay or die, visionaries like Lord Ashfield and Frank Pick were making London Transport a model for the world. Now, in cities all over the North American continent, they are admitting

[1] C. D. Foster, 'Surplus Criteria for Investment', *Bulletin of the Oxford Institute of Statistics*, 22 (1960), 337–57. See also D. W. Glassborow, 'The Road Research Laboratory's Investment Criterion Examined', *ibid.*, 327–35.

[2] *Report from the Select Committee on Nationalised Industries: British Railways* (H.M.S.O. 1960), paras. 206–25.

[3] Cf. W. H. Glanville, 'Individual and Mass Transport in Urban Areas', *Traffic Engineering and Control*, 2 (1960–1), 412.

[4] L. C. Hawkins, *op. cit.*, 107.

their mistake, and planning to renew mass transport systems, at astronomical cost: £190 million in Los Angeles, £360 million in San Francisco.[1]

The dilemma of American mass transport is ours also; but it is older and deeper. While London Transport has lost off-peak revenue since about 1950, New York has lost it since about 1930; the impending American four-day week should stifle any hope that the Americans can ever make mass transport pay again. Yet even now, mass transport has to continue carrying the commuters—88 per cent in New York, 78 per cent in Chicago, against 90 per cent in London[2]—and if they ceased to carry these numbers the cost of curing the street congestion would be unbearable. So deficit operations are coming to be accepted as economic good sense.

The same paradox occurs, in milder form, in London with the Victoria line. Parts of the existing underground system and bus system in the West End are now grossly overtaxed, because employment has grown steadily while no new tube has been built since 1907. The Victoria Line, running diagonally under the West End from Victoria to Euston and then on to Walthamstow, will relieve this congestion. The level of interest charges to be carried, plus maintenance expenses, make it certain that it will lose a regular £2·5 to £3 million a year. Yet the saving in congestion on the streets alone will, in terms of social cost-benefit accounting, almost certainly justify a subsidy of this order.[3] Indeed, this is the justification for the existing internal (cross-) subsidization of the existing tube lines and half the central bus routes.[4] We are only just refining our techniques sufficiently to make an accurate cost estimate of these social benefits. Probably for this reason, construction of the Victoria Line was held up for seven years.

But these paradoxes are illusory. They occur only because the street users are not charged the economic cost of the congestion they cause. Once devise an adequate system of charging to 'clear the market', and many deficit operations in mass transport—certainly the Victoria Line—would become surplus operations.

It is all the more important to get investment decisions on a firm footing, because a lot of large-scale investment is likely to be forced on us in the near future. Not merely sections of the central area Underground system, but large parts of the suburban railway system south of the Thames, are working at full physical capacity. Minor improvements, such as longer trains and more frequent signalling devices to

[1] J. S. Gallagher, Jr., 'Urban Transport Developments in the U.S.A.', *British Transport Review*, 6 (1960–1), 93–7.

[2] R. J. Smeed, 'Visit to the United States', *Traffic Engineering and Control*, 2 (1960–1), 96–7; Regional Plan Association, *op. cit.*

[3] Sir John Elliot, 'London Transport—Route C', *Journal of the Institute of Transport*, 26 (1954–6), 318–24; *The Victoria Line* (Report by the London Travel Committee to the Minister of Transport and Civil Aviation), (H.M.S.O. 1959). Cf. C. D. Foster and M. E. Beesley, 'Estimating the Social Benefit of Constructing an Underground Railway in London', *Journal of the Royal Statistical Society*, Series A, 126 (1963), 46–92.

[4] Sir John Elliot, 'Efficiency versus Cost in Public Transport', *Journal of the Institute of Transport*, 27 (1956–8), 335.

reduce headway, create extra capacity which is almost immediately swallowed up in the rush of extra commuters. Thus even the first stage of the Kent Coast electrification did not notably increase capacity, because the track was already fully used. British Railways' estimates of the probable number of commuters on these lines by 1970 show them to be well beyond the capacity of the system without major new construction.[1] I have already argued in Chapter 3 that could we make our social cost and benefit accounts sufficiently sophisticated, we might well find it profitable to limit the growth of commuting into the centre by a system of incentives and disincentives. But the necessity here, as in the more particular question of road versus rail, is to have comparable estimates of the costs and returns of the different courses of action open to us. Otherwise, we will be making a series of intuitive gambles, which may cost us, as a society, dear.

The probable answer is that some expensive new rail capacity is inevitable. The cheapest way to provide this may be to integrate more closely the disparate elements of London's mass transport system. The suburban main line railways in the London area—especially south of the Thames—have mostly been electrified, but independently of the central underground system. As only one result, nearly one-quarter of London's commuters arrive each morning at southern terminals, where they use extremely archaic and unsatisfactory interchange facilities to transfer to the central systems of trains and buses. The aggregate delays, quite apart from the value we place on the strain and inconvenience, are colossal. In 1955, after seven years of nationalization during which integration should have taken place, the Committee of Inquiry into London Transport recommended strongly that facilities for interchange should be improved.[2] Yet still nothing is done. Nor, under the present decentralized regime, is it likely to be, until all the suburban transport services of London region are brought under one authority, as they ought to have been in 1948. Only then will it be possible to extend throughout the region the model of travel which London Transport has carried through in its improvement of the Metropolitan Line between 1939 and 1962: the integration of fast long-distance and slow short-distance trains with cross-platform interchange between the two in the inner suburbs.[3]

Such improvements will be bought at a price. This is right;[4] while the tendency of modern industry is to emphasize service competition rather than price competition, public transport systems in both Britain and America have been obsessed by the necessity to keep prices down, often because of political pressure applied through fares tribunals or similar bodies. Thus the rises in London fares between 1940 and 1960 were much less than the rises in their costs, in general living costs, or in salaries.

[1] P. A. White, 'The Problem of the Peak', *Journal of the Institute of Transport*, 28 (1958-60), 270-1.
[2] *Report of the Committee of Inquiry into London Transport* (H.M.S.O. 1955), paras. 355-6.
[3] A feature of the New York subway system.
[4] This is also the philosophy of Dr. Beeching, as revealed by *The Reshaping of British Railways* (H.M.S.O. 1963).

The same sort of lag in America in the thirties was a major factor in the declining standards of public transport. Only recently in this country have the nationalized transport systems got the right to impose commercial rates. But this does not reach the heart of the dilemma, which is once again the lack of adequate cost comparison between the public and the private sectors of transport. Cure this, and you will at least be in a position to say how much people are willing to pay for better public transport. The economic dice must first be unloaded.

A New Plan for Traffic

To start unchoking the roads, we need again to compare our situation with America's.

Our policy for urban roads has been do-nothing. The result is the most conspicuous example we can offer to Professor Galbraith of public squalor. While in many departments of welfare we have led the world, our city streets resemble nothing so much as a compulsory public health service organized on the basis of the nineteenth-century Poor Law, with no option to pay for anything better.

The American policy, in contrast, has been to do everything: to build roads for the cars wishing to use them regardless of any cost regulator. This has had precisely the same effect as the action of the primitive Bolsheviks, when shortly after the October Revolution they threw open the railway system to all free of charge.

The end result of both policies has been near-chaos, with only differences of detail. The American car commuter drives smoothly at forty miles an hour along the freeway—and then may take an hour to cover six city blocks to his office. His English counterpart groans at fifteen miles an hour along a narrow early nineteenth-century turnpike lined with parked vehicles, milk floats and stray dogs; his transition to the city blocks is less evident.

Today, in the early sixties, we stand on a critical watershed in the history of traffic planning in London. For the first time in decades, the money is being made available for major road building: £10 million a year over the next ten years in the L.C.C. area alone. In the late sixties, as the network of main inter-city long-distance motorways is completed, the pace of urban construction is likely to increase even further. Already, in 1963, work has begun on London's first urban motorway: the M4, to join west London with London Airport and the Great West Road beyond Maidenhead. The seeds of the American vicious circle are thus already sown: construction generates traffic, generates demand for more construction, generates votes, generates election promises, generates more construction. Unless we lay the foundations now of a coherent transport policy for the decades to come, the process bids to overwhelm us—and London.

The elements of such a policy are clear. There must be a *negative* element: a system of rationing of traffic where demand exceeds the supply of road space. I have already argued that the best system of rationing is by price, which does not involve bureaucratic regulation and will also guide our investment decisions. And there must be a *positive* element: reconstruction of London to provide for the traffic that is willing to pay the price; a high rate of investment.

It behoves us, first, to look at what we are likely to do with our money. What are the existing plans? The answer is an extraordinary jumble: of archaic ill-conceived schemes, devised in the days of the horse-drawn vehicle; of utopian plans of vast magnitude, prepared regardless of cost and innocent of information, in the flush of careless wartime enthusiasm; of the total lack of any coherent and considered scheme, based on close observations of traffic flows and projections of future developments, anywhere in the County of London Development Plans. The East End provides just one example of this last failing. Here it has been estimated that a radial motorway, from Aldgate to the Barking by-pass, would save many times its construction costs within a few years, through economies in time and materials. In 1951, when the original L.C.C. Development Plan was prepared, the East End was a bomb-scarred wilderness; the L.C.C. proposed to rebuild it, as a vast New Town for 100,000 people. Since then, with great vision and courage, the L.C.C. have gone far to turning this dream into magnificent reality. But in 1951 they were not allowed by the Government to make any provision for a modern road plan; so the East End has been rebuilt with its nineteenth-century system of roads, which are about as appropriate to it as would be earth closets in the flats. The result will stand for a century as a monument to short-sightedness and failure of the planning imagination.[1]

But because there is still no coherent plan, the L.C.C., at last given the money, are about to repeat the mistake over the face of inner London. They propose to spend £100 million in a decade on ill-conceived piecemeal improvements of no proved traffic value, on tinkerings with the existing Victorian street system. The basic aim, accepted for decades by traffic engineer and town planner alike—that different types of traffic be segregated on different roads—is being ignored. Some of these schemes date back to the year 1910,[2] when the pace of London's traffic was fixed by the horse and cart. They are to be carried through, regardless of good economics or good planning, because no one has the courage to rethink the problem through. When the L.C.C. ends in 1965—as now seems probable—they will provide an ill-fitting epitaph on a great authority.[3]

The first essential in a London Road Plan is to suspend these schemes, as from

[1] The L.C.C. have now announced (Autumn 1962) that the 'East Cross Route' to the Blackwall Tunnel is to be built as a near-motorway.

[2] In the Report of the London Traffic Branch of the Board of Trade, 1910, 32 (*Parliamentary Papers*, 1911, XXXIV). This stressed also (page 33) the need for a single Greater London main roads authority—a need which should be met 55 years later.

[3] Since this was written the L.C.C. have accepted the urban motorway principle for a number of important schemes, including the West Cross Route (Wood Lane–Chelsea), the Western Avenue Extension (Wood Lane–Edgware Road), the Eastern Avenue Extension (City Road–Temple Mills), the East Cross Route (Bow Bridge–Kidbrooke) and the Kent Radial (Lewisham–Eltham). *Highway Times*, April 1963. But existing schemes will be retained.

now, completely. The money should be diverted to cross-country construction until a coherent scheme is devised on the basis of a charging system and a traffic survey.

The Short-Term Solution: Traffic Engineering

While this happens, limited funds should be applied to the sort of improvement that brings proved short-term dividends: large-scale traffic management on the existing streets. In central London, this means extending meter parking, one-way streets, 'jug-handle' routes to cut out right turns across traffic flows, progressive traffic lights, channelization of traffic at junctions, lane demarcation; on the radials leading from the centre, the clearway technique: lane marking, channelization, total waiting bans and peak bans on loading and unloading, one-way routes at important junctions, reversible flows.

These methods have been a commonplace on the Continent, and even in British provincial cities,[1] for decades. But only since the setting-up of the Ministry of Transport's London Traffic Management Unit in 1960 have they been applied on any scale in London. The resulting revolutionary increase in the efficiency of the street system may be judged from the single fact that in 1961, for the first time in many years, the average speed of traffic in central London increased, by no less than 9 per cent.[2]

But there is an important limitation: in 1961, also, the volume of traffic in central London increased 4 per cent: twice the average increase of the fifties.[3] Inevitably, and often quickly, traffic management generates extra traffic to fill the new spaces. This is not to say that traffic management will wither away; however much we reconstruct London to cope with the vehicle, it will remain an essential art, simply because pressure on scarce land will remain at the centre, and it will always be necessary to use that land as economically as possible—which is the basic object of the traffic engineers. The ingenuity of the engineers will develop new techniques of more effective control: in particular, the use of electronics to guide traffic on to less congested streets,[4] where they will automatically be charged a lower rate under an electronic charging system.

Traffic management has a more important limitation. The traffic engineer is paid to make traffic flow; he does just this; other considerations are irrelevant to him. In a city as ill-planned for the motor vehicle as London, the result may be a disaster in terms of true planning. The two most spectacular cases of this so far are the routeing of a main West End traffic stream through London's handsomest surviving Georgian square;[5] and the plan to bring heavy lorries, north-bound from the docks and central

---

[1] In Birmingham since 1933.

[2] Department of Scientific and Industrial Research, *Road Research 1961* (H.M.S.O. 1962), 12.

[3] *Ibid*. These figures relate to working hours.

[4] Department of Scientific and Industrial Research, *Road Research 1960*, 29.

[5] Bedford Square.

markets, through the old village centre of Highgate.[1] But there are many other cases which are no less disturbing, but which get less spectacular publicity because they do not involve aesthetics or because the people affected are less vocal than in Highgate. Any and every residential backwater is now likely to have its peace and privacy ended by the diversion of a main traffic flow.

Based on considerations of traffic flow alone, traffic engineering techniques bid to erode the Londoner's standard of decent civilized living more quickly than any other contemporary development. But based on a careful weighing of costs and benefits to everyone involved—motorists, residents, pedestrian schoolchildren and shoppers—they could point the way to a cheap and quick method of making London a better place to live *and* drive in, until we can spare the resources for more radical reconstruction. That method is *flexible traffic control*. Within each area and at each period of day, traffic must be routed so as to cause the minimum inconvenience to the maximum number. At the morning rush hour, traffic flow must be paramount: residential streets, for short periods, must carry one-way flows, though streets around schools must be sacrosanct. When shoppers crowd the High Street, it must be turned into a precinct reserved for pedestrian shoppers, parked cars, delivery vans; that will demand the use of one residential street, at least, as a relief road. But as soon as the evening rush is over, the High Street can be opened up; and the residential areas must be sealed, for the evening and the night, against through traffic. In other words, flexible control would try to achieve for short periods precisely those conditions, which radical reconstruction would achieve permanently. The techniques of flexible control can be applied to actual situations, where current Ministry of Transport thinking has produced woefully inflexible solutions. True, this will demand more money than the present solution; money for extra traffic lights, indicator signals, traffic police and wardens, crash barriers. But the resulting social benefits would make it a much better proposition in terms of communal welfare. And it must be remembered that, relative to complete reconstruction, all traffic engineering schemes are cheap.

Essentials of a Traffic Plan

I cannot present a blueprint here for the London we need to cope with the problem of the motor vehicle; the detail depends on the traffic survey we do not have. But one can, without presumption, forecast the main outlines. Origin and destination surveys in big cities the world over show three main demands of traffic on land, overlying the myriad and contradictory cross- and scatter-trips. First, strong radial flows, into and out of the central area and other main sub-centres of activity like the docks and industrial areas. Second, an extremely dense and complex pattern of movements within the central business district. Third, demand for parking, waiting

[1] This plan was modified by the Ministry of Transport in January 1963, after considerable protest.

and loading space within the same district and the sub-centres. Each demands first a calculation of likely needs; secondly a programme of physical construction and a policy for making it possible. In the rest of this chapter I am concerned with the needs; construction is only part of the problem of urban renewal, which I take up in Chapter 7.

Rebuilding for Traffic: The Motorway Net

C. D. Buchanan, in the best book likely to be written on Britain's traffic problems, concludes: 'The radials are, in fact, a nasty nagging problem to which there seems to be no satisfactory answer.'[1] But, he admits, investigation might show specially heavy traffic along some of them, justifying motorway construction. Plainly, Buchanan is frightened—he is not alone in this—at the destructive potential of freeway construction on an old city like London. I think this fear misplaced, because it is based too exclusively on the American parallel. Not only have some American cities built freeways indiscriminately; they have built them badly, without any concern for good planning, for their integration into the urban landscape. Even then, their effect is no worse than that of the great Victorian railway lines and yards which scar so much of inner London. But we should be able to do better than the Victorians.

The problem is only one of sensitive design. For here as elsewhere, good traffic engineering equals good planning; the urban motorway is both, because it segregates fast-moving, through-travelling traffic and gives it unimpeded flow. This is good for the traffic and good for the people who formerly suffered the traffic. The urban motorway is also better value for money than the present policy of piecemeal improvement, although initially it might seem expensive. In London there is a direct cost comparison: Finchley Road. The L.C.C. propose to widen it at a cost of some £2 million a mile.[2] In Chapter 1 I have already pointed out the deplorable effects this scheme will have on the neighbourhood. As an all-purpose road its probable capacity (based on American experience) would be 600 vehicles per lane-hour, or 3,600 vehicles per hour with all lanes fully occupied.[3] But the Ministry of Transport already have a tentative scheme for an urban motorway parallel to Finchley Road. The capacity of this road would be the urban motorway average: 1,500 vehicles per lane-hour (9,000 vehicles per hour with all lanes fully occupied), or as high as 2,000 vehicles per lane-hour with traffic management.[4] The estimated cost in 1956 was £3·75

---

[1] C. D. Buchanan, *Mixed Blessing: the Motor in Britain* (1958), 199.

[2] *Roads in England and Wales: Report for the Year 1960–1* (H.M.S.O. 1961), 29; mileage from *Report of the Committee on London Roads* (H.M.S.O. 1959), 21, which gave a lower estimate of cost.

[3] Fred Burggraf in *British Road Federation Bulletin*, 282 (1960), 166.

[4] *Ibid.*; W. H. Glanville and J. F. A. Baker, 'Urban Motorways in Great Britain?' in British Road Federation, *Urban Motorways* (1956), 24; W. Fisher Cassie in *British Road Federation Bulletin*, 284 (1960), 198.

million a mile.[1] Even allowing for rises in costs since 1956,[2] the motorway clearly represents a better way of spending limited funds.

About the probable total cost of a freeway system it is difficult to generalize: there are great variations in construction costs per mile, even along the same road. American extremes are the Hollywood Freeway (early postwar; £2 million a mile) and the Boston Central Artery (1955: £15 million a mile). The Cross-Bronx Expressway, which probably is the closest parallel to a London freeway, cost £8 million a mile; the U.S. Bureau of Public Roads estimate that the urban parts of their proposed inter-state system would cost £1·4 million a mile for 6 lanes;[3] the Association of Metropolitan Borough Engineers and Surveyors estimated in 1960 that a ring motorway about 4 miles from Central London would cost £2½ million a mile.[4]

At a guess, then, we might build at current prices 1½–3 miles a year for, say, £10 million. Thus on the basis of this expenditure between 1970 and 2000 we could build 45–90 miles of urban motorway.

Again pending confirmation from traffic surveys, it seems from experience of other cities that the system would be based on the so-called *radial-tangential* plan: this in contradiction to the most advanced existing plans we have, the County of London and Greater London Plans of 1943–4, which used radials intersected by concentric rings. As Buchanan points out, these plans were based on no survey of traffic movements, but on hunches, many of them unsound.[5] American studies show that around big cities the proportion of traffic approaching the city, but wishing to avoid it, is as low at 10 per cent.[6] So the ring road, built at right angles to the radial, is the least valuable road that could be built. Instead, the system should allow traffic to approach as near as possible to that part of the central area it wants to visit, and then to encourage it to halt there without entering the ordinary street system. This demands a number of routes skirting the city centre tangentially, with frequent junctions between them, and with direct loops to special car parks within walking distance of the objective; the objective already partly realized in Detroit.[7] American city freeways are invariably built on a variant of the radial-tangential system.[8]

But no simple tangential system is possible for a central business district of ten

[1] Glanville and Baker, *ibid.*, 27.

[2] For the section of the same motorway between Aldenham, Herts., and the North Circular Road, which is now a firm proposal, the estimated cost in 1963 was £1·58 m. per mile including all interchanges (some of which would be incurred whether the motorway were built or not) against £1·28 m. per mile in 1956. *The Times*, 12 February 1963.

[3] These figures from W. Owen, *op. cit.*, 49–50.

[4] British Road Federation, *London Needs . . .* (1960), 6.

[5] C. D. Buchanan, *op. cit.*, 157.

[6] Glanville and Baker, *op. cit.*, 29.

[7] R. M. Hare, 'Radials versus Ring Roads', *Traffic Engineering and Control*, 2 (1960–1), 660; W. Fisher Cassie, 'Scientific Approach to Urban Traffic Problems', *ibid.*, 602–4; J. D. McGillis, *op. cit.*, 491.

[8] Plans in B.R.F., *Urban Motorways, op. cit.*

square miles or more.[1] So London's system will depend on multiple tangents running through the central area, dividing it up into sub-areas of high value and high economic concentration; the motorways would be built through lower-value border zones, themselves ripe for early redevelopment.

How dense should this central network be? The most detailed scheme so far proposed—that of R. B. Hounsfield[2]—postulated one per lateral mile: four north-south and four east-west motorways to be built within sixteen years across the central area. This plan assumes peak-hour flows out of the central area of 76,000 vehicles per hour (compared with 25,000 in 1937 and 30,000 in 1956). Hounsfield's detailed plan is too rigid: it makes no allowance for the existence of historical precincts where no radical reconstruction could be tolerated. Another plan—that of J. A. Proudlove, which won the Roads Campaign Council 'New Ways for London' competition in 1959[3]—is based on an outward peak-hour flow of 60,000 vehicles; it leaves the existing street system, somewhat improved, to carry 25,000 people, and puts in twelve or thirteen radial motorways to carry another 43,000.[4] Proudlove accepts the radial-tangential principle, but makes his net tangential to the centre *as a whole*: only one main north-south line (between West End and City) and two branches (tangential to the City) cut through the Central Business District. Elsewhere he relies on improved and new all-purpose streets, one of which cuts through the Bloomsbury University precinct. The motorways are mainly planned along existing streets, widened to 250 feet; the result of which would be as bad as anything in North America. Neither Hounsfield nor Proudlove seem to have succeeded, then, in reconciling engineering with amenity. They also suffer from the fundamental assumption that roads must be built to carry greatly inflated numbers of vehicles, which under a rational pricing system would no longer necessarily be true.

Till we have a pricing system, it is difficult to guess at the system we need. But the following two-stage programme could be suggested tentatively.

First: between 1965 and 1980 a number of radials should connect the London ends of the national cross-country motorways with the edge of the central area. Their precise routes will depend partly on existing needs, as revealed by a traffic survey; partly on the wider plan for urban renewal of the inner areas. To this latter end, the motorways should pass between, but tangentially close to, existing sub-centres of economic concentration in the inner suburbs; and their construction should be coupled with the development of these sub-centres as nodes of a wider central area, as outlined in Chapter 3, and the consequent re-arrangement of land-values, as

---

[1] London's C.B.D. is not yet scientifically determined, as are American examples (see R. E. Murphy and J. E. Vance, 'Delimiting the C.B.D.', *Economic Geography*, 30 (1954), 189–222): see the various *ad hoc* definitions in *Report of the Royal Commission on Local Government in Greater London* (H.M.S.O. 1960), Map 12.

[2] R. B. Hounsfield, *Engineering Aspects of the Transport Problem of London* (1951).

[3] J. A. Proudlove, 'A Traffic Plan for London', *Town Planning Review*, 31 (1960–1), 53–73.

[4] *Ibid.*, 55–6. There is therefore a surplus capacity of 8,000 vehicles per peak hour.

suggested in Chapter 8. The roads should as far as possible run through belts of obsolescent property, ripe for renewal; in many cases the lines of railway tracks will be suitable, since these historically divide neighbourhoods, they are intersected by relatively few cross-streets, property along them is depressed and land values are often low. In some cases the motorways may use main-line railway tracks which are superfluous and no longer remunerative: the line out of Marylebone is an obvious example.[1] In Map 5 I suggest a very tentative motorway net for inner London, based on these considerations and on the few existing firm plans for new construction by the L.C.C.

These first-stage radials should terminate in special car parks on the edge of the central area. After 1980 they should be connected across the central area, tangent-fashion, so as to divide it into sub-centres of concentration. Again they would use zones ripe for redevelopment. This stage of construction could be carried through only as part of the complete comprehensive redevelopment of the central area, which I outline in Chapter 7. The object will be to avoid the American mistake of cutting the motorway as an isolated trench, through the city; it will be integrated into a completely new, multi-level system of circulation, to create a city quite unlike any we know today.

A Parking Plan

Extra carrying capacity, into and out of the central area, demands extra parking capacity, a great deal of it connected directly with the new radials; and at least some extra capacity on the existing network of all-purpose streets in the central area. How much extra will depend on the planned capacity of the radials. Twelve or thirteen radials—a fair target by 2000—would allow for peak flows at the Hounsfield-Proudlove levels (60–76,000 vehicles per maximum peak-hour outward flow), though this might well be more than motorists are willing to pay for under a pricing system; much will depend on how rich we are by 2000. Proudlove implies an eventual parking capacity for 180,000 in the central zone;[2] this would allow for a higher proportion of car commuters than the cities of eastern North America do now.[3] If we catered for one in eight of the present total of central area commuters to arrive by car (as in New York in 1960) with an average of 1·5 people per car, this would require only about 110,000 places.

In 1956, by comparison, there were some 43,000 parked cars on central London streets;[4] in 1959 about 51,000;[5] in 1961, 47,000.[6] By 1964, with complete metering,

---

[1] And the Regent's Canal, which runs for the most part through a belt of massive obsolescence, and which calls for imaginative comprehensive development combining a motorway, industry and open space. Cf. *Highway Times*, April 1963.

[2] Calculated from J. A. Proudlove, *op. cit.*, data on 54 and 63.

[3] P. H. Bendtsen, *op. cit.*, 67.

[4] Ministry of Transport, *Parking Survey of Inner London, Interim Report* (H.M.S.O. 1956), 4.

[5] Hilary Green, 'Parking in Inner London', *The Surveyor*, 120 (1961), 997.

[6] Association of Metropolitan Borough Engineers and Surveyors, *Car Parking Plan for London* (1961), Appendix A.

there may be as few as 20,000, so that 27,000 of the 1961 parkers will be displaced. There is a floating but roughly constant figure of about 4,000 places on bombed sites, or sites awaiting redevelopment; there were about 8,000 places purpose-built in public off-street garages in 1958 and a total of 16,500 off-street places in a 1957 survey;[1] this last was probably an under-estimate. The best estimate then is that in the early sixties there were about 63,000 cars parked in central London on workdays, 47,000 of them on the streets. This was just under 7 per cent of the estimated cars in the Greater London Conurbation at the time: a figure very close to the 6 per cent quoted by Bendtsen for American cities of over one million population.[2]

To provide for 110,000, then, needs 43,000 more places: to provide for 180,000, 113,000; to which, in both cases must be added places for the 27,000 displaced from the streets. This will make very heavy demands on limited and expensive space. The average European car needs 128 square feet if self-parked, 96 square feet if attendant-parked;[3] this gives one acre per 340 cars self-parked and one acre per 450 cars attendant-parked. Thus to provide self-parking for 100,000 cars would take 290 acres, or over two-fifths the area of the City of London. Even with long-term parkers concentrated in four- and five-storey parks, the demands will be considerable and the expense relatively much higher. If the motorists of London demand this space, through the pricing system, it will demand replanning and rebuilding on a scale—administrative, financial, physical—still almost outside our present imaginative grasp.

But the parking problem is not limited to the central area alone. All over the Inner and Suburban Rings, and in the country towns of the Outer Ring, smaller centres of congestion occur. These are most serious where, due to past failure to plan, shopping and parking are mixed with through traffic functions: a problem all too familiar, in areas of Victorian development like Kilburn and Brixton and Wandsworth, in interwar suburbs like Kingsbury and Hendon. Too often the suburbs are not nearly ripe for redevelopment, and will remain a problem for decades yet. But the inner shopping centres,[4] many of them, are ready for immediate renewal; and like the central area they demand thorough-going reconstruction in terms of motor traffic.

The Central Street Network

If we plan to increase the capacity of the radial roads two- or three-fold, it is inevitable that the capacity of the central street network must increase too. The relationship is by no means simple, because many of the extra cars using the new radials would have to be siphoned off into direct-access parks. Nevertheless, some

[1] L.C.C. Development Plan, First Review, 1960, I, 73 and II, 163.

[2] P. H. Bendtsen, op. cit., 69.

[3] E. N. Underwood, 'Multi-Storey Car Parks', The Structural Engineer, 37 (1959), 349.

[4] The Association of Metropolitan Borough Engineers and Surveyors have recommended to the Boroughs' Standing Joint Committee that around such centres street parking should be rigidly controlled, and have suggested capacities and sites for off-street garages. Car Parking Plan, op. cit., 6 and Appendix B.

increase in 'scatter' or 'errand' traffic is inevitable if activity in the central area increases; and it would be sanguine to expect no increase, whatever scheme of incentives or controls we introduce.

On the other hand, it is evident that at critical limiting times of day, many parts of the central street system are even now working at or beyond their economic capacity; only the fact of congestion is limiting that congestion. So long therefore as people are willing to pay the cost, the aim of central reconstruction must be to provide extra street space. This, in an area where there is desperate competition for scarce land, might seem an unlikely prospect. But this again is only because we are imaginatively limited by the concept of the traditional city with its corridor streets, which has dominated mankind for four thousand years. The Americans, in their heroic age of laissez-faire, first discovered the solution to the paradox: where space is shortest and land values highest, there you maximize individual profit by building vertically. We need now to realize that social profit is maximized in the same way. By rearranging land uses—street space, office space, shop space—vertically instead of horizontally, we achieve more space for all these uses at minimum extra cost. This is the solution the private developers already employ within their own buildings. They put shops on the ground floor nearest their customers and their sources of goods, offices higher up, perhaps flats higher still. But because there is now no effective social control, street space cannot be similarly disposed; for the street space is that which was marked out by the first developer of the area, perhaps two centuries ago, perhaps two millennia,[1] in an age without our problems. It is essential to find a way, the least painful way, of imposing that social control; and to turn over, in central London, a whole level of space to the circulation of vehicles.

Given then this free plane for vehicles, what to do with it? That is for the traffic engineers to decide. Available evidence indicates that for central areas, the motorway is not the solution; too many journeys are too short and too random in character. A simple, uniform and easily understood geometric plan, based on the grid-iron streets of American cities, is probably the answer. It might work on a simple plan, alternate streets operating one-way in opposite directions; or it might be sophisticated on two levels, all north-south and south-north traffic on one level, all east-west and west-east on another, with regular communication ramps between the two; on this second alternative there would be no intersections on the same grade. Within the resulting checker-board pattern, the squares would each contain loading space for the commercial or residential buildings above, and short-term 'errand' parking space, connected with the blocks above by ramp or escalator. Long-term parking space would most be connected directly with the urban motorway system at a different level— probably a higher one in most cases. Connections between the two road systems in the central area would be relatively few: certainly not more than every mile, and very probably less.

The vertical solution is not a rigid, total solution, which involves the sudden and

[1] Oxford Street follows a Roman line.

simultaneous reconstruction of London into a model of a Prussian drill-ground. Above the street level, indeed, it frees architects from the tyranny of corridor street planning. The essence of the solution is that it is applicable in parts, as one area and then another is reconstructed; the only element which has to come into being as a whole is the motorways, which is why these can arrive in the central area only when reconstruction is well advanced. And the vertical solution will never be suitable everywhere; it is merely an element in an eclectic solution for London. The art of central planning will be the art of applying it sensitively; which will prove one of the major responsibilities of the next generation of planners. This, and other problems, I take up as part of the wider discussion of urban renewal, in Chapter 7.

Postscript, 1969

When *London 2000* was published, it was still possible to argue that London had no effective transportation planning, either at the most immediate short-term level or at the long-term investment planning level. Since the establishment of the Greater London Council Department of Highways and Transportation, and since the appearance of Part Two of the *London Traffic Survey*, that is a purely historical argument.[1] The policy-making procedures of the Survey itself, it can be argued with some important reservations, are about as carefully structured, and as closely integrated with general strategic planning, as in any major metropolitan region of the world. The sequence of operations—from survey and inventory of facilities, through projections, preparation of alternative plans, evaluation and choice—borrows technically from a decade of experience in North America since the first modern transportation study—that for Detroit—appeared in 1955. But London's study goes far beyond its North American counterparts in its emphasis on a total transportation plan, as opposed to a mere highways plan, and in the integration of that plan within a total strategic development plan. It goes almost without saying that this is possible because London now has what it did not have when *London 2000* was published, and what North American cities still lack: an overall metropolitan area government, responsible for strategic decisions in the fields of planning and transportation.

The Survey stage of the London study was commissioned in 1961, before the reform of London government became an accomplished fact. It was therefore carried through, and published in 1964, under a joint *ad hoc* agreement between the Ministry of Transport and the old London County Council.[2] But the Study Area necessarily covered an area much larger than the old L.C.C.'s 117 square miles; it was bigger even than the Greater Council area which replaced it, extending well into the Green Belt

---

[1] Volumes One (1964) and Two (1966) of this study were published under this title: Volume Three will appear under the new title of the *London Transportation Study*. The results of the Study will be incorporated in the Greater London Development Plan, to be published early in 1969.

[2] *London Traffic Survey*, Volume One, *op. cit.* (London County Council, 1964).

and even beyond. Nevertheless, its outer cordon line was drawn more tightly than in equivalent American studies; it thus excluded most of the fast-growing areas of the Outer Metropolitan Area where transportation planning presents many more imponderables than in the firm built up areas of London. But within these limits, the Study's home interviews and roadside studies tell us more about the movement patterns of London than had ever been known before. This, indeed, was a triumph of applied social science in action.

The most striking point which the Survey illuminated was the critical distinction between the problem of traffic at the morning and evening peak hours, and the problem of traffic at all other times. Still, when the first volume was published in 1964, it was still possible to see the peak as the problem. One-third of the total 1962 flow of traffic occurred in four hours of the two daily peak periods; one tenth actually occurred in the hour of maximum demand.[1] And during those times when all forms of transportation were in greatest demand, it was observable that public transport came into its own. This was true, above all, of the great number of journeys which ended or began in the Central Area. 73 per cent of all internal journeys to the centre by British Railways arrived between 8 and 10; for the underground the figure was 50, and for buses only 35 per cent.[2] The finding accords with the experience of traffic planners in cities the world over. And over 87 per cent of all central arrivals between 8 and 10 are by public transport, compared with 56 per cent of arrivals outside the centre.[3]

These figures are so important, because peak journeys are mainly work journeys, and work was overwhelmingly the most important reason why people made journeys. Over 47 per cent of so called basic journeys, in fact, were journeys to work; the next most important, personal business, accounted for only 12 per cent.[4] But here a critical distinction was observable. In 1964, about 38 per cent of households of the survey area owned a car; under 4 per cent owned two or more.[5] (Very similar results were given nationally by the National Travel Survey of 1965, and by the Census in 1966.) These 38 per cent were responsible for 60 per cent of all internal journeys.[6] And these households make more than twice as many journeys by motor transport as non-car owning households: 6·1 basic internal journeys a day, against 2·5.[7] Strikingly, even people in car-owning households still made 29 per cent of their journeys by public transport.[8] Doubtless, this was a product of many factors: the fact of only one car and several people in the households, the fact that not all family members could drive, and so on. But undoubtedly significant was the great and growing difficulty of driving a car to work at the peak hours, above all to central London. This would work as a

[1] *London Traffic Survey*, Vol. I, *op. cit.*, paras. 9, 21 (p. 158).   [2] *Ibid.*, paras. 6, 31 (p. 101).
[3] *Ibid.*, para. 6.34 (p. 103).   [4] *Ibid.*, para. 6.44 (p. 104), para. 6.46 (p. 105).
[5] *Ibid.*, para. 6.43 (p. 78), para. 6.44 (p. 79).
[6] *Ibid.*, para. 6.49 (p. 105).
[7] *Ibid.*, Table 7–1 (p. 127).
[8] *Ibid.*, para. 6.52 (p. 106).

permanent disincentive to the use of the car at these times. But it would not stop people driving their cars at other times: above all, in the evening and weekend leisure hours.

These journeys passed over an extraordinary diffuse and complex road network—compared, that is, with average European or North American cities, where a few high capacity arteries carry a high proportion of total traffic. The reason was the simple lack of capacity on London's roads. Only one really high capacity route then existed, the Great West Road; and significantly it was carrying the highest recorded volumes over any appreciable distance, 56,000 vehicles a day.[1] For the future, as car ownership levels increased, this lack of capacity would clearly represent an increasing problem. And the distinction already observed, between the behaviour of the car owners and the non-car owners, merely underlined the point.

TABLE 26

INTERNAL BASIC TRIPS, BY PURPOSE: 1962 and 1981

	1962	1981	1962–1981 Number	increase per cent
Work	5,377,200	5,906,900	529,700	9·9
Personal business	1,383,700	2,831,800	1,448,100	104·6
Social	812,400	1,414,800	602,400	74·2
Shopping—convenience	659,700	1,250,200	590,500	89·5
School	549,700	1,224,900	675,200	122·8
Other home-based	1,209,800	2,047,000	837,200	69·2
Total home-based	9,992,500	14,675,600	4,683,100	46·9
Non home-based	1,339,800	2,017,100	677,300	50·6
Total all purposes	11,332,300	16,692,700	5,360,400	47·3

Source: *London Traffic Survey*, Vol. 2, Table 13.5

It received statistical expression in Volume Two of the Study, published by the GLC in July, 1966. Here the central aim was to project future traffic volumes by establishing firm statistical relationships between travel patterns and a host of factors that might be assumed to affect these patterns—factors like density, the density of population in an area, its distance from the centre, and the average income of its residents. All of these affected car ownership; and additionally, density had its own effect on people's propensity to make journeys, whether they owned cars or not. Among these factors, few striking changes were likely to occur in total population (which was expected to grow by only 4 per cent between 1962 and 1981), or in employment (which was expected to increase by 11 per cent in the same period); but big changes were forecast in incomes (a 60 per cent increase) and hence in car ownership (a doubling, with exceptionally big increases in the inner suburbs). Because car

[1] *Ibid.*, para. 2 (10, p. 13).

154

TABLE 27

INTERNAL JOURNEYS, BY TRAVEL MODE AND PURPOSE: 1962/1981

		Work Trips			Other Home-based Trips			Non Home-based Trips			All Trips		
		Central Area	Non Central Area	Total	Central Area	Non Central Area	Total	Central Area	Non Central Area	Total	Central Area	Non Central Area	Total
Drivers	1962	220	1323	1543	110	1591	1701	117	758	875	447	3672	4119
	1981	321	2359	2680	272	4538	4810	184	1301	1485	777	8198	8975
Bus Passengers	1962	578	1467	2044	157	1512	1669	63	114	177	798	3093	3890
	1981	560	717	1277	121	1197	1318	42	82	124	723	1996	2719
Rail Passengers	1962	1000	399	1399	135	204	339	53	44	96	1188	646	1834
	1981	1019	340	1359	125	156	281	33	22	55	1177	518	1695
Other Passengers	1962	72	320	390	87	820	907	44	148	192	201	1288	1489
	1981	90	500	590	161	2199	2360	71	292	353	322	298	3303
Total	1962	1868	3509	5377	488	4127	4615	277	1063	1340	2633	8699	11332
	1981	1990	3916	5906	679	8090	8769	330	1687	2017	2999	13693	16692

Source: *London Traffic Survey*, Vol. 2, Tables 14–15 and 14–18.

ownership gives mobility, the effect of this last increase on journeys should be dramatic: in less than twenty years, internal trips will have increased 50 per cent. But of this
growth, only a small part will represent journeys to work; these are expected to grow
10 per cent, compared with a 96 per cent growth for the home-based, non-work trips.
Personal business trips will double, shopping trips will nearly double, trips to school
more than double; social trips will go up about three quarters. Thus, while in 1962
work journeys were nearly one-half all journeys, by 1981 they will only represent
one-third.

There is a similar disproportion in the places where the extra journeys will happen.
Central Area trips will rise only 14 per cent; trips to places outside the centre will rise
by 57 per cent. Thus by 1981 almost five trips will be made to the suburbs for every one
trip to the centre—a fact which has profound implications for the way the trip is
made. Likewise, there will be a shift in the timing of journeys. While peak journeys
are expected to rise one third, because of a small increase in work journeys and a big
increase in school ones, off-peak trips will rise one half. Taken together, the effect of
these changes will be a profound shift in the character of travel. Non-work trips, non-
central trips, non-peak trips are all more prone to go by car if a car is available; and
for 68 per cent of all households by 1981, as compared with only 38 per cent in 1962,
it is expected to be available. Therefore, the Survey forecasts that though trips by rail
will hardly alter between 1962 and 1981, their proportion will fall from one-sixth to
one-tenth. Whereas one-third of all journeys were made by car drivers in 1962,
by 1981 that share is likely to be one-half. In the words of Volume Two of the Study:

'The total number of trips undertaken on the normal weekday will have increased
by nearly half, but, of these, work trips will do little more than reflect the slightly
greater number of jobs, and the great increase will be in shopping, social, school and
other personal trips, for which there will be almost double the number of cars available
as compared with 1962. This will result in a high density of traffic over almost the
whole of the former County of London, and will involve many trips from suburb to
suburb across (or round) the Central Area. Peak-hour traffic will increase by one-
third but off-peak traffic will increase by almost half. The roads will be almost
continuously busy.'[1]

This enormous increase, the Study declared in its conclusions on Volume Two, could
be met—at a cost. A network of high-capacity, high-speed primary routes could take
up to three-quarters of the extra traffic—though in turn it would generate some extra
traffic, because of the easier accessibility it would convey. This enhanced accessibility
would in the main not cater for wholly external trips, passing through London; these
tended to avoid London anyway, and this would be even truer when adequate orbital
roads were completed. Neither would it cater for trips to the centre, which would not
grow very rapidly and would be served in large measure by public transport. Rather,
it would cater for the enormous projected increase in internal trips from suburb to
suburb, across London—much of it in the form of off-peak, social trips by car. To

[1] *London Traffic Survey*, Vol. 2, *op. cit.*, Preface.

this end, the projected network took the form of circular routes connected to the main radials leading out from London. The two outer ones, the 'D' and the 'C' rings, are actually inherited from the Abercrombie Greater London Plan of 1944: the 'D' ring passes through the outermost suburbs, and the 'C' ring through the heart of the internal suburban areas. North of the river. The 'C' ring is the existing North Circular Road, which will be upgraded.

The most radical proposal in the plan, and the most controversial, is the innermost ring: the so-called Motorway Box. Roughly on the line of Abercrombie's 'B' ring, and mainly following existing railway tracks to minimize social disruption and physical dislocation, the Box will pass through the inner Victorian suburbs of London at an average distance of about four miles from the centre. It will have to cater for very large, some say unrealistically large, traffic volumes: 339,000 vehicles per day, in the extreme case, on the West Cross Route between Shepherd's Bush and the River Thames.[1] The shorter west and east legs were programmed first, and seem certain to be virtually complete by the early 1970s. Most controversy therefore concerns the long north and south legs, particularly the stretch of the north leg through Belsize Park and the stretch of the south leg through Blackheath Village. In both places residents have called for construction in deep tunnels to minimize dislocation and demolition; the Greater London Council have replied by pointing out the physical difficulty and very high cost of building the large-bore tunnels involved, given the geological character of the London basin.[2]

Even without the tunnels, the cost of the whole primary route system is astronomic: almost certainly, the largest single civil investment package ever presented for one area of Britain. As compared with an average of £50 million for a major airport or a 70-mile stretch of rural motorway, the London programme has been officially costed out at £840 million. A two-stage construction programme will allow this cost to be cut, for Stage One, to £650 million—though this will add £56 million to the final bill. In addition, £210 million is needed for secondary roads. This is the budget from 1967 up to the early 1980s.[3]

Meanwhile, the years since 1963 have seen a radical improvement in the planning of public transport and its co-ordination with the highways programme. The 1968 Transport Act, for the the first time, gives the Ministry of Transport powers to give grants to local authorities for investments in public transport, on the same basis as grants for roads. This ends the anomalous situation whereby the Ministry were empowered to give grants that might help pour more cars into city centres, but not to give grants that might reduce the numbers. At the same time a White Paper has announced agreement between the Ministry of Transport and the Greater London

[1] *Ibid.*, Figs. 17–19.

[2] J. S. Moulder, 'Route Integration in a Built-up Environment', Transportation Engineering Conference, *Institution of Civil Engineers* (1968) pp 79–90.

[3] Joint Report of Highways and Traffic Committee and Planning and Communications Committee, *Greater London Council Minutes*, 21st November 1967, pp. 697–8.

Council on the transfer of responsibility for London Transport to the GLC.[1] Concurrently the GLC will get extra powers over traffic, to make it the supreme transport and traffic planning authority for London—an authority which had been exercised since 1966 through the unwieldly medium of a joint Transport Co-ordinating Council for London representing the different interests of the Ministry, GLC, London Transport, the Users' Consultation Committee and the Boroughs. The transfer of London Transport has to start by recognizing its difficult financial position. Though in 1967 the authority managed to halt the loss of passengers that had plagued it for a decade, its finances deteriorated further, with a working deficit of £3·7 million and a total deficit (after allowing for interest charges) of £10·9 million.[2] Therefore, in order to wipe the slate clean for the transfer, the Government have had to agree to pay off 90 per cent of London Transport's accumulated deficit at the point of transfer.[3] Thereafter, in effect, London Transport will be the affair of Londoners: the system will no longer be subsidized by British taxpayers at large. The GLC will have to decide whether to support the system out of the rates, or whether to run it so that it pays its way. But support will come from the Government, through the GLC, for major investments like new tube lines—provided always the Government agree on the wisdom of the investments.[4]

One complication, in all this, concerns the relationship of London Transport to the Prices and Incomes Board. London Transport have repeatedly complained about the delays in approving fare increases, which they say have frustrated their efforts to get the system on a self-supporting basis. If PIB proved as restrictive on this point as the old Transport Tribunal were on occasion, this could mean a considerable degree of interference in the GLC's freedom to pursue the policies they thought right. But PIB recognize fully, as do the London Transport management, the difficulty of reconciling a fares policy for London Transport with a situation whereby private motorists do not pay the full social costs of the congestion they cause. The Joint Review of London Transport by the Ministry and London Transport officials, published as an Appendix to the 1968 White Paper, heavily underlines this point,[5] thus echoing the PIB's own emphasis on a study of social costs in the running of London Transport.[6]

There is no doubt that in recent years, some small progress has been made in the direction of levying social costs on the motorist. Parking meters now cover ten miles of London's central area, save only for the wholesale markets, and are now extending outwards into mixed residential and commercial areas like Belgravia. The GLC are

[1] Ministry of Transport, *Transport in London*. Cmnd. 3686 (H.M.S.O. 1968), paras. 46–54 (pp. 10–13).

[2] *London Transport in 1967* (H.M.S.O. 1968), para. 32 (p. 7).

[3] *Transport in London, op. cit.*, para. 50 (p. 12).

[4] *Ibid.*

[5] *Ibid.*, Appendix, paras. 136–141 (pp. 56–7).

[6] National Board for Prices and Incomes, *Proposals by the London Transport Board . . . for Fare Increases in the London Area* (Report No. 56), Cmnd. 3561 (H.M.S.O. 1968), pp. 22–25.

still pressing ahead with their proposal for a 40-square-mile area covering the whole of inner London, as far as the motorway box,[1] and in early 1968 announced a proposal to extend it even beyond this line;[2] progress in implementation has been slow, chiefly because of financial restrictions imposed by the central government. But parking controls and parking charges are a very limited and imperfect means of reflecting the social costs of congestion, as almost every report on the subject has recognized; and this is particularly the case in London, where large areas of private parking space attached to new office developments represent in effect a public subsidy to commuting by private car. In their 1968 report on parking, the GLC have at last recognized the absurdity of this point, and intend to try to remedy it. But this will take time. Meanwhile, the clear evidence is that as parking controls spread, the effect is merely to transfer the zone of free off-street parking, and of associated congestion, from the central area to the zones around tube stations in the inner suburbs—and eventually, perhaps, the outer suburbs too. Between 1966 and 1967, there was a decrease of 3 per cent in vehicles entering central London by road during the 7 a.m.–10 a.m. rush period; but during the same period, there was an increase of no less than 10 per cent in cars approaching the North and South Circular Roads.[3] The GLC's only hope, in their 1968 parking policy report, is to deal with this on a piecemeal basis, by parking controls and charges round suburban stations.

TABLE 28

PASSENGERS ENTERING CENTRAL LONDON DAILY BETWEEN
07.00 AND 10.00 HOURS, 1957–67

	1957	1962	1963	1964	1965	1966	1967
	000	000	000	000	000	000	000
By Public Transport							
British Railways	418	450	444	454	449	443	448
L.T. Railways	471	545	527	520	524	519	524
Total Rail*	785	883	860	860	861	852	860
Buses and Coaches	258	215	191†	191	180	175	172
Total—Public Transport	1,043	1,097	1,051†	1,052	1,041	1,026	1,032
By Private Transport							
Private Cars	69	94	95	98	99	100	98
Motor Cycles, etc.	20	29	25	22	18	15	13
Total—Private Transport	89	123	120	120	117	115	111
TOTAL	1,132	1,220	1,171†	1,172	1,157	1,142	1,143

The figures in this table are rounded and may not cast to totals.
  * Excludes double counting of passengers who travel both by British Railways and London Transport Railways.   † Affected by ban on overtime and rest-day working.

[1] Greater London Council, *Parking Policy in Central London* (February 1966), *passim*.
[2] *Greater London Council Minutes*, 7th May 1968, p. 260.
[3] *London Transport in 1967, op. cit.*, para. 130 (p. 28).

But in the longer run, only full road pricing can meet the situation. And it is here that progress has been unaccountably slowest. Already at the time of the Smeed report in 1964,[1] the prototype technical equipment was available and it was possible to calculate an approximate scale of charges that would be necessary to compensate for the costs of congestion. But between then and the official report on *Better Use of Town Roads*,[2] in 1967, little progress seems to have been made. The Ministry continues to talk of work on prototype machinery and of devising a suitable experiment, but is slow in issuing concrete details. The Isle of Wight, the City of Portsmouth and Greater London have all been suggested as ideal sites for the experiment; the first two because of their island situation, which makes monitoring easier, the last for the obvious reason that its problem is unique. Certainly, because of the scale of the problem, road pricing would probably prove politically more acceptable in London than anywhere else in the country. And this, there can be little doubt, is the chief force that is inhibiting the Ministry over road pricing.

Until this happens, as transportation economists well recognized, all discussion of priorities in transportation investment is likely to be fundamentally confused. The GLC quote rates of 'Social Return' on the London primary route system of 20 per cent,[3] though the details of the calculation do not seem to have been published, and Douglas Jay has questioned it.[4] There is as yet no parallel calculation for alternative transportation investments, like the projected Fleet underground line which would cross London diagonally from north west to south east. The case for the Motorway Box rests in large measure on this assumed rate of return, which would necessarily be affected by a road pricing policy. The difficulty is that it rests also on the gain in amenity to residential areas now affected by heavy traffic, which would profit from the channelization of these vehicles on to the primary route system: and as the Ministry of Transport's own Economic Planning Directorate have shown in their searching analysis of Road Track Costs, to evaluate amenity proves in practice to be virtually impossible.[5] All that can be said is that public transport investments, like new underground lines, prove to be much more effective than motorways in carrying large peak-hour flows, but perhaps not so effective overall in that they are underused outside these peak hours. The first stretch of genuine urban motorway to be built in inner London, the $2\frac{1}{2}$-mile Western Avenue extension and spur to the West Cross Route, will cost £27 million: about £11 million per mile. This is almost exactly double the cost per mile of the Victoria tube line from Walthamstow to Victoria, which will open during 1968–9. But whereas the Western Avenue extension will carry a maximum of about 6000 cars per hour (or, say, 9000 people at current rates of car occupation) in to London at the morning peak hour, the Victoria Line will carry up to 40,000. On

---

[1] Ministry of Transport, *Road Pricing: The Economic and Technical Possibilities* (H.M.S.O. 1964).
[2] Ministry of Transport, *Better Use of Town Roads* (H.M.S.O. 1967).
[3] GLC Minutes, 21st November 1967, *op. cit.*, p. 696.
[4] *The Guardian*, 12th August 1968.
[5] Ministry of Transport, *Road Track Costs* (H.M.S.O. 1968), paras. 24–28 (pp. 7–8).

the other hand, the motorway will carry heavy flows of traffic also on Saturday nights and Sunday afternoons, when the tube will be relatively little used. To stress merely the superior peak capacity of the tube is to ignore the superior overall capacity of the motorway; and this, at a time when peak journeys will rise little and off peak journeys will rise a great deal, is short sighted indeed.

In other words, on the most basic questions of all—the questions of how we make our planning decisions—the years from 1963 to 1968 have seen a great advance in our understanding. But paradoxically, one of the main effects has been to bring home just how much we do not know, and are unlikely soon to know, about the rationale of our investment decisions. If this is accepted, it merely underlines the central point of the transportation chapter in *London 2000*: until we have an approximation to a consistent pricing policy, our planning will lack any firm base. It would be possible to question many details in this chapter of *London 2000*; I would question them now myself, notably the proposal for motorways across central London. But this would not be the central point: the point is the *raison d'etre* of our recommendations and our decisions.

Part III · BUILDING THE NEW LONDON

CHAPTER 6

New Towns and Old

In Chapter 4 I concluded that within London Region there would be a million and a half extra people, in half a million households, between 1961 and 1980; and another million and three-quarter extra people, in half a million households, between 1980 and 2000. We saw that for economic reasons, the homes for these people would virtually all have to be built on previously undeveloped land, which now rests under crops and grass and woodland in the outer parts of London Region —thirty to fifty miles from central London—and a little beyond. Broadly, we can get these homes built in three different ways.

Three Choices

First, we could leave initiative to the private builder, and ask the local planning authorities to make enough land available for him to do the job. This has been basic Government policy since 1951. I think, and most planners think, that it is a wrong policy because in practice it does not secure adequate planning and design.

Second, we can create machinery for the rapid and large-scale planned expansion of existing towns in the zone between thirty and one hundred miles from London. Abercrombie, we saw, made this one of the main elements of his policy; but up to now it has not worked satisfactorily. In practice, 'town expansion' takes place through agreement between an 'exporting' authority with an overspill problem and a 'receiving' authority willing to receive the overspill population. This was the solution envisaged by the Town Development Act of 1952. But this Act has failed to get houses built in anything like sufficient quantity, and there are no indications that matters will suddenly improve. And even if it did get houses built, it is unlikely to get them built in sufficient numbers in any one place to create a proper urban life, or even to attract necessary industry. Up to the large-scale Basingstoke expansion, announced in 1961 as a palliative to the L.C.C. for the loss of their proposed New

Town at Hook, the largest projected expansion was 20,000 at Swindon, and the majority were between three and ten thousand. And if the receiving authority itself undertakes development (a 'nomination' scheme), it is very unlikely to be big enough to afford the skill and expertise necessary to produce a good job of detailed planning.

Third, we can build more New Towns. By this I mean not merely towns built on virgin sites by Development Corporations, but also town expansions by such Corporations (as happened at Hemel Hempstead) and all sorts of large-scale development by a single authority (for instance the L.C.C.'s Hook project). The New Town method, whether on virgin or expansion sites, has proved itself on every count the most effective way of providing for the overspill population of London. It alone permits real planning because one authority—perhaps a Development Corporation, perhaps an exporting authority, perhaps even, in the future, a private company[1] or a new sort of national corporation—provides all the needs of the population in an integrated scheme: jobs, homes, schools, shops, pubs, entertainments, community service buildings. It allows much freedom to experiment. It is by no means inimical to the interests of the good private builder, as many of them are now finding in the original New Towns. It has helped, and will help, to promote a higher level of design than any other method of development we know, among public and private developers alike.

For the expanded London of 2000, then, a two-pronged policy is essential. One is to find more effective ways of expanding existing towns, by a substantial amount, quickly. The other is to find the sites for a large number of New Towns. Assume, from Chapter 4, that we must house three and a quarter million extra people in the London region by 2000; assume that half go into expanded towns and half into New Towns. What are the detailed implications?

The Need for Town Expansion

To 'expand' a town, rather than build a 'New' Town, is really a matter of degree. A New Town might involve the expansion of an existing settlement from anything between 500 and 15,000 people to a figure between 50,000 and 150,000; while an 'expansion' would involve smaller increases, in relative terms: the growth of a village, say, from 1500 to 4000, or a town from 75,000 to 150,000. Because of the scale of the expansion, a New Town needs a separate external authority to carry out the operation; expansion on the smaller scale need not, but will almost certainly benefit from it. For this latter case, we should *first* keep the existing machinery of the Town Development Act, 1952, but greatly strengthen its financial provisions, especially the inducements offered to employers to move.[2] But *second*, a new type of public

---

[1] A private enterprise New Town is being built at Cramlington (Northumberland) to provide for Newcastle overspill.

[2] See Chapter 3, pages 68–9.

corporation should be established, should work to a central policy, and should build extensively in certain existing centres chosen for expansion schemes.

The great weakness of the 1952 Act in practice is that it has not provided enough incentive for the movement of employment. This could be remedied if a public corporation were subsidized, out of a payroll tax imposed on inner London, to build factories and offices for lease at low rentals. The same public corporation could take a great deal of the financial burden off the receiving authority by providing houses at low repayment rates for the critical first few years when the burden of investment is heaviest. I have objected to subsidizing high buildings in the central and inner parts of London,[1] which I think contrary to good planning principles. But subsidy applied to overspill housing in the right place is subsidy rightly applied. It is public money used to counteract the imbalance between social cost and private benefit at the centre. It should be the counterpart of financial measures designed to make activity at the centre less attractive to the private entrepreneur; it should be met out of the proceeds of payroll tax.

Better Designs and Lower Costs: The Need for a Development Corporation

In housing developments of all sorts—not merely new developments, but also in urban renewal—there is a pressing need for an organization which would improve the general level of design, and lower costs; which would develop and use methods of standardization, prefabrication, bulk purchase, long runs, advance planning, in which most firms in the British building industry are today so backward; which would do the research, at present so seriously lacking, into the possibility of technical improvement.[2] We do know that dramatic improvements are possible both in costs and quality, because they have been made in school-building: first through the exhortations of a progressive group in the Ministry of Education just after the war, and then through the highly successful CLASP (Consortium of Local Authorities Special Programme). Three northern cities, Sheffield, Leeds and Hull, have arranged a joint research programme for housing on the lines of CLASP; in summer 1962 the Ministry of Housing and Local Government announced plans for fostering similar consortia among Lancashire housing authorities with slum-clearance problems, with the help of Ministry architects; in autumn 1962 the Ministry of Public Building and Works announced a research programme to help a Government drive to modernize the building industry. But in London, the L.C.C. Architect's Department, which made preliminary experiments in new methods of construction, faces virtual dismemberment as a house-building authority. And local authority schemes, though

---

[1] See Chapter 4, pages 97–103.

[2] During 1962 the Department of Scientific and Industrial Research announced that Manchester College of Science and Technology would begin a three-year study into the structure and economy of the building industry.

they may help to improve quality and lower costs in the public housing sector, do nothing to improve standards in private speculative building—which is one of the major problems of London Region. Here, Government research may help; but it will face the traditional conservatism of the small builder.

A way out of this difficulty would be to create a new type of public corporation. It would be modelled on the New Town Development Corporation, which in general organization—including accountability to Parliament on broad policy, through an annual report which can be debated—resembles a nationalized industry. There could be one Development Corporation for the whole country, as originally suggested in the policy statement *The Face of Britain*;[1] or regional corporations; or *ad hoc* corporations up and down the country for particular pieces of development or redevelopment, as suggested by the Civic Trust.[2] The case for a National Corporation is now less strong because the necessary centralized research is to be undertaken by the Ministry of Public Building and Works. A mixture of regional and *ad hoc* corporations might best meet varying needs.

A Development Corporation would not take over the existing building industry in its area (though it might buy out existing firms in the free market); it would compete with private undertakings, large and small. It would simultaneously perform several functions.

First, and very importantly, it would build houses and flats for sale and to rent. It could build these with a direct labour force, or use commercial contractors.

Secondly, it could offer expertise in planning to local authorities which lacked the resources to plan major developments. It could either prepare plans merely; or carry the development out itself as agent for the authority, in which case the authority would enjoy the advantages of greater efficiency and lower costs.

Thirdly, it could perform similar work for commercial organizations wishing to invest in housing, and to co-operative housing organizations.

Fourthly, it could lay out and lease land for individually designed homes.

By its nature the Corporation would not be a public housing authority. If it sold, or rented, it would do so as a commercial undertaking. It would not administer any subsidies, though it could receive them and pass them on. It would in every respect be a nationalized industry in the new image, pursuing an aggressive commercial policy in competition with private enterprise. But it should do what the best private firms manage to do in their fields: establish a reputation for quality and low price which would allow it to lead the industry, forcing the existing private firms to reorganize themselves and raising standards generally.

Nor could the Corporation be an overall planning authority. Although it would prepare detailed plans of estates or even whole towns, and although one of its chief responsibilities would be to raise the general level of planning design, it would have to submit its plans to a planning authority for approval. In particular, it could

[1] *Socialist Commentary*, September 1961, xiv–xv.
[2] *Urban Redevelopment* (1962), 47–8.

not be left with the decision as to where development would occur. To do that would be to expect too much of the public-spiritedness of the executives of a public corporation.

Where to Develop

The siting of the new development, within the London Region and South-East England, involves major decisions; and it is a very vexed question as to what sort and size of planning authority should make them. In Chapter 9 of this book I argue for regional authorities, much larger in scale than anything we know in local government today. But the implications of the growth of London extend beyond any manageable London regional government. Even in 1962, arrangements are being made to receive London's overspill population in towns up to a hundred miles from Charing Cross. This means that there will almost certainly be delicate conflicts of interest to resolve. So there must be a strong power at the centre. The Ministry of Housing and Local Government must become once again a true Ministry of Town and Country Planning. It must build up its research staff to a level where detailed research can be undertaken on the siting of development.[1] The siting of a New Town should not depend on a conflict of wills among various authorities. Without threatening local or regional autonomy, the Ministry will therefore have to blandish, cajole, woo, threaten. It must stand with a planning authority in its fight to stop development in the wrong places; it must be ready to attack when this hardens into a refusal to allow development at all.

Candidates for Expansion

A true regional plan for London would at least name the existing main centres which would be candidates for expansion. It seems clear that, as the Town and Country Planning Association have argued, it is least painful and disruptive to expand the existing large centres in the belt between forty and a hundred miles from London. They include Canterbury, Dover, the major south coast resorts, Hastings, Eastbourne, Brighton, Worthing, Portsmouth, Southampton, Reading, Swindon, Oxford, Northampton, Bedford, Kettering, Peterborough, Cambridge, Norwich and Ipswich. Some of these are County Boroughs, and so under the existing planning structure are completely autonomous planning authorities. Possibly some of these cannot be expanded because of landscape amenity in the surrounding area—for instance Brighton; others because of the need to preserve their traditional character—for instance Cambridge, though I think that much of this danger can be obviated by careful local planning.[2] But there would be no harm and no difficulty in the imaginative

[1] The Ministry staff are currently (early 1963) making a regional survey of South-eastern England, from which a new Regional Plan will emerge.

[2] In the particular case of Cambridge, expansion of the Fitzroy Street shopping area to the east of the main shopping centre (as the University suggest) coupled with expansion of the City towards the east.

expansion of Norwich, Peterborough or Northampton, by 100,000 and more people apiece. Indeed, it would provide a tremendous planning challenge of precisely the sort that bomb-devastated Coventry faced, and so triumphantly met, in the early postwar years: the double challenge of creating new neighbourhoods to provide for a vast influx of population,[1] while simultaneously recreating the city centre according to a new model. Some of these southern English centres urgently demand this treatment. They are traditional market centres which were suddenly enlarged by the coming of the railways, at a period when domestic and commercial architecture was at its dullest. Apart from a few Georgian showpieces, their town centres are often monuments of tedium, completely obsolescent and lacking in distinguished architecture or urban liveliness.[2] Because of the general industrial expansion of South-east England and the increased prosperity of their surrounding rural areas in the postwar years, these centres are bursting at their seams. Within a very few years they will either get rebuilt in a piecemeal and inadequate fashion; or they will be rebuilt on a larger scale by the major property interests, which will be better than nothing; or they can be rebuilt, totally, coherently and imaginatively, as part of a plan of town expansion.

Through expansion we should aim to house about a million extra people in the major centres of South-east England, and another half a million in minor expansions. These minor expansions will be in the zone of the new New Towns[3] and a little way beyond, between thirty and seventy miles from London; they will not involve increases of more than about twenty per cent above the 1961 populations. The major expansions, on the other hand, should take substantial towns farther out, between sixty and one hundred and ten miles from London—as far as the hypothetical 'Solent-Wash line'—and should expand them in most cases two- or three-fold. Below I give some very tentative estimates, merely as illustrations, of the order of expansion we should visualize. Some of these may seem very sensational increases for a forty-year period. But let me emphasize: if the estimates of Chapter 4 are at all valid—if we need sites for one million[4] new houses in the outer parts of the region, and beyond, in forty years—we have to get used to figures of this order; or give up planning altogether, and let the population spill where it will over the face of the Home Counties.

---

[1] The population of Coventry rose by 127,000 in the thirty years 1931–61, and by 85,000 in 1939–61 alone.

[2] Pevsner on Peterborough: 'There is surprisingly little of interest in the town, in spite of its age. It is hard to make up a perambulation.' (*Northamptonshire* (1961), 372.) And on Cambridge: 'There is not enough in the following to make up into a coherent picture.' (*Cambridgeshire* (1954), 187.)

[3] See page 138.

[4] This takes no account of need to accommodate overspill arising from the redevelopment of obsolescent property.

Centre	Status	Miles from London	1961 population	Suggested Ultimate population	Suggested Expansion by 2000
				(All figures in thousands)	
Northampton	C.B.	66	105	250	145
Kettering	M.B.	75	39	80	41
Peterborough[1]	M.B.	81	62	200	138
Cambridge	M.B.	54	95	125	30
Norwich	C.B.	111	120	250	130
Lowestoft	M.B.	116	46	80	34
Clacton	M.B.	69	28	80	52
Ipswich[1]	C.B.	72	117	250	133
Dover	M.B.	72	35	100	65
Hastings	C.B.	63	66	150	84
Winchester	M.B.	65	29	60	31
Salisbury	M.B.	84	35	100	65
Swindon	M.B.	79	92	200	108
Newbury	M.B.	56	20	80	60

C.B. = County Borough   M.B. = Municipal Borough

In making these estimates I have considered the existing character of the town; its nearness to rival service centres; and the character of the surrounding agricultural land. It is almost certain, as with the New Towns, that more detailed survey will show some of these towns to be unsuitable for such large-scale expansion, in which case more people will have to be housed in smaller expansions, or in extra New Towns. But the essential is that there is a regional policy for overspill; and that the region concerned is the whole of South-east England. Unless the multifarious needs of this region are considered *as a whole* in relation to the problem of London overspill, it is almost certain that bad decisions will be taken simply as a result of the triumph of one pressure over another.

A New Town Survey

This still leaves about one and three-quarter million people to be housed, over the next forty years, in New Town schemes within and around the London Region. A first essential, therefore, is a detailed New Town survey. What Abercrombie did in 1943–4 for the area just outside the original Metropolitan Green Belt, we need to do again for the areas farther out. The L.C.C.'s analysis of the selection of their Hook New Town site[2] shows the amount of work that must go into a complete survey. It needs the combined resources of a big team of location economists, transport

[1] Since this was written the Minister of Housing and Local Government has announced that official studies are to be undertaken of the possible expansion of Peterborough and Ipswich. The order of expansion to be considered is smaller than that indicated here—50 or 100 per cent.

[2] L.C.C., *The Planning of a New Town* (1961), 13.

specialists, geologists, hydrologists, agricultural experts, practical planners, engineers and architects; working within a government department, a local or regional planning office or a special university unit.

But this is something that the wit of our administrators has not supplied for us. So *faute de mieux*, I outline below some of the factors that a New Town survey must take into account; and on that basis propose tentatively twenty-five possible sites to serve as the basis of fuller investigation. Throughout, I assume that development will follow the 'new model' New Towns such as Cumbernauld or Hook: towns holding about 100,000 people at a net residential density of about 60 persons per acre, on compact sites of about six square miles each. Seventeen of these, on the assumptions above, would be needed in the years up to 2000 in the London Region.

The factors that must be considered are these.

(1) *General Area of Location.* The new New Towns are meant to cater for London overspill. So they must be located in South-East England, south and east of a line drawn roughly from the Wash to the Solent. This limitation is especially important to the north-west of London, where at a distance of about seventy miles from Charing Cross we arrive at the border of the London and the Birmingham spheres of influence.

But now two contradictory principles emerge. On the one hand, sensitive spacing of the New Towns is vital if we are to keep the right balance between town and country in the outer parts of London region. The original New Towns are in the zone between twenty-one and thirty-two miles from central London. In this zone population growth has been fastest in the decade 1951–61, not only due to the New Towns themselves, but also due to the very rapid private development. With some exceptions, we can regard this zone as nearly full up, at any rate for the purposes of New Towns. So our new New Towns will have to be set somewhere in the zone between forty and (say) sixty miles from London; and some extending perhaps into the 'Fringe Zone' beyond the London Region—a belt variable in width, between sixty and a hundred miles from the centre of London. But, on the other hand, these towns are specifically planned as overspill centres for Londoners in the first instance; the jobs will mostly come from London too; we can safely presume that many of the enterprises will retain close links with London. This is the more sure, in that we want especially to encourage decentralization of office jobs into the new New Towns. So we have to insist on a second factor:

(2) *Good Communications*—with the London-Birmingham axis of growth, and with a possible extension south-east towards a Channel link. The sites of the old New Towns were chosen with both rail and road access in mind. In the event, their industry has proved to depend mainly on road transport. But office decentralization should emphasize the importance of fast rail links; and it is sensible therefore to restrict investigation to sites within ninety minutes of London by a reasonably frequent rail service. This requirement limits the choice of sites very radically, because of the very marked finger-pattern of rail access from London (Map 4A). In addition, though, it is necessary to allow for the fact that many firms may want to use fast road transport,

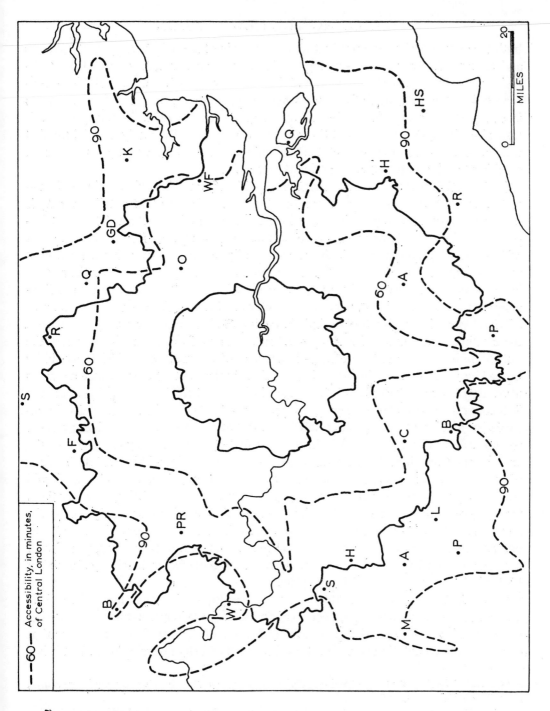

Map 4.
Factors in New Town Location

A. Accessibility
by Rail from
Central London

---60--- Accessibility, in minutes,
of Central London

90

MILES
0   20

173

both to carry materials and products (these occur in office as in factory undertakings) and to carry key personnel—managers, directors, executives, key specialized technicians, salesmen. So the sites should be within reasonable access of high-speed road links from the centre of London when the present programme of improvements is substantially complete—which should happen about 1970. In many cases, it transpires from Maps 4B and C that the fast road links will closely parallel the fast rail links. I assume throughout that manufacturers will be equally interested in reaching London and the wider national market.

(3) *Essential Services.* The site must be capable of provision with basic services—water, drainage and sewerage—at reasonable cost. It is here that detailed survey is most necessary, and any preliminary investigation will be weakest. The most important and costly of the services will be water supply; yet as I write the only area of South-East England for which we have really detailed surveys is the north-east sector, comprising the basins of the Great Ouse and the Essex rivers. For the rest we have to rely on the extremely general and speculative estimates made by the Sub-committee on the Growing Demand for Water in 1959[1]—estimates which in the case of the Essex rivers give too optimistic an impression. For what they are worth, these estimates are mapped in Map 4D.[2] In the case of the Essex rivers, where the Sub-committee estimated that thirty-six per cent of the mean annual yield would be tapped by 1965,[3] detailed investigation has since indicated that there will be a serious *water deficiency* by 1980. On this basis the whole area of the Thames basin (where the Sub-committee estimated 40 per cent tappage for 1965) should certainly also be regarded as an area of serious water deficiency. But at this point a much wider problem emerges. Is it in fact possible within the next forty years to supply the needs of the extra population within the London Region from the supplies within it? If the Thames offers no extra resources, then the answer is almost certainly no. In this case it will be necessary to embark upon extremely expensive schemes for bringing water from the western, wetter side of Britain into the London Region—probably across the Severn-Thames watershed somewhere between Gloucester and Oxford—and all our basic assumptions about water deficiencies may be altered. In the survey, therefore, I have not excluded potential sites on the grounds of local water deficiency alone; but I have indicated that the deficiency exists.

(4) *Agricultural Land.* The site should not occupy agricultural land of the best quality. This is done for no good economic reason: the evidence available shows that the value of even very good agricultural land is one of the least important items that can enter into calculation of the costs and benefits of urban development. But it is a

---

[1] Central Advisory Water Committee, *Sub-Committee on the Growing Demand for Water, First Report* (H.M.S.O. 1959).

[2] *Ibid.,* Figs. 6 and 7, pp. 26–7. The estimates were based on Surveys by Ministry of Housing and Local Government engineers from 1945 onwards. See *Report*, para. 26, for limitations of the method; it is described as a "first step in comparing . . . resources".

[3] And that this would produce a surplus of 37 million gallons per day over expected demand.

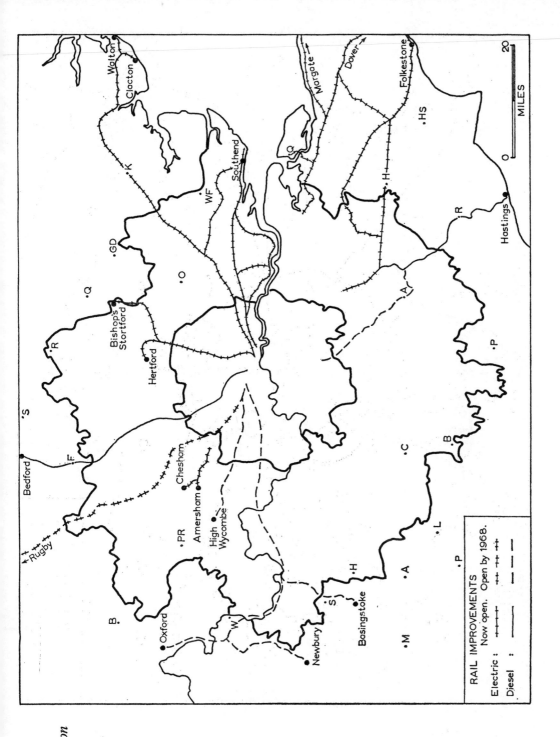

Map 4.
Factors in
New Town Location
B. Recent and
Projected Rail
Improvements

175

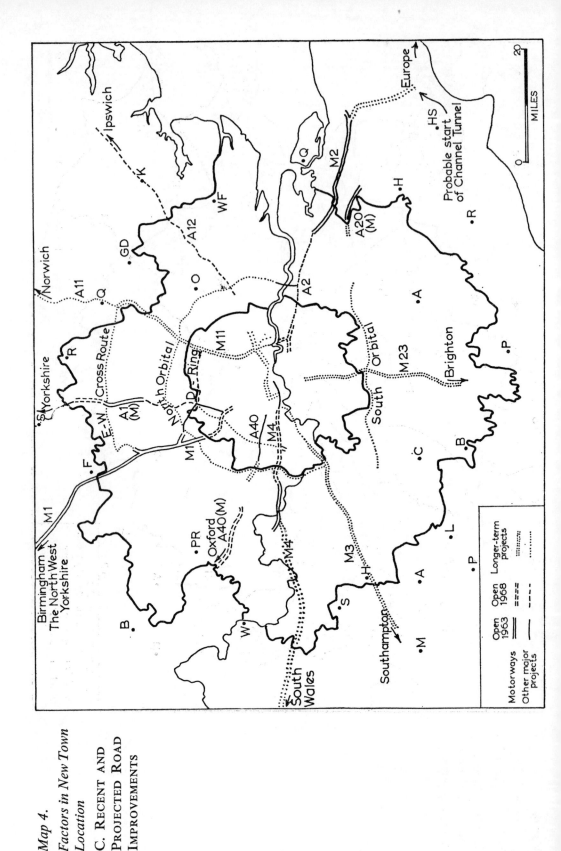

Map 4.
Factors in New Town Location

C. RECENT AND PROJECTED ROAD IMPROVEMENTS

176

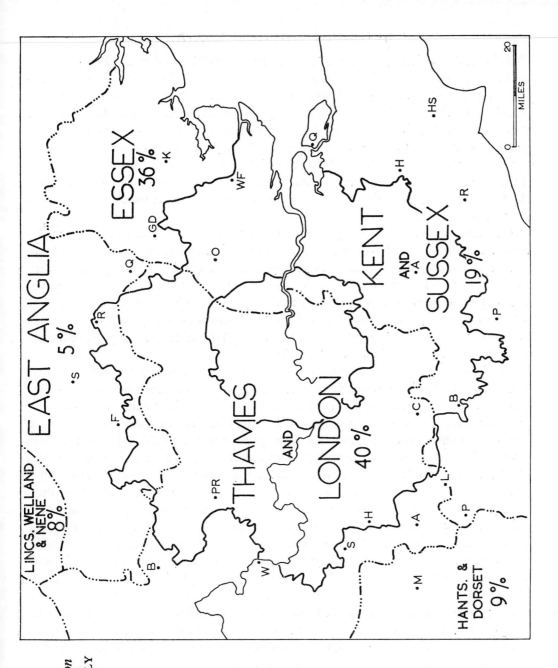

Map 4.
Factors in
New Town Location

D. WATER SUPPLY
Percentage Mean
Annual Supply
Tapped,
Estimate for
1965

177

burning political issue; politics is the art of the possible; and in the last resort the politicians will have to take the decisions. So I have avoided all first-class agricultural land, as classified by the Land Utilization Survey of Britain; and I have been cautious in siting on land described as 'good' (that is, Grades II to IV of the Survey).[1] The distribution of the major classes is shown in Map 4E. But if we completely exclude good land, it is almost certainly impossible to find enough sites, for the simple reason that so much of the land within seventy miles of London, especially to the north and east, is classified as good. In fact, several of the original eight London New Towns in the northern sector are on good land; which seems a satisfactory precedent.

(5) *Landscape Value*. The site should exclude all land of landscape or scientific value. Admitted, this is often a highly arbitrary category, depending to a large extent on the prejudices of the local planning officer; and when these prejudices are coupled with others against receiving metropolitan overspill, the diagonal green shading which marks the 'V-land' may spill very freely across a County Development Map, as Map 4F shows. Despite this, I think it behoves us to pay even more respect to this sort of land than to agricultural land. The 'V-land' represents possible amenity to millions, and should not lightly be invaded.

On the other hand, the Metropolitan Green Belt should not be regarded as sacrosanct. First tentatively devised before the 1939–45 War, the Green Belt was made by Abercrombie into an integral part of his solution for London; and this solution, as we have seen, has been no solution at all, simply because the basic assumption of the plan—a stationary population for the region—has not been fulfilled. In the fast-growing London Region of the post-1945 period, there is in fact a serious danger that the Green Belt may become a device of anti-planning, used by the counties around the Conurbation—which are understandably reluctant to take more overspill than they can help—to make sure that the London émigrés go anywhere rather than their sacred plot.[2] The alternative solution, which I think essential for the proper regional planning of South-East England in the next forty years, is for the *whole region* outside the present built-up area of the Conurbation to be declared green *in principle*, and then for a single central authority to decide where the holes in the green curtain should be shot. This and this alone would allow consideration on merit of the case for expanding (say) a small market town in the inner, original part of the Green Belt.

These factors are the most important in the siting of any New Town. Of course there are many others: perhaps the most complete analysis of factors in development,

[1] Based on the 1 : 650,000 *Land Classification Map* (Ordnance Survey, 1944), supplemented by material in Land Utilization Survey Reports. For the basis of the Land Classification Survey see L. Dudley Stamp, *The Land of Britain: Its Use and Misuse* (1948, 1962), ch. 17.

[2] Cf. the Herbert Commission on Local Government in Greater London, on the revision of the Surrey Development Plan: 'The main object of these revisions is to bring the greater part of Surrey into the green belt with the object of ensuring that if London's population overleaps the green belt, as it clearly is doing, the emigrants shall alight, say, in Hampshire or Sussex, rather than in Surrey.' *Report*, Cmnd. 1164 (H.M.S.O. 1960), para. 719.

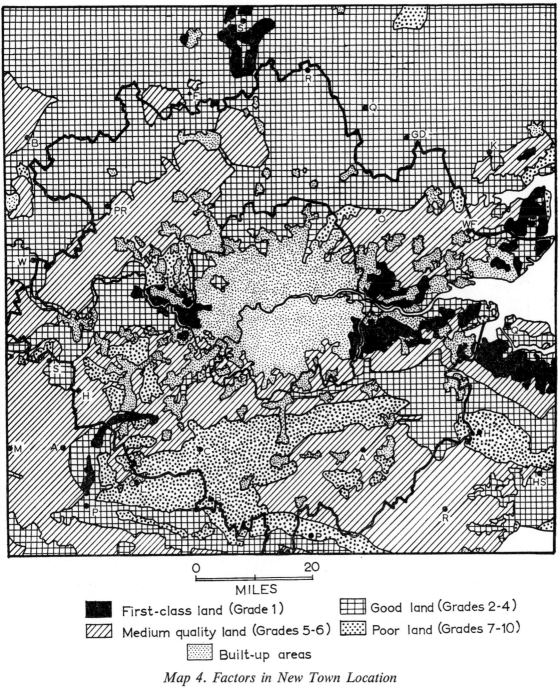

MILES

0   20

◼ First-class land (Grade 1)   ▦ Good land (Grades 2-4)

▨ Medium quality land (Grades 5-6)   ⬚ Poor land (Grades 7-10)

⬚ Built-up areas

Map 4. Factors in New Town Location

E. AGRICULTURAL LAND: GRADING

Based on the Ordnance Survey Map with the sanction o the Controller of H.M. Stationery Office. Crown Copyright Reserved.

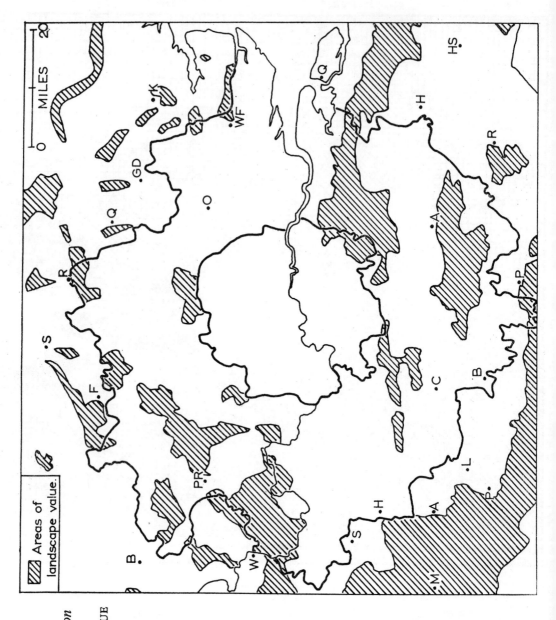

Map 4.
Factors in
New Town Location
F. Land of
Landscape Value

the East Sussex County Analysis of 1953, listed no less than thirty-one, and mapped them all to boot. But this is a later, more sophisticated stage of the investigation.

The preliminary survey shows twenty-five potential sites, which are shown in Map 4G and described in detail in the Appendix to this chapter.

NORTH OF THE THAMES	SOUTH OF THE THAMES
1 Wallingford (Berks.)	12 Queenborough-Minster (Sheppey) (Kent)
2 Bicester (Oxford)	13 Hamstreet (Kent)
3 Princes Risborough (Bucks.)	14 Headcorn (Kent)
4 Flitwick (Beds.)	15 Ashurst (Kent)
5 Sandy (Beds.)	16 Robertsbridge (East Sussex)
6 Royston (Herts.)	17 Plumpton (East Sussex)
7 Quendon (Essex)	18 Billingshurst (West Sussex)
8 Great Dunmow (Essex)	19 Cranleigh (Surrey)
9 Ongar (Essex)	20 Liphook (Hants.)
10 Kelvedon (Essex)	21 Alton (Hants.)
11 Woodham Ferrers (Essex)	22 Micheldelver (Hants.)
	23 Hook (Hants.)
	24 Silchester (Hants.)
	25 Petersfield (Hants.)

The Costs of Decentralization

To some, the proposals in this chapter may have a utopian air. It may be said: this is what we would do, if our economic problems were solved, if as a community we had unlimited resources; and not otherwise. This view is dangerously mistaken. Given the continuation of present social and economic trends in London Region, decentralization of this order is *inevitable* over the next forty years. If the community does not plan it, private anarchy will ensure it happens somehow.

And anarchy is not necessarily cheaper. The very detailed cost estimates made by the L.C.C. for their Hook project showed that the country, and London, would have got a very good bargain for their money. At 1960 prices, the probable gross capital cost of this New Town for 100,000 people would have been £156,600,000 over 50 years—£1,560 per person. This simple sum is complicated on the one hand by the need to pay interest on the money borrowed—the L.C.C. estimated 5 per cent over 60 years for the houses—and on the other by state subsidy payments for houses and roads. On the housing account alone, the L.C.C.'s calculations show that, including interest, the cost of a dwelling over the 60-year repayment period might have been £9,360 (including management costs). The Council would have got back just over £2,000 from the State in subsidies; and by charging an average rent of just over £2 a week in the fifteenth year of operation, it thought it could break even. The State

181

Map 4.
Factors in
New Town Location
G. SITES OF THE SUGGESTED 25 NEW TOWNS, AND DISTANCES FROM LONDON

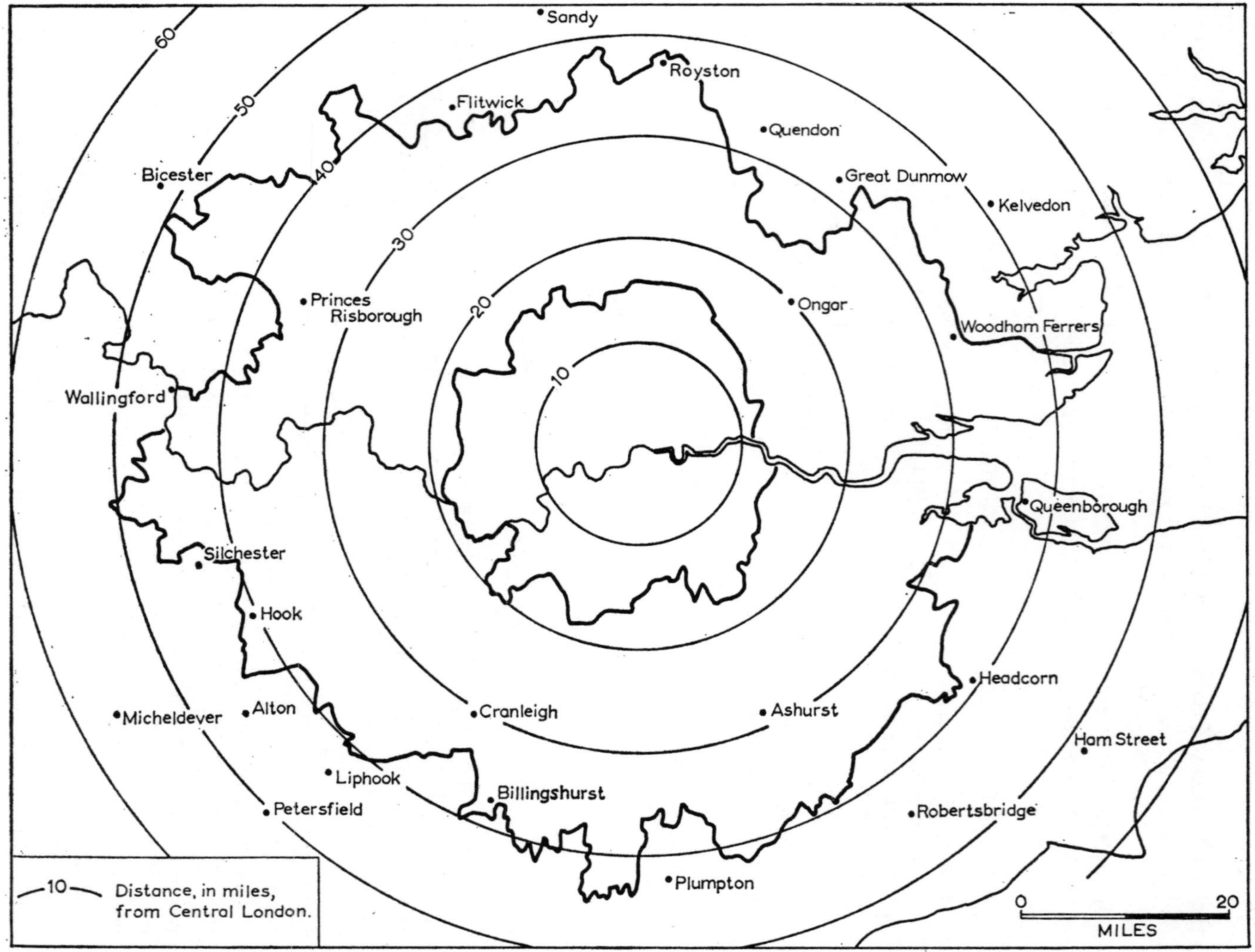

Sandy
Royston
Flitwick
Quendon
Bicester
Great Dunmow
Kelvedon
Princes Risborough
Ongar
Woodham Ferrers
Wallingford
Queenborough
Silchester
Hook
Headcorn
Micheldever
Alton
Cranleigh
Ashurst
Ham Street
Liphook
Billingshurst
Petersfield
Robertsbridge
Plumpton
10
20
30
40
50
60
10 Distance, in miles, from Central London.
0
20
MILES

would be paying over a 60-year period some £66 million in housing subsidies.[1] The cost to the community is then the cost of State subsidy: some £1·16 million a year for 100,000 people.[2] On this basis, to decentralize four million people by properly planned development would cost the community (over and above private costs), £64 million a year up to 2020, at 1960 prices. This is almost exactly the same as the annual subsidy paid to British farmers on cereal production in the early sixties. It is based on normal commercial accounting criteria, and takes no account of communal savings from lower congestion, quicker and easier journey to work, greater economic efficiency of firms in the planned centres: savings which simply would not be present on the social balance sheet, or only in much smaller quantities, if we leave anarchy to do the job.

So good planning is good economics, or good hard-headed common business sense. Why then is it not certain to happen? Simply because of our remaining rooted aversion to public expenditure and public management. In real terms of pounds per person, planning is unlikely to cost more than anarchy, and may well cost less; but it will involve a transfer of resources from the private to the public sector of spending; it may mean higher taxation (with higher benefits back, of course); and in the process it may well mean transfers of wealth from one part of the community to another. It is more than high time that, as a prosperous society, we were willing and even desirous that these things should happen. For Galbraith applies to us, too, albeit in smaller measure than in the United States; and nowhere more than in housing and the total urban environment. A system that produces unlimited television sets and washing machines to put into slum houses, or that tolerates massive investment in badly-planned new housing, needs condemnation on the grounds of sheer social inefficiency: it does not maximize welfare; and needs replanning by a system which comes nearer to it.

Postscript, 1969

In the five years between publication of *London 2000* and the writing of this post-script, many things about the book have dated. But none so fundamentally than its central policy prescription: the proposal for some 25 new towns, each of about 100,000 people on the model of the abandoned scheme for Hook new town, lying at various distances between 24 miles and 61 miles from London. Of all the fundamental criticisms made of the book, I think this was the most telling: that it put forward an enlarged version of the traditional new town of two decades before, without any

[1] These calculations are made from L.C.C., *The Planning of a New Town* (1961), Tables 7–9 and Appendices W and Y.

[2] Another state subsidy, for roads—estimated at £3·4 million—is not included, since it is assumed that this would be incurred in any development. It must be emphasized that the sum of £1·16 m. is merely a transfer payment, not a real cost, and that it is incurred in respect of the public housing at Hook; New Towns built with houses for sale or rent on a commercial basis would not incur such costs.

realization of the fact that economic changes, and social changes, were making the idea completely archaic. In the event, the failing was soon enough exposed.

In the process, three distinct stages can be traced. The first dates from publication of the official *South East Study*, in March 1964. Earlier we noticed that the *Study*, purely as a policy exercise and without any consideration of how far the target was likely to be achieved, called for a shift in the distribution of population within the South East: a much bigger proportion of the total growth, amounting to nearly half the growth in what is now known as the South East Planning Region, was to be diverted to the areas beyond the forty-mile ring from Central London or into planned developments outside the boundaries of the Region. In practice, this meant that the area within the forty-mile ring was to be reserved mainly for 'spontaneous' migration, that is migration into speculatively-built private housing; the planned developments, that is those which were to be planned by Government for the public overspill schemes, were with one exception to be located well outside the 40-mile ring, and in some cases even beyond the boundary of the South East Region. The precise figures, insofar as they can be calculated from the *Study*,[1] are set out below.

	Outer Metropolitan Area	Rest of South East	Outside Planning Region	Total
Spontaneous	1,385,000	584,000	266,000	2,235,000
Planned	220,000	600,000	240,000	1,060,000
Total	1,605,000	1,184,000	506,000	3,295,000

This balance was itself very different from anything in *London 2000*, where most of the proposed new towns were inside the Outer Metropolitan Area or only just beyond the forty-mile ring. In the event, the proposals in the *South East Study* proved in most cases not to be merely outside the Metropolitan Area, but well outside it: most were between 55 and 80 miles from London. This was deliberate: the intention, rightly or wrongly, realistically or unrealistically, was to put them well beyond the commuting influence of London. But this, in turn, helped to condition thinking about their size. If the new developments were to be farther from the London labour market, that suggested they should be big enough to be independent. The authors of the *Study* also thought that big towns would have cheaper public services, per head of population; they also argued that only a big town could support adequate shops, schools and entertainments. Lastly, they stressed the importance of not dissipating the efforts of the planners and architects on too many small schemes. At the same time, there were practical limitations in the building programme which made it impossible to concentrate all the effort on to a few very large cities. The conclusion pointed inescapably to something bigger than any previous new town, but not something many times

[1] Calculated from *The South East Study* (H.M.S.O. 1964), Table IV, p. 73 and Table VI, p. 86. Transfers have been made from the Rest of the South East to Outside Planning Region, to follow the more restrictive definition of the South East Region excluding East Anglia.

bigger: in other words to towns with total populations of anything up to a quarter of a million people (Map 5).

True, as the *Study* finally emerged, there were proposals of the old conventional kind: for a new town of 100,000 next to the proposed airport at Stansted, for instance, or for modest expansions of towns like Aylesbury, Chelmsford or the Medway Towns. But arising from the now emphasis on large scale, the *Study* also puts forward three sets of proposals which were, in greater or lesser measure, revolutionary. The first was to take existing market towns, all of them outside the Metropolitan Area and some of them outside the South East Region altogether, and expand them to a target size far in excess of the original new towns. Two of these proposals involved the expansion of what were then fairly small towns, Newbury in Berkshire and Ashford in Kent, to target sizes of 100,000 or 150,000; interestingly, though for different reasons, both these proposals were later dropped. The others were more revolutionary in that they each took a substantial county town, with between 60,000 and 110,000 people, and grafted a new town of 50,000 or more people on to it. Thus, in addition to their own natural increase, Northampton (100,000) was to receive an eventual 100,000 people; Peterborough (60,000) 50,000 or more; and Ipswich (120,000) 60,000 or more.[1] The logic of this was simple: it was to avoid the problems of the first generation new towns, which had had to grow to a substantial size without adequate shopping, entertainment and other services. It was to avoid also the problem of providing special services, like primary schools, to deal with the sudden population bulges which arose when a new town was built up from scratch. In any rapid growth of a new town, of course, these problems are inherent; but in an existing town with a well-developed school or shopping structure, at least they will not seem so overwhelming. At any rate, this was the hope of the authors of the *Study*. At the same time, it was evident that the old town-new town combination would involve a different and more complex organizational structure than the simple new town designated in the 1940s. All these old towns were important places; two were county boroughs, exercising all planning powers in their own right. It would not be possible, therefore, to create an autonomous development corporation, independent of local authority control, to plan and manage the new town operation. Some form of joint management would be necessary.

The second revolutionary element appeared to avoid most, if not all, of these organizational problems. It was the proposal to create a new town *de novo*, much bigger than any new town built before; so much bigger, that it should properly be called a new city. Such a city, with an eventual population of more than 170,000, was proposed for the Bletchley area of north Buckinghamshire. This site had already been the subject of an imaginative new city design by Mr. Fred Pooley, the county planning officer, which became celebrated for its reliance on a monorail system coupled with moderately high-density housing layouts.[2] In the event, the Government laid it down

[1] *South East Study, op. cit.*, Table IV (p. 73).
[2] County of Buckingham, *Review of Development Plan 1963, passim.*

that they were not going to be bound by any existing plan. The city, renamed Milton Keynes after a local village,[1] was put into the hands of a Development Corporation in 1967, and consultants have been set to work with a remit to produce their own master plan.

The third, and most revolutionary, of the new ideas in the *Study* was the proposal to link the cities of Southampton and Portsmouth into a new urban complex. This South Hampshire area, with an existing population of 750,000 in 1961, would receive an addition of 250,000 people together with nearly 150,000 natural increase. An operation on this scale, the creation in effect of a planned conurbation, had no precedent. In July 1966 a consultant's report from Professor Colin Buchanan gave some very detailed advice.[2] It concluded, first, that growth on this scale was quite feasible; indeed, by the end of the century it was reasonable to think of accommodating a total of 1,750,000 people in the area without violence to the fine landscapes of the Hampshire Downs and the New Forest, which border the two cities. Secondly, if recent trends continued, it concluded that growth on very nearly this scale would occur anyway, through spontaneous migration into the area plus natural increase; thus the job was not to plan an overspill operation from London, as the authors of the *Study* had indicated, but to plan a structure to accommodate the growth which would occur whether the planners intervened positively or not. Thirdly, it proposed that the growth should be mainly accommodated in a more or less continuous urban corridor running east-to-west and linking the cities of Southampton and Portsmouth. And fourthly, after a very detailed and sophisticated study of alternative urban structures, it put forward a preferred structure: a 'directional grid', composed of a hierarchy of roads with a dominant east-west element, within which a hierarchy of urban service centres could be set at intersections of the road system. This notion is a revolutionary one, and repays very close study, not merely for the South Hampshire area, but generally. It breaks clean away from the old notion of a rigid master plan: it suggests instead that once a network of roads is laid down the urban structure can develop and change more or less naturally, in response to social needs and to the pattern of accessibility the roads convey (Map 5).

The Buchanan study, in effect, put forward a series of challenges to almost everyone: to traditionalist town planners, to countryside preservationists, and above all to those concerned with regional planning in the Government ministries. For South Hampshire had been thought of as a key element in the planned overspill of Londoners on the London housing lists; and, in terms of Government policies, this is a very different matter from planning to accommodate spontaneous migration, which would find housing for sale anyway. Now, it can be argued that this is a false and even a pernicious distinction: that rapid population growth needs comprehensive

---

[1] It would be pleasant to think that this name was chosen to commemorate two great Englishmen: but actually that was an incidental bonus. In fact it was chosen to eliminate rivalry between the existing small towns in the area.

[2] Ministry of Housing and Local Government, *The South Hampshire Study* (H.M.S.O. 1966).

Fig. 5.
STRATEGIES :
REGIONAL AND
SUB–REGIONAL,
1964–7.
The South East
Study proposals
(March 1964)
represented the first
positive regional
strategy for two
decades. The
emphasis was on
counter magnets
50–80 miles from
London, with little
indication as to
future plans for the
Outer Metropolitan
Area. Detailed
consultants' propo-
sals for South
Hampshire (July
1967) are based on an
east–west 'directional
grid' of roads.

187

structural planning, whether it is to accommodate people from the London housing lists or not. This, indeed, is a case I tried to make in *London 2000*; and it is a case that has been met in part, by the Ministry of Housing's new policy that 50 per cent of all houses in further new towns should be for owner-occupiers. Nevertheless, the shift in emphasis in Buchanan's *South Hampshire Study* does almost certainly entail a smaller government commitment, in terms of investment in infrastructure, than in the case of an overspill development in the strict sense. And it does mean that the case for a development corporation type of administrative structure, which might be needed to provide the public overspill housing, is destroyed. Indeed, in a large and complex region like this, this case would not have been strong anyway: the experience of Basingstoke and Andover, where the GLC have worked in a joint partnership with local authorities, has shown conclusively that an extremely high level of planning and design can be maintained without a Development Corporation formula. In the event, the Government gave their blessing in July 1968 to an agreement that the South Hampshire area should be developed through a plan to be drawn up by a technical unit of the local authorities concerned; the county of Hampshire, and the cities of Southampton and Portsmouth. Significantly, the 'possibility' of accommodating 60,000 overspilled Londoners was left open, as a matter for study by the technical unit.

Meanwhile, the notion of the planned agglomeration was taking root elsewhere in the region too. As early as 1965, the consultants Wilson and Womersley had completed their study for the Ministry of Housing of the co-ordinated development of the whole region including Northampton, Bedford and North Buckinghamshire.[1] They found that this region, with an existing population of 427,000 in 1661, was almost certain to increase to over a million in the late twentieth century under the impact of the schemes in the *South East Study*: the plan for the new city later known as Milton Keynes, the expansion of Northampton, and the more modest expansions of Wellingborough (already agreed between London and the local authority before the Study) and Bedford. Like Buchanan in South Hampshire, the Wilson-Womersley team considered different forms which could be used to bind the area into a planned agglomeration; tentatively they emerged with a series of thin corridors of growth following public transport lines, along which strings of small settlements could be strung. As with South Hampshire, this suggestion is nowhere yet incorporated into government or local authority policy. Nevertheless, as in South Hampshire, it seems clear that by the end of the century this will be a single region in functional terms, whatever the physical reality will be. In other words: there will be an area in the form of a rough square with sides 20 miles long, and with relatively easy communications. At the four corners will stand towns and cities of different sizes, but all substantial places. Though many people will live, work and shop within the boundaries of one of these towns, substantial and increasing numbers will commute and travel to shop

[1] Ministry of Housing and Local Government, *Northampton, Bedford and North Bucks Study* (H.M.S.O. 1965).

between them; the area will have become a unified market for jobs, shopping and entertainment, and it will have a population of over one million—equivalent to a conurbation like Tyneside today.

Thus we are faced with the virtually certain prospect of two planned agglomerations in the South East, in addition to the existing mass of Greater London, by the end of this century: one, with a million and three quarter people, seventy miles south-west of London; the other, with over a million, between 50 and 70 miles north-west of London. To complete the picture, in their *Strategy for the South East* the South East Economic Planning Council have called for the development of a third agglomeration at the borders of the South East and East Anglian regions, to be based on the planned growth of Colchester, Ipswich and the Haven Ports of Harwich and Felixstowe.[1] Centred as it would be on the green heart formed by the Stour Valley and by the Stour and Blackwater estuaries, this proposal offers unique possibilities for a new urban region based on the co-ordination of economic planning and recreational planning. The South East Council suggested that it should take third priority behind Southampton-Portsmouth and the Northampton-Milton Keynes developments, and should get under way when these were reaching maturity; say, in the last decade of the century.

In only four years since publication of the *South East Study*, then, its proposals have been transformed. The original notion of a number of free-standing large new towns and town expansions has gone, leaving survivals only in the firm agreement to expand Swindon and Peterborough. In its place has come the notion of three major planned agglomerations, all at or near the edge of the South East region, and all on major lines of communications radiating out from London. But what is still missing, in this revised philosophy, is any coherent notion of how to provide for the very large numbers of people, estimated in 1967 at over 700,000, who will have to be housed between 1961 and 1981, with many more beyond that date, in the outer metropolitan area. It was here that both the *Study* and the later *Review* of the *Study*, were conspicuously silent; this was a job which the local planning authorities could be left to do. And considering that some of the biggest pressures were likely to occur across local authority boundaries, the likelihood of any coherent planning seemed small.

During 1966 and 1967, two different regional bodies in the South East were wrestling with the problem of filling this anomalous gap. The first, the Standing Conference on London and South East Regional Planning, had been enlarged in 1966 to take in exactly the same boundaries as the South East Economic Planning Region. Essentially a confederation of all the local planning authorities in that region, the Conference was served by a technical panel of very able officials who provided a mass of statistical analysis about population and employment trends in the region as a firm basis for the development of a regional strategy. These analyses, which started as early as 1963, culminated in July and November 1966 in an important document to serve

[1] South East Economic Planning Council, *A Strategy for the South East* (H.M.S.O. 1967), para. 42 (p. 12).

as a basis for policy thinking, *The Conference Area in the Long-Term*.[1] Its authors argued that the concept of a self-contained town or community had broken down, to be replaced by the notion of different communities welded into an organized pattern of inter-relationships. Therefore, they argued, a study of communications and of movement patterns was fundamental to preparation of a strategic plan. This pointed to the fact that any plan must be related, first to plans for major regional, inter-regional and international routes, so that non-local movements could be catered for efficiently; and secondly, to developing clusters of settlements closely related to transport routes. They concluded:

'This may point to the advantages of establishing corridors (on regional or sub-regional scales) in which road and rail routes and services would be closely associated with axes of urban development (existing and new). The needs for access to areas for open-air recreation would have to be considered. As has been noted, such corridors are already in existence in many places in the Conference area.'[2]

Curiously, given this obvious lead, the thinking of the Conference then went in a quite different direction. The next major statement, of August 1967, set out three maps illustrating different ways of developing the region up to the end of the century; but significantly, none represented the corridor or axis principle of growth.[3] The accompanying report said that the Conference preferred the idea of accommodating most of the growth in a few specially selected areas, each with a considerable popula-tion, so that large tracts of rather thinly-populated countryside could be preserved between them. This, the Conference thought, would be efficient industrially, would represent the increasing scale of social organization, would help preserve agriculture and open countryside, and would cut long commuter journeys to a minimum. But all, the Conference admitted, would involve heavy investment in new road routes, which would not follow the existing dominant radial lines out of London. In fact, all their preferred alternatives incorporate three major new lines: one, running from Oxford to the west of and south west of London, to communicate with a line to the Channel ports; and two others, running diagonally across the South Midlands from London towards Bedford and Cambridge.

Within this framework, the three plans give some common elements, but very many different ones. All accept some development in the Outer Metropolitan Area north-west, west and south-west of London, though in different places; all allow some development of the north bank of the lower Thames round Southend, and two of them put development on the south bank too; all have major development in South Hampshire, and to some degree on the Sussex coast; all foresee growth in the Milton Keynes-Bedford area. There similarity ends. In the first alternative, the emphasis is on development in the Outer Metropolitan Area, especially north-west, south-west and

---

[1] Standing Conference on London and South East Regional Planning, *The Conference Area in the Long-Term* (L.R.P. 680. London, 20th July and 23rd November, 1966).   [2] *Ibid.*, para. 13 (pp. 9–10).
[3] Standing Conference on London and South East Regional Planning, *Planning London and the South East up to 2000 A.D.* (Press Release), 2nd August 1967, Maps A, B, and C.

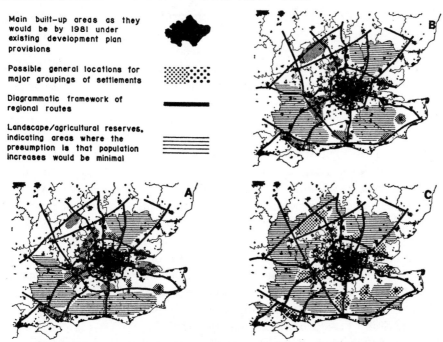

Main built-up areas as they would be by 1981 under existing development plan provisions

Possible general locations for major groupings of settlements

Diagrammatic framework of regional routes

Landscape/agricultural reserves, indicating areas where the presumption is that population increases would be minimal

Fig. 6. ALTERNATIVE REGIONAL STRATEGIES, 1966–7. The Standing Conference alternatives (July 1966, above) were all variants of 'cluster plans'. Plan A put these clusters near London, Plan B put them further out; Plan C was a variant of Plan B with more scatter. Conspicuously lacking was a sector or corridor strategy, which earlier work from the Technical Panel had suggested. The Regional Planning Council's *Strategy* (November 1967, below) put forward a schematic proposal for development in sectors radiating from London.

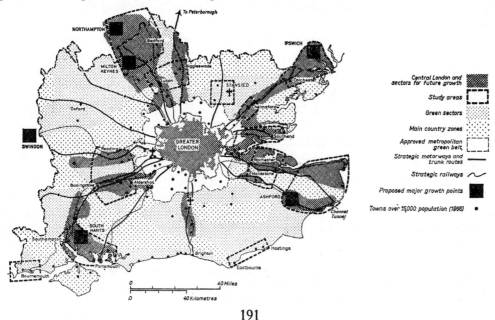

Central London and sectors for future growth

Study areas

Green sectors

Main country zones

Approved metropolitan green belt

Strategic motorways and trunk routes

Strategic railways

Proposed major growth points

Towns over 15,000 population (1966) •

east of London. In the second, there is much more emphasis on Milton Keynes-Bedford and on a series of developments in mid-Kent and mid-Sussex. The third alternative rather closely resembles the second, but with much looser groupings of population. All three, the Conference reported in 1967, had some unsatisfactory features: the Technical Panel would try to produce an acceptable refinement (Map 6).

In the event, this never became publicly available. Meanwhile, the other regional body—the South East Regional Economic Planning Council, set up in 1966 as an advisory body to the First Secretary of State for Economic Affairs—was at work on its own strategy. Such a strategy was called for in the remit to all the Regional Councils; and since the South East Council started with the benefit of the existing *Study* and *Review*, it could proceed immediately to prepare it as a first priority. Very early on in this work, it became clear that in a region growing so rapidly as the South East, any economic strategy must contain a large physical element: in other words, it must be centred upon proposals for the actual location of new investment in roads, housing and other elements of the urban infrastructure. In the event, this was to become a source of great confusion, since many physical planners did not consider this to be part of an Economic Planning Council's job. But in the particular circumstances of the South East, it could not be otherwise.

With a curious irony, the Council's thinking evolved from the important initial analysis by the Technical Panel of the Standing Conference. It also drew heavily on a comparative analysis of the regional development plans of other major metropolitan areas in Europe and elsewhere, which I was making at that time.[1] It received preliminary expression in a plan for the region which was published by the *Weekend Telegraph* magazine in March 1967,[2] after an intensive series of meetings by a working group under the chairmanship of Lord Redmayne, to which Leslie Lane and I (both members of the Regional Council) contributed. After very intensive comment and criticism from members of the Council and from Government departments, the proposals were modified both in form and in terminology before their incorporation in the Council's strategy as published in November 1967.

As thus modified, the essential principle of the *Strategy* is that development should be concentrated, as far as possible, into a series of sectors radiating out from London along main lines of communication. The name 'sector' was deliberately chosen in preference to 'corridor' to indicate that the urban area would have breadth as well as length. 'Major sectors' would be wider, and would lead normally to planned 'counter-magnets' in the form of planned agglomerations of people as already described. There would be four of these major sectors: one leading south-westwards to Southampton-Portsmouth, one north-westwards towards Northampton-Milton Keynes, one north-eastwards towards Colchester-Ipswich, and a last leading south-

[1] For a detailed account see Peter Hall, Planning for Urban Growth: Metropolitan Area Plans and their implications for South East England. *Regional Studies*, 1 (1967), pp. 101–134.
[2] London 1990, *Weekend Telegraph*, 17th March 1967.

eastwards towards Canterbury. Each of these would be paralleled by a planned 'minor sector' which would be narrower. These would also lead towards 'counter-magnets' but in these cases they would be the smaller, free-standing towns. Thus a western sector would lead to Swindon, a northern one to Peterborough, a north-eastern one to an expanded Basildon and Southend, and a south-eastern one to Ashford (a project later abandoned). Lastly, an isolated minor sector would run along the main radial road and rail lines to Brighton. The form of these sectors would leave very wide green sectors embodying much of the best landscapes of the region; these would receive a specially-protected status as 'country zones'. Lastly, and most importantly (though not always sufficiently realized by the public who read the *Strategy*) the sectors were not designed for continuous urbanization. The form of development was rather to resemble beads, of very different size, along a string. Clearly, in many cases the urban pattern would be punctuated, sometimes for con-siderable distances; as in the Hampshire downs, for instance, between Basingstoke and Winchester, or in the fine Greensand country of Woburn Sands, between Luton and Milton Keynes[1] (Map 6).

The rationale behind the sector strategy was simple and clear enough. Though it was far from trend planning in the pejorative sense, it recognized a number of realities. The first was that a large amount of investment was committed, through the 1970s, in the form of forward plans for improved communications, above all motor-ways and trunk roads. It made sense to utilize this investment as far as possible, by relating other urban investment—in houses, schools and shops—to it. The second was the existing commitment, inherited from the *Study*, to counter-magnets 50–70 miles from London. The third was that all experience showed that industrialists seeking factory sites, and following them developers seeking office sites, sought places with good communications, above all to London. They also sought a good catchment area for their staff—which also spelt the need for efficient communications. The fourth was the need, which everyone accepts, to preserve large tracts of unspoiled countryside, above all for the recreation of the town dweller. If, as already in North America, driving for pleasure is to be the major single form of recreation for a large part of the population, that merely underlines the point of keeping the undeveloped areas as large and as unspoilt as possible. By concentrating development in only three sets of corridors, with a very minor fourth one, the Council achieved this end to about the maximum feasible degree. To have gone further would have meant a single east-west sector, probably in the form of two parallel axes, on the lines of the Paris development plan of 1965; but in the circumstances of the London region, that would just have ignored the reality of the critical main industrial axis of England which runs from London up to Birmingham and beyond.

In this discussion of the Planning Council's *Strategy for the South East*, I have dealt in passing with the main criticisms since its publication in November 1967; but it is useful perhaps to summarize them. The first is the criticism that the Council did the

[1] The strategy is set out in more detail in *A Strategy for the South East, op. cit.*, Ch. 3 *passim*.

wrong job: that, appointed to do an economic planning job, they produced a physical plan instead. I have argued than an economic strategy, in a region like the South East, necessarily has a physical component. The second is the criticism that the Council put too much weight on the restrictions imposed by investments in infrastructure, especially roads; this criticism goes on to say that the Council should have been much freer in suggesting alternative forms of development that involved new investment in transportation. In view of the recurrent economic crises which rack all public expenditure projects in this country, I offer no apology here. The third is the criticism that the Council are proposing continuous corridors of urbanization, seventy or more miles long. This, I hope it is now clear, is based on a wilful misreading of the proposals. The fourth is that there would have been advantage in combining all development into a single east-west axis. This, I would argue, completely ignores the reality of existing development, and of the planned complex of counter-magnets around Northampton and Milton Keynes—which the Council inherited from earlier official plans when it began its task.

There is, though, one fifth and fundamental criticism, which I think is justified and in which I would join. It is that the *Strategy* was presented as a single physical sketch, without presentation of alternatives or an attempt at evaluation. In the circumstances, given the timetable and the restrictions on supporting staff, that was probably inevitable. But it did help to conceal many of the steps in the argument, which led to our selection of the corridor Strategy as the most efficient and the most economic one. We did admit that our chosen strategy required testing and evaluation, which axiomatically required the setting up of alternatives; but we were not in a position to do it ourselves.

In the event, the Government in May 1968 announced that this process would be undertaken by an independent Study team, under the direction of the Chief Planner at the Ministry of Housing and Local Government, Dr. Wilfred Burns. This will start by considering the Council's strategy, as well as the alternatives put forward by the Standing Conference. Against a review of population trends and the possibility of moving employment, it will try to evaluate these, and other possible alternative strategies. From preliminary statements, it seems clear that this evaluation will in some places be quantitative, in others only qualitative. The transportation implications of the different strategies, for instance, are capable of being assessed in a fairly precise way; the implications for the preservation of countryside, given the present state of the art, probably are not.

There are many question marks about the latest Study. The most obvious is why no one did it before. Since the original *South East Study* was being prepared inside the Ministry of Housing in 1962 and 1963, there have been seven years of continuous activity in and around Whitehall, involving the expenditure of countless thousands of highly-skilled man hours. A *Study* has been followed by a *Review*, and then by a *Strategy*. Now, there is another *Study*—which, since by now the Government appears to have run out of terms, can only be described as a Study Mark Two. This is not a story of conscious planning; it is a melancholy story of conspicuous failure to plan. If the Government had really wanted a plan, the original *South East Study* authors were fully capable of producing one; the suspicion remains that large parts of their report were censored out of existence by the Government, because they proved politically unpalatable. Between them, the South East Council and Board were fully capable of producing an adequate plan; but they were denied the resources to do the job. As a result, the job they did was rightly criticized as half-baked. The public was right in its criticisms, but wrong in laying them at the Council's door. Now, at last, the Government has brought into being a team capable of the job; but of course, it had done that seven years before. All that any rational man can hope for, now, is first that the Burns team proves worthy of its commission and secondly that the Government has the courage to accept its report when finally it appears.

Therefore, there are elements of a strategy. But too many elements are still un-integrated. Neither the Planning Council, nor the Standing Conference, mention the Greater London Development Plan, which is due early in 1969 and must form a major element of any strategic plan.[1] Neither can deal adequately with the question of a third London airport, where the Government—after over a year of trying to force through a decision to build on the much-criticized site at Stansted in Essex —announced a Planning Commission to reconsider the whole subject.

[1] On the plan, see the final postscript, p. 276.

APPENDIX TO CHAPTER 6

Twenty-five New Towns for London

SITE 1. WALLINGFORD (Berks.)

Location. 47 miles London. 13 miles Oxford.

Present Population. Approx. 5,000.

Rail Access. Cholsey Station, 95 minutes Central London. If expresses stopped, 65 minutes.

Road Access. Excellent. A 423 (Trunk) to Henley (by-pass projected) and M4; also to Oxford, Midlands.

Agricultural Land. Grades 2 and 4. Possible difficult drainage on latter.

V-Land. Clear.

Water. Probably difficult (Thames).

SITE 2. BICESTER (Oxfordshire)[1]

Location. 57 miles London. 13 miles Oxford.

Present Population. Approx. 5,500.

Rail Access. 80 minutes Central London. Frequency poor.

Road Access. Good. To M1 via Buckingham and Stony Stratford. To Birmingham also via B4030 and A34. To Southampton via Oxford by-passes and A34.

Agricultural Land. Border of Grades 4 and 5. Agriculturally this region is not prosperous.

V-Land. Clear.

Water. Near Thames-Ouse watershed. The upper Ouse is a deficiency area and the upper Thames is also unlikely to have a surplus.

Comment. This site seems unsuitable for office decentralization.

[1] This site has previously been suggested for a New Town or Town Expansion in the Town and Country Planning Association Map of South-Eastern England for their Regional Conference, on 7 March 1961.

SITE 3. PRINCES RISBOROUGH (Bucks.)

Location. 40 miles London. 9 miles High Wycombe.

Present Population. About 4,000.

Rail Access. 60–70 minutes Central London. Service excellent.

Road Access. Excellent. A4010, thence A40 to London. Needed: a spur to connect A4010 with projected High Wycombe by-pass; an east-west cross road giving access to A34 and M1.

Agricultural Land. Thin mixed soils of Chilterns, Grades 5–6.

V-Land. Clear.

Water. Difficult (Thames Basin).

SITE 4. FLITWICK (Beds.)

Location. 43 miles London. 8 miles Bedford.

Present Population. About 3,000.

Rail Access. 66 minutes Central London. Service excellent.

Road Access. Excellent. A5120 connects with M1, 5 miles to south.

Agricultural Land. Mixed Grades 2 and 4.

V-Land. Woburn Park area to west, on medium (Grade 6) land.

Water. In water surplus stretch of the Great Ouse basin.[1]

SITE 5. SANDY (Beds.-Hunts.)

Location. 49 miles London (New Town site two miles north of old town, 51 miles from London). Biggleswade 4 miles. Bedford 8 miles.

Present Population. About 4,000.

Rail Access. About 90 minutes Central London. Service adequate; rather variable.

Road Access. Excellent. On A1. A603 to Bedford, thence via Newport Pagnell to M1.

Agricultural Land. Adjacent to the old town is Grade 1 land. The New Town would stand on Grade 2 and Grade 4 land to the north-east.

V-Land. Clear, except for a patch to the east of the present village which would provide a public open space.

Water. In the upper middle Ouse, which has a water surplus.[2]

SITE 6. ROYSTON (Herts.-Cambs.)

Location. 41 miles London. 14 miles Cambridge.

Present Population. About 6,000.

Rail Access. 85–95 minutes Central London. Service good.

Road Access. 10 miles from A1 (proposed Baldock by-pass). A603 a few miles north gives access to West Midlands and north-west.

[1] Ministry of Housing and Local Government, *River Great Ouse Basin: Hydrological Survey* (Hydrometric Area No. 33) (H.M.S.O. 1960). [2] *Ibid.*

Agricultural Land. The New Town would be built on Grade 2 land to the north of the present town, in the County of Cambridgeshire.

V-Land. The downland to the south, providing public open space.

Water. In water-surplus Ely Ouse section of the Great Ouse Basin.[1]

SITE 7. QUENDON (Essex)[2]

Location. 38 miles London. 8 miles Bishops Stortford.

Present Population. About 1,000.

Rail Access. 70 minutes Central London; but new station needed. Service moderate.

Road Access. Excellent. M11 and extensions, about 1968, to London; improvement of E.–W. cross-road necessary to give access to M1 and Midlands.

Agricultural Land. Grade 2.

V-Land. Considerable areas to north, would provide open space.

Water. In Upper Lea catchment area, deficient.[3] But to north Ouse Basin undoubtedly contains large ground-water reserves.[4]

Note. Access to Stansted, proposed third airport for London.

SITE 8. GREAT DUNMOW (Essex)

Location. 39 miles London. 10 miles Bishops Stortford. 13 miles Chelmsford.

Present Population. About 4,000.

Rail Access. Line at present closed to passenger traffic. If re-opened, London would be within 70 minutes (via Bishops Stortford).

Road Access. M11 to London, by-passes Stortford on the Dunmow side. E.–W. cross-route necessary to Midlands.

Agricultural Land. Grade 2. To south of existing town is classic (Rodings) area. Expansion would take place to north on less distinguished land.

V-Land. A tongue, would provide open space.

Water. Deficiency area.

Note. Access to Stansted Airport.

SITE 9. ONGAR (Essex)

Location. 24 miles London. 7 miles Epping. Within the original Metropolitan Green Belt.

Present Population. About 1,000.

---

[1] *Ibid.*

[2] This is close to the 'Saffron Walden' site indicated by the Town and Country Planning Association in March 1961, *op. cit.*

[3] Ministry of Housing and Local Government, *River Lee Basin: Hydrological Survey* (Hydrometric Area No. 38) (H.M.S.O. 1962).

[4] River Great Ouse, *op. cit.*

Rail Access. Central Line, 60 minutes Central London.

Road Access. A113, not a heavily trafficked road, to London. Construction of North Orbital Road would give access to Midlands, Channel Ports.

Agricultural Land. Expansion would take place on Grade 6 land: heavy London Clay and poor stony glacial till.

V-Land. To the south-east of the proposed New Town.

Water. Deficiency area.[1]

SITE 10. KELVEDON (Essex)[2]

Location. 44 miles London. 13 miles Chelmsford. 10 miles Colchester.

Present Population. 3,000.

Rail Access. 80 minutes Central London. Good service; probably improved if New Town built.

Road Access. On A12 to London, planned by-pass; improvement of E.–W. cross-route necessary for access to Midlands.

Agricultural Land. Grade 2.

V-Land. To south-west, attractive sandy area which would be open space.

Water. Deficiency area.

SITE 11. WOODHAM FERRERS (Essex)

Location. 35 miles London.

Present Population. About 2,000.

Rail Access. 60 minutes Central London. Single-track but service good.

Road Access. B1012 leads south to Southend Arterial Road (A127) for London; Midlands link (via Chelmsford and east-west route) needs improvement.

Agricultural Land. Grade 6, heavy infertile London Clay grassland.

V-Land. Shores of Crouch estuary to the south.

Water. Deficiency area.

Comment. Near Southend Airport.

SITE 12. QUEENBOROUGH – MINSTER (SHEPPEY) (Kent)

Location. 49 miles London. 4 miles Sheerness.

Present Population. 3,300.

Rail Access. 80–95 minutes Central London. Service good.

Road Access. A249 via new Queenborough Bridge to M2 for London, Dartford-Purfleet tunnel, eventually Channel ports. The port at Sheerness could be developed.

---

[1] Ministry of Housing and Local Government, *Essex Rivers and Stour: Hydrological Survey* (Hydrometric Areas Nos. 36 and 37) (H.M.S.O. 1961).

[2] This is close to the 'Witham' site indicated by the Town and Country Planning Association in March 1961, *op. cit.*

Agricultural Land. Grade 6 land around Minster; Grade 2 adjacent to Queen-borough. The main development on the medium-grade land.
V-Land. Clear.
Water. Expected deficiency.

SITE 13. HAMSTREET (Kent)

Location. 61 miles London. 7 miles Ashford.
Present Population. Negligible.
Rail Access. 95–105 minutes Central London. Present service barely adequate, but presumably could be improved.*
Road Access. A20 London or Channel link (would need new link roads east of Ashford as part of the plan).
Agricultural Land. Grades 6–7, poor to medium.
V-Land. Clear.
Water. Evidence indicates a surplus.
Note. Exceptional potentiality for Channel crossing.

SITE 14. HEADCORN (Kent)

Location. 45 miles London. 11 miles Ashford.
Present Population. 2,000.
Rail Access. 90 minutes Central London. Service adequate.
Road Access. B2163 to Maidstone by-pass, London and projected S. Orbital; or to Channel ports.
Agricultural Land. Grades 6–7, medium-poor quality; very mixed.
V-Land. Clear.
Water. Believed good.

SITE 15. ASHURST (Kent)

Location. 32 miles London. 8 miles Tunbridge Wells.
Present Population. Negligible.
Rail Access. About 90 minutes Central London. Service good.
Road Access. B2026 to Westerham. Thence A233 to London.
Agricultural Land. Grade 6.
V-Land. Clear.
Water. Believed good.

SITE 16. ROBERTSBRIDGE (Sussex)

Location. 52 miles London. 12 miles Hastings.
Present Population. Negligible.
Rail Access. About 90 minutes Central London. Service excellent.
Road Access. A21 to London or South Orbital.

Agricultural Land. Medium quality, Grade 6. Grassland on Hastings Sands. Very varied soils.

V-Land. Clear.

Water. Good (big collecting area).

SITE 17. PLUMPTON (Sussex)

Location. 44 miles London. 8 miles Lewes.

Present Population. Negligible.

Rail Access. 80 minutes Central London. Service good except late night.*

Road Access. A275 to Forest Row and then A22, planned for improvement, to London; or A272 and M23.

Agricultural Land. Very mixed, including some poor quality soils, Grades 6–7.

V-Land. Clear. South Downs immediately to south of town.

Water. Presumed good.

SITE 18. BILLINGSHURST (Sussex)

Location. 43 miles London. 7 miles Horsham.

Present Population. 3,000.

Rail Access. 75–85 minutes Central London. Service excellent.

Road Access. A29 to London, connects with Orbital system. Good access to Midlands.

Agricultural Land. Very mixed, Grades 6–7. Grassland on Weald Clay, with arable and some woodland.

V-Land. Clear.

Water. Presumed good.

SITE 19. CRANLEIGH (Surrey)

Location. 37 miles London. 9 miles Guildford.

Present Population. About 5,000.

Rail Access. About 70 minutes Central London. Service rather poor.*

Road Access. A281 to Guildford, thence to Midlands (but improvements necessary); A29 to London.

Agricultural Land. Varies, medium-poor, Grades 6 and 7.

V-Land. Clear.

Water. Presumed good.

SITE 20. LIPHOOK (Hants.)

Location. 46 miles London.

Present Population. Negligible.

Rail Access. 80 minutes Central London. Service excellent.

Road Access. On A3. Access to Midlands via B roads to A32 and A332 at Alton.
Agricultural Land. Grades 6–7, medium to poor.
V-Land. Would be built to north of existing village, on Forestry Commission land.
Water. Presumed excellent.
Note. Longmoor military camp one mile distant.

SITE 21. ALTON (Hants.)

Location. 49 miles London. 12 miles Basingstoke.
Present Population. 9,000.
Rail Access. Central London 90 minutes.
Road Access. A31 London, under improvement. A by-pass necessary; also for A32 (to Midlands) which intersects.
Agricultural Land. Medium grade, downland, Grade 5.
V-Land. On edge according to revised Hampshire Development Plan.[1]
Water. Presumed ample.

SITE 22. MICHELDELVER (Hants.)

Location. 59 miles London. 7 miles Winchester.
Present Population. 1,300.
Rail Access. Central London 84 minutes. Service adequate.
Road Access. M3 to London. A34 to Midlands.
Agricultural Land. Downland, medium quality, Grade 5.
V-Land. Indicated on revised Hampshire Development Plan, together with *all* chalklands west of Basingstoke.[2]
Water. Presumed adequate.

SITE 23. HOOK (Hants.)

Location. 41 miles London. 6 miles Basingstoke.
Present Population. 1,200.
Rail Access. 80 minutes Central London. Service good.
Road Access. New M3 to London. Easy access northwards to A34 and Midlands.
Agricultural Land. Medium quality, Grade 6.
V-Land. Clear.
Water. Presumed adequate.
Note. This is the L.C.C. site, abandoned in favour of a series of Town Expansions. The proposal should be restored.

[1] The revised Plan was submitted in August 1961, after the original New Town survey was conducted.
[2] *Ibid.*

SITE 24. SILCHESTER (Hants.)

Location. 47 miles London. 9 miles Reading. 10 miles Basingstoke.

Present Population. 421.

Rail Access. Mortimer Station, 75–85 minutes Central London. Service adequate.

Road Access. About one mile from line of M4.[1] To north a new link would lead to this and give access to A340 at Theale, thence via A417 to A34 at Harwell.

Agricultural Land. Mixed, medium-poor, Grades 6–9.

V-Land. Clear.

Water. Probably deficient (Thames Basin).

Note. The Roman remains give exceptional opportunity for an imaginative town design.

SITE 25. PETERSFIELD (Hants.)

Location. 54 miles London. 17 miles Portsmouth.

Present Population. 7,379.

Rail Access. 85 minutes Central London. Service excellent.

Road Access. Excellent. A3 to London. Via A272 to A34 at Winchester (by-pass at Winchester planned).

Agricultural Land. Grades 2–4. An alternative site about 4 miles south of the existing town on Grade 5 land, but possible landscape value.

V-Land. Indicated on revised Hampshire map (together with most of western Hampshire).[2]

Water. Presumed adequate. (Hampshire basin, surplus.)

[1] The Ministry of Transport have subsequently proposed (January 1963) a line for M4 running *north* of Reading (Map 3C). This is probably the least suitable line for any New Town development.

[2] Hampshire Plan, *op. cit.*

* British Railways have subsequently proposed the closure of the stations at these places. *The Reshaping of British Railways* (H.M.S.O. 1963).

CHAPTER 7

Renewing The Fabric

In the years up to 2000, the London Region will contain two areas of rapid physical change, where the planner must above all be active. One, we have seen in Chapter 6, is the Outer Ring, where must be provided virtually all the homes and services, and as much as possible of the factory and office space, needed for the new households which will be generated naturally within the region and arrive from elsewhere. But parallel to this tremendous programme of construction, between thirty-five and sixty miles from central London, is another: the complete physical renewal of great stretches of central and inner London, the area roughly within a seven-mile radius of Charing Cross.

Here, at first sight the problem might seem to be simply massive obsolescence. In the central zone, slum offices and workshops and warehouses, carved out of converted dwelling houses, without adequate daylight, ventilation, heating, sanitary facilities: alike inconvenient for the employer, degrading for the worker. In the inner zone, the legacy of hastily built and inadequate Victorian housing, for a population poorer than ours: the insanitary, cramped labourers' cottages of Stepney and Bermondsey, now in process of being swept away; the horrors of early charitable building for industrious artisans, the barracks along the highways which the Victorians drove so ruthlessly through the teeming rookeries of Clerkenwell and Shoreditch; and the biggest problems of all, the speculative failures built for the Victorian middle class in Paddington and North Kensington, Brixton and Battersea. The extent of obsolescence within this zone, I have already tried to calculate.[1] Some of it might be cured by improvement techniques; we do not know. And obsolescence of housing is accompanied by obsolescence of all necessary community services; inadequate open space, too few and too cramped swimming-baths or playing fields, libraries and clinics tucked in corners of draughty dark old houses, poky insanitary corner shops.

But obsolescence is itself a rather elementary problem. You cure it by diverting

[1] Chapter 4, pages 93–5.

resources to reconstruction: either away from other ends, or, preferably, by generating new resources. In the next chapter, I discuss a financial technique which should achieve the latter. But given the money, you may spend it well, in terms of social weal, or foolishly. Since 1945 we have built a good deal in central and inner London, but much of it represents relative waste of resources, because it is innocent of real planning. I gave examples in Chapter 1; they were only representative of a very widespread failure of our techniques and our imaginations. In internal planning, in external appearance—considered individually—the buildings are some good, some bad, most adequate; but they were planned on one thousand separate drawing boards; functionally and aesthetically, they relate to each other in no coherent way.

This is because no one is being paid, and given the power, to see that they relate. But, it will be said, we have Planning Departments. Unfortunately, this fact is meaningless. For under the system of permissive land-use planning created under the 1947 Town and Country Planning Act, the Planning Department is everywhere emasculated. Over 95 per cent of the area of inner London, it performs a merely passive role: it waits for initiatives to come from a multitude of individual developers, and is then limited to saying yea or nay, or suggesting minor modifications, on the basis of very generalized rules about permitted densities and permitted land uses.

The exception—it applies to only 4,000 acres out of London County Council's 75,000[1]—is provided by the Comprehensive Development Areas. Here, and here alone, the Planning Authority engages in positive planning: it wipes the slate clean and creates anew the pattern of roads and footpaths, flats and houses and gardens and open spaces, libraries and schools and clinics, shops and banks and garages. The private developer is not excluded in the areas of Comprehensive Development—in some, such as the Barbican, which are commercial areas, he has a very important part to play. But he is limited to doing what the Planning Authority specifies: the roles are reversed. This is the essence of real planning. It has produced what is, despite its omissions, the greatest triumph of planning so far in London: the reconstruction of the East End, one of the greatest coherent pieces of urban renewal in the world, now well under way. It can produce many more. But only when it is allowed to be not the exception, but the invariable rule.

In the rest of this chapter, therefore, I want to ask: what, specifically, is the present machinery failing to achieve? what different sort of planning do we need, and how will it work better than the present one? in other words, why is it worth having? Having—I hope—proved the case, I go on in the next chapter to ask, *inter alia*: what sort of machinery—administrative, legal, financial, technical—do we need to achieve the new sort of planning?

Planning for Circulation

The need for planning is permanent. But its objectives change, according to the social problems uppermost in men's minds.

[1] In 1960. *L.C.C. Development Plan, First Review* 1960 (County Planning Report, vol. I), para 610.

Until 1945, and after, planners in England were dominated by *sanitary* considerations.[1] They were carrying through the tail-end of the great revolution in environmental health, which Edwin Chadwick had initiated in the eighteen-forties. Fresh air, fresh food, the healing touch of nature were the essentials. This is why—rightly —the 1947 system of planning is obsessed by density standards and the need to separate homes from noisome workshops; this is why—ironically—the New Towns contain acres of untended gardens intended to allow the inhabitants to grow their own cabbages,[2] while streets are jammed with garageless Ford Populars.

The problems of sanitation are not all solved yet: a walk round London's West Side on a summer evening will make that clear. But they have become secondary; road accidents now kill nearly twice as many people as tuberculosis. The central planning problem of our age has become the motor vehicle, and our urban reconstruction must be based on this fact. The essential is now almost a journalistic commonplace: *segregation*.[3] You need to keep vehicles away from where people eat and sleep and work and think and talk and shop; and put them where they belong, in pipes sealed off from the rest of the system, like bottled genies ready to perform the miracles we ask of them. At present, in an Aladdinesque nightmare, they have run amok.

But segregation is precisely what, under the 1947 system, we are incapable of achieving. Even in the most radical Comprehensive Development Plans, the ideas about traffic circulation are exceedingly primitive. There is only one belated scheme for a segregated motor road in the vast Stepney-Poplar reconstruction area. In the smaller schemes where there is insufficient space to achieve proper rearrangement of functions, the planners are even putting shop windows facing on to busy traffic routes—as at the Elephant and Castle, and Lewisham—and hoping to deal with the resulting chaos by a few subways.

Outside the Comprehensive Development Areas, virtually no segregation is possible at all. Since 1955 large parts of the central business district of London—especially at the fringes, as at Fitzrovia or Victoria—have been reconstructed. But at most, the L.C.C. have used comprehensive techniques to achieve minor improvements of road junctions; over wide areas, the development has been completely piecemeal. I quoted the example of Fitzrovia in Chapter 1. Map 7 shows in detail what has happened in this area in the space of eight years. It is an eloquent testimony to the opportunities we have lost. Given the most elementary social control, this reconstruction could have been carried through—at little extra cost—to provide a completely new environment for the thousands of people who live and work in Fitzrovia: both a better machine for working in and a better place for living in.

[1] See the account in W. Ashworth, *The Genesis of Modern British Town Planning* (1954).
[2] The idea dates back to Raymond Unwin (see his *Town Planning in Practice* (1909), 320) and his 1903 design for Letchworth. Unwin influenced Barry Parker, who designed Wythenshawe, which in turn powerfully influenced the New Towns.
[3] H. G. Wells applied the word to traffic as early as 1901 (*Anticipations*, Fifth Edition, p. 17) when forecasting, with uncanny accuracy, the coming of motorways.

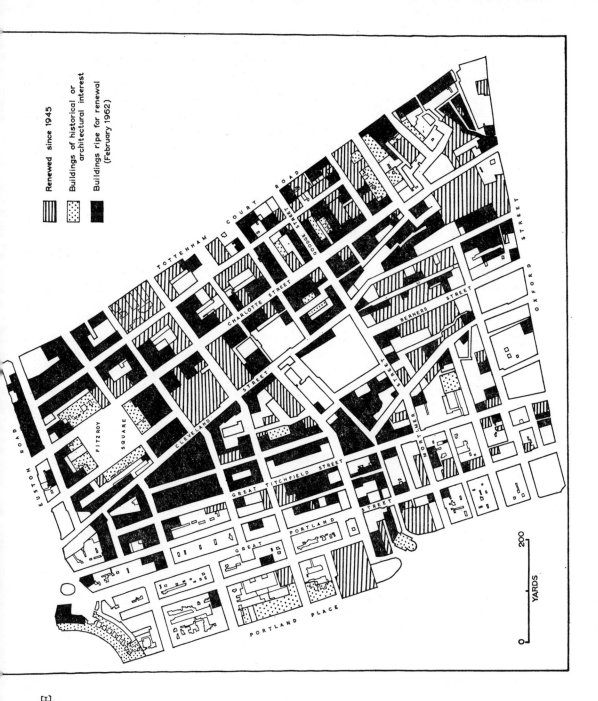

Map 7.
FITZROVIA:
OBSOLESCENCE
AND
RENEWAL
(February 1962)

Renewed since 1945

Buildings of historical or
architectural interest

Buildings ripe for renewal
(February 1962)

207

The same thing occurs in the slum-clearance building which has taken place on such a widespread scale over large areas of inner Victorian London since 1955. Traverse, street by street, the triangles made by any two of the main radial roads in this zone—between New North Road and Kingsland Road in the north-east, between Old Kent Road and Camberwell Road in the south, between Wandsworth Road and Clapham Road in the south-west—and the same pattern recurs. As at the centre, a large part of the urban fabric has been renewed; but piecemeal. Under the slum clearance programme, which has operated since 1955, the local authorities have been limited to clearing and rebuilding the narrowly defined slum sites, a block or two at a time; at most a minor rearrangement of the street pattern is possible, a stopping-up here, a diversion there. Still pedestrians cross the path of the stray motorist un-awares, still they emerge from their blocks to find themselves exposed to the hazards of main-road traffic. And because these are strictly *housing* schemes, the main roads are often untouched: here traditional commercial prejudices, enshrined in the pattern of local land values, ensure that every time they shop, the people from the new blocks are exposed to maximum inconvenience and maximum hazard. Since 1955 also, with the great boom in retail trade, major reconstruction of inner-suburban shopping centres has taken place—as at Notting Hill Gate[1] or Swiss Cottage—on the traditional pattern, facing on to main radial traffic routes, with the acquiescence of the L.C.C.: a measure of the complete inadequacy of our present planning machinery.

The P-Solution and the V-Solution

The solution we should be applying in these areas depends on the amount of traffic generated by land use. I have already pointed out[2] that we know next to nothing about this, though the Americans have advanced as far as producing mathematical generalizations from studies or particular cases. The broad rules, though, are evident. Work generates more traffic than homes; within residential areas, densest traffic is generated round shopping and service centres; within work areas, certain industries—newspaper printing or women's clothing—are exceptionally high generators. These rules are likely to remain true, whatever conceivable technical development occurs in the coming decades.

For comprehensive planning, then, the first essential is a projection of the amount of traffic likely to be generated by the proposed land uses. From this, the planner will have one of two solutions open to him.[3]

The first is where traffic generation is light: residential areas and those work areas where transmission of bulky goods is not important. This alternative, the simpler, is *Horizontal Segregation*, or the *Precinctual Solution* (*P-Solution*). The idea of the

[1] See the criticism and pictures in the *Architectural Review*, February 1962.
[2] Chapter 5, pages 105–6.
[3] The best account of the two solutions, with examples, is Kenneth Browne and Henryk Blachnyki, 'Over and Under', *Architectural Review*, May 1961.

precinct has been instinctively applied by builders and architects for centuries, in the Oxford and Cambridge Colleges, in London's Inns of Court, in the original plans for Bloomsbury where through traffic was kept out by gates: wherever, in fact, it was essential to get peace, for living or scholarly working, from the urban bustle outside. But as a deliberate policy for urban reconstruction in the age of the motor vehicle, it seems to have originated from a police expert on London traffic, Sir Alker Tripp, in 1942.[1] It became the basis of Abercrombie's famous (and ill-fated) Westminster and Bloomsbury precincts, in the County of London Plan a year later. But Tripp did not intend it merely as a special solution to the needs of rather peculiar areas; it was to be applied widely through all areas like inner London, where the ground plan is suitable, with main roads at fairly wide intervals about a mile apart. (Tripp's original example was the Hackney Road-Bethnal Green Road area.) Within a block enclosed by main roads, the street pattern was to be remodelled so that through traffic would find it virtually impossible to penetrate. This meant the closing of certain streets leading on to the main roads, and their replacement by pedestrian malls; narrowing of others; frequent corners. The design of the whole system would be made suitable for only very slow-moving traffic. To compensate, the bounding main roads should be made really capable of performing their true function. This meant widening where necessary; the removal of all impediments such as parked vehicles, loading and unloading, by the transfer of commercial uses away from the main roads—where, historically, they tended to concentrate—into special zones within the precincts. Shopping centres, for instance, would no longer face main roads, but turn inwards to face the precinct whence their customers came.

Evidently, this operation would require very powerful planning machinery, which the 1947 Act failed to supply. Only in the big comprehensive development areas, therefore, has it been thoroughly applied in the postwar rebuilding of London. Travel along the main radial roads of the East End—Commercial Road and East India Dock Road, for instance—and you will immediately appreciate, by the contrast between reconstructed and unreconstructed areas, the difference in traffic flow and environment which results. The first essential, then, is to apply the P-Solution to all reconstruction areas where it will provide an adequate answer.

This may however not be in every respect the precise precinctual solution which Abercrombie foresaw. A valid criticism of Abercrombie's planning is that he paid too little regard to costs. Under virtually any conceivable system of compensation to owners, it will invariably prove more expensive to shift shopping centres from their existing positions along main roads, than it would be to drive a relief road through cheaper property parallel to the main road and then turn the old main road into a pedestrian and parking precinct, sealed off from through traffic. The economy will be even more striking if there is need for a completely new motorway parallel to the

[1] H. Alker Tripp, *Town Planning and Road Traffic* (1942), 78. Tripp also advocated vertical segregation: *ibid.*, 27 and 68. C. D. Buchanan has pointed out the importance of Tripp's contribution to planning, which is not generally appreciated.

BUILDING THE NEW LONDON

main road—an aspect too often ignored in the County of London Plan—for then construction of relief road and motorway may be combined. In this way, as Map 8 shows, different sorts of traffic can be completely segregated: through traffic on the motorway, intermediate traffic on the relief road, purely local traffic parked within the precinct or adjacent to it.

City centre redevelopment poses a more complex problem. Until recently, even the most radical central replanning schemes have been conceived in terms of the precinctual solution; standard manuals of planning practice still recommend it.[1] And it has produced the pedestrian shopping malls, which are among the greatest successes of postwar planning: central Coventry, Stevenage, Lijnbaan in Rotterdam, Hötorget in Stockholm, Kettwiger Strasse in Essen, Salzstrasse in Münster. But there are difficulties and defects. All are essentially small-scale solutions, based on a single street or place, or at most a complex of two or three streets. (Thus Coventry's centre is cruciform.) The reason is that vehicle access must be provided at the back of all the premises, for loading and unloading goods. In addition there must be car parks within reasonable walking distance of any shop. These demands mean the virtual sterilization of large areas of land immediately around the shopping precincts, and produce aesthetic problems which have not yet been satisfactorily met; the desolation of the 'back sides' of central Coventry, or central Stevenage, detracts very seriously from the merits of the whole conception. The root of these problems is that in the city centre, the amounts of traffic generated are simply too great for a one-level solution to be practicable. It is necessary to increase the total amount of space available to vehicles and pedestrians on each acre of the city centre, by multi-level planning. *Vertical Segregation*—the *V-Solution*—becomes inevitable.

Like the precinct, the idea of V-segregation is not new. Leonardo understood it; in the Adelphi scheme, the brothers Adam used it; it was incorporated in railway building from the start.[2] But very few city rebuilding schemes, anywhere in the world, have yet had the imaginative grasp to accept it wholeheartedly. An exception is the most radical piece of urban renewal being carried out in London since 1945: the southern part of the Barbican comprehensive redevelopment area, which is being built on a three-level basis: parking at underground level, traffic at ground level and pedestrians on continuous walkways at upper level. The Barbican and the Holford plan for the comprehensive redevelopment of Piccadilly Circus[3] represent the biggest breakthrough in planning since Ebenezer Howard invented the Garden City.

In Chapter 5 I have already outlined the essentials of the traffic flow in a system of vertical segregation. I now want to develop three points: the degree to which the solution can be sophisticated; the extent to which it can be applied in an old city

[1] F. Gibberd, *Town Design* (1959 edition), 57. Gibberd is best known as architect of Harlow New Town.
[2] See G. A. Jellicoe, *Motopia* (1961), 78–9, 121–3.
[3] London County Council, *Piccadilly Circus Future Development* (1962).

210

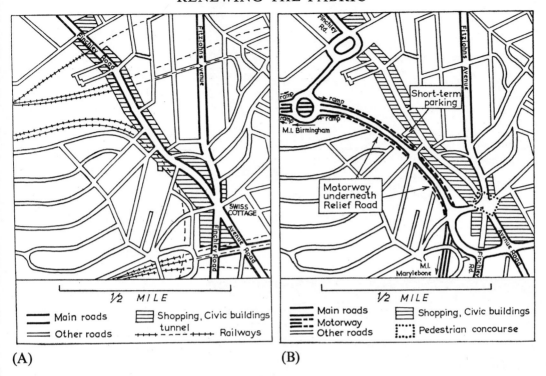

(A)   (B)

Map 8

MAIN ROAD REPLANNING—RIGHT AND WRONG
An example from Finchley Road

Map A shows Finchley Road in 1963. It presents in extreme form the problems of ribbon shopping development along a main radial road, which has to perform simultaneously three irreconcilable functions: arterial road (main outlet from the West End to the M1), main road for journeys of intermediate length, and local shopping street. The solution currently proposed is merely to widen the road; this will simply intensify the existing conflict of functions. The 'precinctual' solution would be to widen the road and seal off side access, while removing the shops elsewhere; this is very expensive (because of compensation) and does not provide the best solution for traffic. *Map B* shows a third alternative which clearly separates the three functions. A motorway (for which official Ministry plans exist) takes the through traffic; intermediate traffic is diverted on to a relief road, which runs in part above the motorway; the existing main road is sealed off to form a shopping precinct for pedestrians and parked cars.

(A)   *Courtesy L.C.C.*

(B)   *Courtesy L.C.C.*

THE 'VERTICAL SOLUTION'

The L.C.C. Plan for Hook New Town (A and B) would have created a large pedestrian deck spanning the entire central area of the town. Moving traffic, car parks, bus stands and goods loading facilities would have been provided at ground level, linked to the pedestrian deck by escalators, stairs, ramps and lifts. The southern part of the Barbican Comprehensive Redevelopment Area in the City of London (C) uses a more open version of the same plan: pedestrian decks at upper level are joined by bridges over the streets. The vertical solution to the problem of vehicle-pedestrian conflict is necessary in central business districts, where the pressure of traffic on space is greatest; it is possible in completely new towns and in large-scale comprehensive redevelopments of old ones.

(C)   *Courtesy L.C.C.*

212

like London; and what can be done to apply it in areas where the opportunity has been lost since 1945.

In 1963, as you walk through the Barbican, looking at the pedestrian walkways that extend crazily to temporary termini on the north side of London Wall, or peer at the model of the future Piccadilly Circus, it is hard enough to grasp the revolutionary implications of the new way of city building. But the Barbican and Piccadilly will prove in not many years to have been very tentative and elementary beginnings. Once we accept the principle, it is capable of infinite sophistication. The architect-planner no longer works in two dimensions, but in three; he has a series of blocks to fit into spaces, in an infinite number of surprising combinations. Not merely three levels are possible, as along London Wall, but six, seven, eight, all carrying separate functions.[1] Some of these would be enclosed spaces enclosing people at work or play. Some would be for walking. Some would be for the parked vehicle, others for the moving private vehicle, others for the commercial vehicle performing its essential urban functions, perhaps another altogether for the public service vehicle. The hazards and the discomforts of the old city streets would be replaced by a new scheme of specialized spaces. The advance would be as great as that from the one-room hovel in which our ancestors lived, ate, slept, cooked, to the suburban home of the English today. But it must not take us as long.

No planner would suggest that the V-Solution is capable of uniform application over the face of an old city like London. Wherever there are major concentrations of buildings of historic or architectural interest, the wholesale reconstruction involved will be out of question. Map 9, which is partly based on the Ministry of Housing and Local Government's official maps of these buildings, shows in a very general way the sub-areas of central London which are amenable to a V-Solution and those where the precinctual method is enjoined. Some of the historic areas are fortunately not major traffic generators, but some—the Harley Street–Wimpole Street area, for instance—are. Such areas present some of our least tractable problems of central area planning.

Lastly, what is to be done with areas like Fitzrovia, where we have missed such a precious opportunity since 1945? Even now, to adapt such areas to the motor age is not beyond our technical or financial means. The new buildings that have gone up are highly standardized curtain wall structures built to the same general dimensions. When they have depreciated somewhat—about twenty years after their erection—there is no reason why they should not be adapted, with the aid of grants, to two-level circulation. Where possible the lower levels below the pedestrian level will be given over to parking and warehousing functions; the loss will be compensated by extra stories on top. In other cases, the lower floors will remain in their present uses such as offices; new high-level access will be forged from the back or side of the building, and the pedestrian level will be less continuous. This is a compromise solution

[1] The plans of Graeme Shankland's group for the St. John's Precinct in central Liverpool, announced in September 1962, already show a sophistication of the principle.

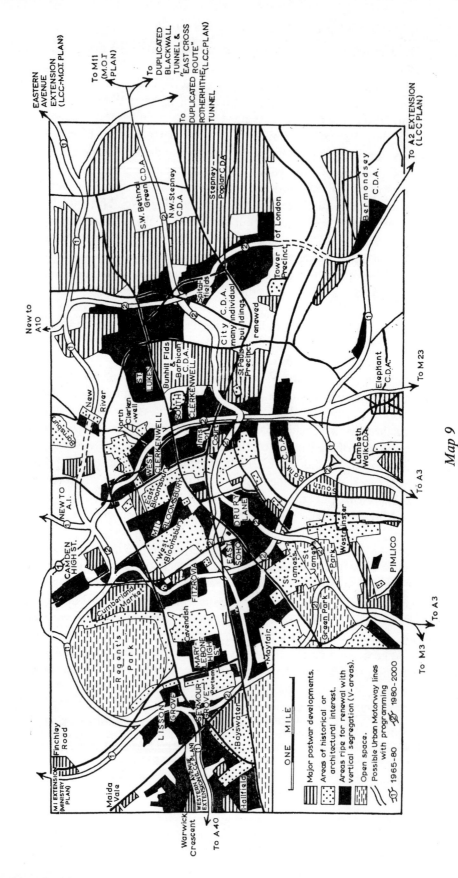

Map 9

RENEWAL ZONES FOR CENTRAL LONDON, AND AN URBAN MOTORWAY PLAN

which leaves the worker still in conflict, to some extent, with the vehicle. It is the price we will continue to pay, in Fitzrovia and elsewhere, for past lack of foresight.

Preparing the Master Plan

Under the new planning, the 'comprehensive development area' as understood since 1945, would disappear. *All* development would be carried through on comprehensive principles.

But within inner London, the authority would for convenience of planning divide the whole area up into units for redevelopment. The boundaries of these units would so far as possible enclose areas which were expected to fall ripe for redevelopment at about the same time. This is likelier to be far commoner than it is now if the financial proposals, which I suggest in Chapter 8, come into operation.

The master plan for London would then be prepared in two stages. From the start, in every area, the future broad pattern of land use and traffic circulation would be laid down, as today; save that, since the machinery of positive planning will be effective, the planning authority will be less inhibited in proposing radical reconstruction than at present. Any development in advance of general reconstruction would therefore at least fit the future circulation pattern. A new office block would, for instance, enclose a precinct rather than block the line of a new motorway.[1]

The second, detailed stage would be prepared a few years before the area was ripe for redevelopment. It would be a complete three-dimensional design, prepared on the basis of consultation with those directly interested and after discussion with a wider public. It would specify the kinds and amounts of buildings to be provided (homes, offices, shops, communal services of various kinds); the broad massing of the buildings in their three-dimensional relationship; the amount of space to be provided for open space, for parked vehicles, for pedestrians and vehicles; and the patterns of circulation. But the physical implementation of the planning requirements—the creative job of planning design—will be left, insofar as he accepts the job, in the hands of the individual developer.[2]

This is broadly the policy now recommended by the Ministries of Housing and Local Government and Transport in their joint planning bulletin on town centre renewal,[3] issued for the guidance of local authorities. The first-stage design will appear as a 'town centre map' which will not be part of the statutory development plan but which will allow separate proposals to be co-ordinated into an overall scheme of development. As the statutory plan is revised, the main features of the

---

[1] As has happened in the case of Torquay House, an office block in West London, which the L.C.C. will have to demolish after about seven years' use.

[2] This procedure is the one we advocated in the *Socialist Commentary* pamphlet, *The Face of Britain* (September 1961).

[3] *Town Centres: Approach to Renewal*. Planning Bulletin No. 1. Ministry of Housing and Local Government and Ministry of Transport (H.M.S.O. 1962).

town centre map can be transferred on to it. As far as it goes, the Ministry's advice is excellent. But it seems to have been specifically designed to meet the planning problems of a small- or medium-sized town, with a town centre small enough to be manageable in terms of a fairly simple plan. The areas needing precinctual treatment, or comprehensive multi-level rebuilding, are even smaller: individual buildings or streets. The Ministry bulletin does not really pretend to deal with the problems offered by Bloomsbury, or Fitzrovia. Here, nothing less than comprehensive re-development powers, and a technique for simultaneous large-scale redevelopment, will suffice. In the next chapter I turn to an attempt to find such a technique.

Postscript, 1969

As so many times elsewhere in the book, to go back to the chapter on renewal in *London 2000* is apparently to go back into history; so much has happened since it was written. But it is of the essence of renewal that it takes a long time to generate; therefore, the advances have been less in physical pieces of renewal actually achieved than in our notions of how to plan future renewal.

Physically, the achievements are modest enough. The first, commercial stage of the Barbican is long since finished (though many of the shops are unoccupied until the arrival of the residents makes them viable); the second, and much bigger, residential-plus-cultural stage is well under way. When finished it will constitute the biggest piece of postwar urban renewal (save for reconstruction of war damage) in Europe and perhaps in the world, dwarfing even La Défense in Paris and Lower Norrmalm in Stockholm. The Paternoster precinct to the north of St. Paul's is complete, and has disappointed a lot of people who find it monolithic and lumpy; plans for the south side have been prepared, and should be realized by the early 1970s; the Tower of London precinct is nearly finished. The City Planning Authorities (who owe the idea to the old L.C.C. Planners) have an ambitious scheme to link these precincts up by a network of high-level walkways across the City, which should be substantially realized by the 1980s unless restrictions on office building thwart them; this should rival the underground pedestrian subways of the new downtown Montreal, for the title of the most extensive system of pedestrian circulation in any major city centre of the world.

These are the shining exceptions. Elsewhere, the developments mainly realize plans dating from the bad old days of the 1950s, and show consequent lack of imagination. The appalling Finchley Road reconstruction, whose decisive merit for the old L.C.C. engineers was that it was a quick job even though it was a bad job, will not be finished until 1970. On the South Bank site, in the centre of a roundabout at a critical point, the engineers managed to create a vast pedestrian concourse entirely devoid of a single point of interest. Pressed at question time on plans, the relevant Chairman replied obscurely that they were considering the rival merits of a pub and a church for the site; since then, a few small trees have been planted. Major road schemes are still being completed with the same dreary engineers' subways as in the much-criticized Park Lane scheme; in north Kensington, with its critical shortage of play space, the Western Avenue extension viaduct is being built with car parking underneath, though a protest from local residents may bring a change. In Barnsbury, protests from local residents about traffic management schemes brought an official study of how to treat this as an environmental area; the residents continued to protest that this study was being mishandled, and it is due to emerge in its final version only in the autumn of 1968.

The long-term prospects are better; but the question is, as always, how long is long-term. There is no doubt about the chief reason for the most optimistic climate; it is the all-pervasive influence of the Buchanan report.[1] For a long time after its appearance in November 1963, Buchanan was over-praised and over-attacked. Five years later, a balanced verdict is possible: the principles Buchanan put forward were not always clearly enough defined to be operational, and even if they had been they would probably have proved too stringent to be generally acceptable; but in a wider and vaguer sense the influence of the report was both enormous, and almost wholly good. The central principle of the Buchanan report was simple enough, but too often misunderstood and misquoted: it was that there is a precise and intimate relationship between the environmental capacity of cities, the amount spent on reconstruction, and the amount of traffic that planners could admit. It is critical to the Buchanan report that the capacity of a city to take traffic should not be the *traffic flow* capacity (which, with traffic management, can be high), but the *environmental* capacity, defined in terms of qualities like noise, smell, accidents and visual intrusion (which is invariably far lower). Once this is determined, the urban community has a simple twofold choice: more traffic for more money spent on comprehensive reconstruction; or less money but less traffic. Thus there is no 'cost of Buchanan', in the simple sense: the often-quoted calculation of Christopher Foster, that the cost of Buchanan style reconstruction would be something like £18,000 million (£6,000 million of which would be in London)[2] is the calculated cost of reconstructing the whole urban fabric of Britain to the standard involved in the exercises on Newbury and Leeds in *Traffic in Towns*. The community can spend less, while maintaining its environmental standards, if it is willing to accept less traffic.

It is here that the criticisms crowd in. Nowhere in the report are the 'environmental standards' precisely defined; so as a precise guide to local authority action *Traffic in Towns* is self-confessedly useless. Since its publication, a research team at Imperial College, under Professor Buchanan's direction, has been trying to define the standards; but no comprehensive guide has emerged. Secondly, the report complicates its own case by making a very arbitrary distinction between 'essential' and 'optional' traffic, ignoring that virtually all traffic (except, conceivably, fire engines and ambulances) is an inextricable mixture of both these elements. From this comes the rather

[1] *Traffic in Towns* (H.M.S.O. 1963). [2] *The Statist*, 183 (1964), 549–51.

startling projection of essential goods traffic in cities like Leeds and London, which apparently requires a very considerable minimum amount of reconstruction to cope with it, and hence provides a basis for the argument that there is, in fact, a minimum 'cost of Buchanan'. Thirdly, these projections have been heavily criticized from an expert technical viewpoint, in an important article which argued that the Buchanan team totally ignored the tendencies to decentralization in modern western cities. Thus in Leeds, for example, the projections of future traffic flows in the central area were said to be quite unrealistically high.[1]

Thus it can be legitimately argued that *Traffic in Towns* lacks precision at critical points; that when it has precision, it is too often unjustified or wrong. But having said all this, it still remains that the report has exercised an incalculable and quite beneficient influence in a more general sense. It mattered not so much that engineers and planners could not quantify environmental standards; it mattered a good deal that planners could at least argue that some environmental standards existed, and that they should have their weight as against the brute principle of traffic flow. It is impossible (or so we can believe), any more, that engineers can destroy whole neighbourhoods for the principle of carrying more cars from A to B, without considering the wider implications of what they are doing. People, and not just planners, are aware: the engineers, if slowly, are being educated. In at least one university department, transportation and environmental planning are taught together; in the GLC's 1968 committee reconstruction, environmental planning and transportation planning were combined under a single committee chief, who has established his reputation as a staunch defender of environmental standards. All this is a great advance on 1961, when the L.C.C. engineers could win their battle with the L.C.C. planners on the widening of Finchley Road, simply because it was a quick solution.

The fact is that there is a new attitude abroad. In *London 2000* I still had to argue that the piecemeal reconstruction of central London, without radical reconstitution of the circulation system, was wrong; that what was needed was a general structural plan, within which detailed plans for the reconstruction of particular areas should be fitted. Since the 1965 report of the Planning Advisory Group,[2] and the 1968 Planning Act, that is not merely orthodoxy but law. 'Structure plans' and 'action area plans' are the new basis of the whole development planning system. And even before this Act was passed, the authorities in London have anticipated it. The new plans for Piccadilly Circus, unveiled jointly by the GLC and the City of Westminster in the summer of 1968, fit into a new system of segregated pedestrian walkways which are shown linking up the whole West End, from Regent Street to Covent Garden. Consultants are considering the future redevelopment of Regent Street along these lines, fully twenty years before the process may begin. It is not too fanciful, within fifteen years, to forsee the West End walkways linking up with those of the City, to

[1] M. E. Beesley and J. F. Kain, 'Urban Form, Car Ownership and Public Policy: An Appraisal of Traffic in Towns', *Urban Studies*, 1 (1964), pp. 174–203.
[2] *The Future of Development Plans* (H.M.S.O. 1965).

form the most magnificent system of unhampered pedestrian movement in the world. What is most significant here is that one great myth has been scotched: that to achieve the principles of comprehensive development, the whole formal apparatus of comprehensive development areas was necessary. The fact is that developers want to develop; they look to the planners to plan. As the City planners began to find ten years ago, if developers are told to incorporate walkways, and are then told precisely where to incorporate them, they simply do what they are told; they are too interested to go ahead quickly, to be concerned about arguing. And although the piece of walkway may be useless as it stands, providing it is in an area where commercial pressures for redevelopment are strong, before long it will link up with others into a continuous system.

This goes above all for London's ten-square-mile central area. Increasingly, it must go too for the inner and outer suburban shopping centres of Greater London, some of which are as big in terms of sales as the centres of major provincial towns. In *London 2000* I was still pointing out how the L.C.C. had allowed the reconstruction of at least two of these—Swiss Cottage and Notting Hill Gate—on completely conventional lines, without any attempt to create a new environment for pedestrians. Here again, by 1968 it is almost impossible to conceive that such blunders could occur again. The bold and imaginative scheme by the Lambeth borough architect-planner's department, for the reconstruction of the town centre of Brixton around the juxtaposition of tube terminus, suburban and main line railway, motorway box and shops, shows precisely what can be done. Ironically, it is bad planning in only one respect; it jumps the gun by appearing in advance of the Greater London Development Plan, which will provide the basic planning structure for the detailed action area plans of the boroughs. Until this appears no one knows what is to be the role of Brixton, or of any other centre, within the total hierarchy of centres in Greater London. But as *London 2000* also assumed a major role for Brixton, perhaps I am the last person who ought to point that out.

There will still be one great bugbear: money. Percy Johnson-Marshall, in *Rebuilding Cities*, has chronicled how in a development like the Elephant and Castle, all far-seeing ideas were excluded because of financial stringencies.[1] It was not the planners who failed, but the civil servants who controlled the purse strings and who wanted to see cheap solutions. But even here, we have advanced. It is far more difficult in 1968, than it was in 1958, to use lack of finance as an excuse for bad planning; if the money is not there, then it is more likely to lead simply to postponement of the scheme until it can be done properly. This advance, we owe in no small measure to Buchanan; may his message not be forgotten quickly. Still, there is one critical change that can affect the pace of renewal, and that is the price of renewal land. Thus the Land Commission (which is discussed in more detail in the postscript to Chapter 8) is important. But precisely how important, it will take some time to find out. Sir Henry Wells, Chairman of the Commission, has pointed out that to acquire developed land is

[1] Percy Johnson-Marshall, *Rebuilding Cities* (Edinburgh 1966), pp. 186–7.

expensive in money and administrative resources. And except in the relatively rare town centre schemes, the financial return may actually be negative, or small and long-delayed. Therefore, the Land Commission is not going to operate on any scale in the renewal business for several years. Not until then will it do what many supporters thought would be its most important function: help in the assembly of fragmented sites, which is often the biggest problem confronting the urban renewer.

Part IV · RUNNING THE NEW LONDON

CHAPTER 8

Cutting the Gordian Knot

In this chapter I turn to two problems which are among the most basic, and the least tractable, in all city planning. One is the problem of securing adequate comprehensive development—whether new development, or redevelopment of older city areas—to replace the chaotic piecemeal development which at the present time is preventing proper planning at all in many parts of the London Region. This follows particularly from the discussion of urban renewal in the last chapter. The other is the problem of land values and the associated question of how to pay for redevelopment.

By 'the problem of land values' we may in fact mean two problems. The first of these concerns the map of land values in a city, and the changes that occur in that map over time. In a normal big city, like London, land values are higher near the centre. But the values of land used for some purposes (shops, offices) rise faster towards the centre than the value of land used for others (houses, flats). Therefore, if the city expands and its economic activity increases (as with London), land near the centre formerly used for lower value uses will be 'bid out' of the centre. If—as in London since 1947—the process is accompanied by a limitation on the total amount of land available for all urban functions, the result will be a great general increase in the values of land used for all purposes, and a real shortage of land.

The first 'land value problem' is not the one that interests me here. That is because it is not a primary problem, capable of solution in its own terms. The map of urban land values is merely a reflection of competition for the most accessible sites, as the American economist R. M. Haig pointed out as long ago as 1926,[1] and the only reason why the planner should be interested in it—as Haig also emphasized—is to correct an imbalance between private and social costs and benefits:

'It is important to establish a sufficient degree of social control over land utilization

[1] R. M. Haig, 'Toward an Understanding of the Metropolis', *Quarterly Journal of Economics*, 40 (1925–6), 179–208, 402–34.

to make sure that the decisions on points of precedence are socially sound—that all the costs properly chargeable to an activity are assumed by it, and that no activity shall be given the decision on the basis of accounts which fail to include, as costs, the losses suffered by neighbors or the community as a whole. . . . The truth is that an individual simply by buying title to a single lot should not be given the right to use it as he chooses, whenever by merely buying a lot he does not meet his full site costs.'[1]

On the basis of such considerations the planner would work to reshuffle the relative accessibility of different points so as to achieve a greater total social benefit. This would demand in the first place a complete re-orientation of the present transport and communications system, with its heavy concentration on a small central business district, so as to achieve a number of nodes of concentration within a much wider central district. This is the policy I have advocated in Chapters 3 and 5.

Betterment and the Uthwatt Report

In contrast, the other sort of land value problem—the one that concerns me here—is an extremely narrow and technical one. It concerns the rises in land values, which accrue to individuals; the right of the community to take part or all of these rises in value; and, given this, the best way of collecting them for the community.

The community's right to these increases has long been enshrined in the concept of *betterment*, which was thus defined in 1942 in the final report of the Expert Committee on Compensation and Betterment (the Uthwatt Committee):

'. . . while the term "betterment" is not specifically defined in any general Act, it may now be taken, in its technical sense, to mean any increase in the value of land (including the buildings thereon) arising from central or local government action, whether positive, *e.g.*, by the execution of public works or improvements, or negative, *e.g.*, by the imposition of restrictions on other land. . . . The term is not, however, generally understood to include enhancement in the value of property arising from general community influences, such as the growth of urban populations.'[2]

Briefly: betterment is the community's contribution, and the community should get it back. But this is a concept extremely difficult to apply in practice: how do we determine, in any particular case, the share of an increase in land values which should pass to the community? This was the problem which vexed the Uthwatt Committee, who, after searching for an answer in the history of betterment from Henry VI onwards, concluded:

'We are forced to the conclusion that no *ad hoc* search for "betterment" in its present strict sense can ever succeed, and that the only way of solving the problem is to cut the Gordian knot by taking for the community some fixed proportion of the whole

---

[1] *Ibid.*, 431–3.

[2] Uthwatt Report (*Final Report of the Expert Committee on Compensation and Betterment*, Cmd. 6386, H.M.S.O. 1942), para. 260.

of any increase in site values without any attempt at precise analysis of the causes to which it may be due.'[1]

So the Committee called for a periodic levy, based on a special valuation of the *site alone* of every developed property or hereditament, to be made by the rating authority as part of its regular quinquennial valuation;[2] the increase in value between assessments to be taxed at (say) 75 per cent.[3]

In other words, the Committee wanted a capital gains tax on gains from land. But, be it noted, a capital gains tax of a very unusual kind. It would be imposed on all increases that 'have been realised or enjoyed or be realisable';[4] in other words, on unrealized as well as realized gains, an idea which even the most radical advocates of capital gains taxation have dismissed as inequitable.[5] The only predictable results of the Committee's proposal, in fact, would be a revolutionary increase in the mobility of owner-occupiers and an orgy of speculation in land, to avoid any possibility of unrealized profit.

So the Coalition Government in 1944, and the Labour Government in 1947, were driven to find alternative solutions. The one finally embodied in the 1947 Town and Country Planning Act was very original, very ingenious, and quite misconceived. It depended on a forced marriage between two features of earlier plans. One was the Uthwatt Committee's proposal for the special case of land being developed for the first time (for instance, agricultural land being developed for houses): that the State should nationalize not the land, but the right to develop it. The 1947 drafters seized on this and applied it to all land. Thereby they achieved a particularly ingenious solution to the problem of compensating people who expected to be able to develop their land, who perhaps had bought it for that purpose, and who were refused permission to do so under the new system of land-use planning: a solution which was essential if land-use planning was to work at all. The solution was this: compensation was to be paid on a 'once-for-all' basis to existing owners for their lost development rights, whether they would ever have exerted them or not, out of a £300 million fund which was the best estimate of all the development values in the country, scaled down to exclude double counting.[6] Compensation was made not as of right, but because of possible hardship.

For this solution, which has survived the subsequent vicissitudes of the 1947 Act, we have good reason to thank its drafters. Where they went wrong was in their treatment of the development values which they had thus acquired for the State. To provide a moral-legal justification for the State's collection of betterment, the Act

[1] *Ibid.*, para. 308.
[2] Then. Since 1950 valuations for the whole country have been made by the Inland Revenue.
[3] *Ibid.*, para. 311.
[4] *Ibid.*, para. 310.
[5] Cf. the memorandum of dissent to the *Radcliffe Commission Report* (the Royal Commission on the Taxation of Profits and Income, Cmd. 9474, H.M.S.O. 1955), paras. 53–5.
[6] That is, to compensate for the 'floating value' which may attach itself to more than one parcel of land.

related it to the State's purchase of the development rights. Henceforth, anyone who was granted permission to develop must purchase the development rights back from the State, by paying a Development Charge: that is, a professional valuer's estimate of the difference between the value of the land in its previous use and its value in the new use.

This solution worked badly, for two reasons: one necessary, one contingent. First, Development Charge could by its nature be imposed only when permission to develop was granted. But rises in land values do not occur merely at development; they occur also through the lifetime of the development, and this second, and most important element, the 1947 Act left untouched, though the Uthwatt Committee had already rejected the idea of a Development Charge specifically on that ground.[1] The second defect was not even written into the Act, but appeared only in the regulations for operation in 1948: this was the fixing of the Charge at 100 per cent of the rise in value.[2] In the late forties, with severe shortages of materials, close licensing of building, and a general feeling among owners and developers that the good times were not yet, the effect was simply to shut off the land market on its supply side. This was the pretext for the Conservative Government's abolition of Development Charge, through the 1953 Planning Act, which was accompanied by the end of building licensing and the great speculative building boom of the late fifties. How, in these changed conditions, would Development Charge have worked? The answer, in conditions of inflation and easy profits, would probably have been that the Development Charge would have been doubly paid: once to the State and once to the seller. The charge would have become a surcharge, willingly borne; there would no longer have been any relation between the official estimate of existing use value and the market estimate.[3] This, however, need not have worried the State, as long as it collected the money.

The Present Impasse: Conservative Answers

In 1963 we are almost back where we started. Development Charge is abandoned; all that has taken its place is an extremely limited tax on short-term speculative gains. In one respect only is the problem simpler than it was for Uthwatt in 1942: development rights are nationalized; to that extent the compensation problem is largely solved. The question has become acute because of the enormous gains that have gone into private pockets as a result of the land boom since 1955.

Official Government policy has produced no answer to these developments. But on the more radical wing of the Conservative Party, disquiet has produced two pamphlets containing solutions: that of the Bow Group[4] and that of Mr. Butler's

[1] Uthwatt Report, *op. cit.*, para. 307.

[2] See the interesting account in C. M. Haar, *Land Planning Law in a Free Society* (Cambridge, Mass., 1951), 110–11.

[3] This was happening as early as 1950: see Haar, *ibid.*, 162.

[4] *Let our Cities Live* (Conservative Political Centre, 1960).

advisory committee.[1] As Conservative contributions they are united in one point: after redevelopment, the land is left in private hands; but during redevelopment, it is of necessity collectivized. The important question is: who initiates and manages the collectivization process? Here the Bow Group is uncompromising: the job is left to private enterprise. In any area defined as a 'redevelopment block', a pooling company can be formed on the decision of half the owners in any site, or the owners of half the site. As Cullingworth has commented,[2] this would create an extraordinary situation: powerful private interests could bulldoze through redevelopment which other owners did not want—perhaps even, on many sites, a majority of the individual owners. And though there are certainly cases where owners should be made, or induced, to accept redevelopment, social decisions of this importance should certainly not be left to private property interests. The same objection, curiously, seems to apply to H. R. Parker's Fabian pamphlet of 1959,[3] which proposed compulsory purchase by local authorities on the initiative of a developer. But at least here the local authority might act as guardian of the legitimate interests of other owners and occupiers.

Mr. Butler's committee, on the other hand, put the initiative firmly in the hands of the local authority, which would buy compulsorily an area for comprehensive redevelopment and then resell it to competing bidders, the bids to include fixed premiums to cover the essential costs of the local authority. Even this scheme hardly provides for full justice to owners who might find themselves in a weak bidding position, though there is a rather vague suggestion that developers might be given obligations to rehouse some former owners. A central objection to both schemes, then, is one of social justice. The likely effect of both is that a sharp contrast would emerge between profitable central sites—which would pass, more quickly than now, into the hands of big property companies—and the unattractive inner areas of 'urban blight' which neither scheme would really help, because private enterprise will inevitably find the job unlucrative. This indeed is the basic dilemma for the Conservatives; and it drove some members of Mr. Butler's group to support the idea first put forward in 1960 by Mr. Henry Wells and the Civic Trust, which would replace the local authority by a nation-wide land-holding agency big enough to use profits from one scheme to support unprofitable (but desirable) schemes elsewhere.

Two Socialist Solutions

It is not surprising then that Socialists, emphasizing the problem of replacement of 'urban blight', have fallen back on land nationalization as a device which might simultaneously solve the development problem, the land value problem and the problem of investment capital. This simultaneous quality is the strength of the nationalization schemes—or their weakness, as I shall try to show. Two deserve

[1] *Change and Challenge* (*ibid.*, 1962).
[2] *New Towns for Old* (Fabian Research Series 229, 1962), 20.
[3] *Paying for Urban Development* (Fabian Research Series 207), 17–18.

227

attention: the Labour Party's scheme for partial nationalization, contained in the policy document *Signposts for the Sixties*; and the total nationalization scheme of the *Socialist Commentary* group (of which I was a member), published in the pamphlet *The Face of Britain*.[1]

The official Labour scheme is extremely pragmatic in that it nationalizes only building land: that is, land which it is proposed to develop or redevelop. No permission for development would be granted until a Land Commission had bought the land (or until it was decided that the development was too small to worry about). The Commission would pay current use value, plus something to cover contingent losses by the owner and to encourage the willing sale of land. Then it would lease the site to the developer on terms which ensured that the community received the benefit of any future rises in the value of the land: that is, the lease would contain a periodical rent revision clause. In this way, Labour's policy-makers claim, not only will the community take a fair share of rises in values; effective comprehensive development will also be possible.

Neither of these claims seems justified. For many years, the community would get only a small part of the rises in land values: that part occurring on land developed under the scheme. What share of these increases would actually come into the public purse is doubtful, since it would depend wholly on the Land Commissioners' capacity to bargain with private developers in extremely artificial conditions. The proposal, elsewhere in *Signposts for the Sixties*, for a capital gains tax, seems to show that Labour has a reserve power in mind, but it remains unclear from the evidence how far the two pieces of policy are related at all. But even more seriously, Labour's scheme does not begin to provide the essential conditions for comprehensive development. The initiative is to come from private individuals; the Land Commission will buy land piecemeal, when development is imminent; sites will come up for individual development, over a long period of years; we should be left with exactly the present mess. Unless, that is, Labour really intends the extensive use in practice of compulsory purchase powers, which was the Uthwatt solution for securing comprehensive development in 1942.

Against this official plan the drafters of the *Socialist Commentary* pamphlet advocated a completely new method of total land nationalization. This depended on the concept, long understood in property valuation, that buildings are not immortal, but have a useful 'life'. From a vesting day, a public owning authority would become ground landlord of all Britain's land. This authority would begin a long process of valuation, which would give every building a 'life', depending on age, condition, amenities and fitness for purpose. The life would vary from nil to a maximum of eighty years, which was considered to be the usual maximum useful life of a building, For the term of the 'life' former freeholders would remain in possession as State leaseholders. Their leases would contain a rent revision clause which would enable the community, at intervals of seven years, to recover a share (say fifty per

[1] *Socialist Commentary*, September 1961.

cent) of the increase in land value that had taken place since the last assessment. At the end of the 'life' the owner would be compensated for loss of freehold rights, on the basis of the original site value plus (say) fifty per cent of the increase in the value of *site alone* since vesting day (the building by definition being valueless). Then the State would decide whether to give the building another 'life'; or to demolish it immediately, granting then an eighty-year building lease for a new building.

As a signatory of the *Socialist Commentary* plan, I—and most commentators on it—agree that it would do the essential jobs: it would collect a fair share of the rises in land values, which could be used, in whole or in part, to provide finance for unprofitable schemes or in unprofitable early stages of schemes; and it would achieve proper comprehensive development because the 'lives' of buildings over big city areas would tend to end simultaneously, allowing large-scale redevelopment. The difficulty is political. To get it accepted, we recognized, would need a massive job of political education over the next few years. But since the publication of the plan the Labour Party has shown few signs of willingness to help perform this job. In the political circumstances of the sixties, this is understandable enough. But meanwhile, time and chance happeneth to London and to our other great cities; and if we do not quickly get into operation some effective machinery, we shall have done worse than lose a share in the speculative gains: we shall have lost a precious chance to rebuild London for generations to come.

For this reason, I now ask: is there a way of achieving our objectives by less radical means? We have seen that there are two main objectives. But the *Socialist Commentary* scheme added a very important subsidiary one: to speed up the rate of renewal, by declaring buildings obsolescent. I now want to suggest that these objectives can be dealt with separately and pragmatically. The Gordian knot can be cut, not by one great sweep but by three accurate incisions. The result will be less tidy than land nationalization or the 1947 Act; but it will be no less effective, and, I would argue, it will be acceptable to the electorate.

The Cure for Obsolescence

The *Socialist Commentary* scheme attempts to cure obsolescence by order: it takes the decisions out of the hands of private landlords and puts them into the hands of the State. But the State can achieve the same ends by providing incentives and disincentives, of which the simplest and most effective are financial. In this particular case that means an *obsolescence tax*.

The concept of depreciation is accepted, albeit far from fully, in the tax structure of this and other advanced industrial countries. We give tax relief on industrial buildings so that they can be written off after fifty years; that is, we allow 2 per cent of the value per annum.[1] The Radcliffe Commission recommended in 1955 that the

[1] The changes in depreciation allowances announced on 5 November 1962 do not affect industrial buildings except those used for research, which receive special treatment.

scheme should be extended to commercial buildings, though the Board of Inland Revenue had argued against it on some rather bizarre grounds, chief among which was that it would give them more work.[1] Nothing, nevertheless, has been done to implement the recommendation by 1963. The Radcliffe Commission's final report rejected the proposal to make the allowance vary over different periods of years according to the type of building;[2] accordingly, nothing has been done here either. And lastly, there is no penalty on the man who gets his tax allowance and keeps the building up long after the Inland Revenue say it is fully depreciated.

The depreciation allowance technique could, I suggest, be extended and radically modified so as to speed up the appallingly slow renewal of buildings, which observers from advanced countries have long noted as one of the more depressing features of our economy.

First, it would be extended not merely to commercial but to *all* property; though different rates of relief might be given on different classes of property. Secondly, it would be operated on a much more elastic basis. The Inland Revenue would be given the responsibility of calculating the remaining life of all the buildings in Britain, as advocated in the *Socialist Commentary* scheme, beginning with the oldest. Thirdly, when any building had outlived its allotted time, the system would begin to work in reverse: the depreciation allowance would become an obsolescence tax. The rate of tax would depend on the desirable rate of urban renewal, which in turn would depend on the general economic climate. But the desirable scale would begin gently at the end of the life, and then rise very sharply; otherwise, there is a danger of buildings decaying slowly as they pay moderate rates of tax over long periods.

The effect of the tax would be that large areas of our cities, built at about the same time, would simultaneously begin to pay heavy tax—in many parts of London, this would happen immediately—and would become an unprofitable investment. As the tax would be payable on unoccupied buildings, too, owners would soon find it profitable to redevelop or sell out—at the value of the bare site—to someone who can.

One reservation must be entered at this stage. The operation of the tax does not mean the establishment of a rigid, sixty- or eighty-year building cycle, in which London is torn down and renewed. It only means that the *possibility* of complete replanning recurs periodically. What the planners then do is their responsibility. I have already argued that in certain historic precincts of London no large-scale demolition should be permitted. In addition we are now learning from the mistakes of American urban renewal[3] that the complete removal of old buildings can have disastrous effects on the vitality of cities, because some important land uses, which ought to be in cities, depend on old low-rent premises. To maintain what is good in cities, what makes them worth living in, while making them more efficient and less

[1] Radcliffe Commission, *op. cit.*, paras. 381–2.

[2] *Ibid.*, paras. 377–8.

[3] Notably from Jane Jacobs' *The Death and Life of Great American Cities* (1962), which contains much of great relevance for the replanning of London.

frustrating and better to look at; this is the essential creative art of the planners. The present chapter aims merely to give them an essential tool for redevelopment, which it is their job to use sensitively.

Community Redevelopment

At this point, the second problem becomes acute. How is society to intervene to guarantee that the development of large urban areas is carried through on comprehensive principles?

The minimum requirement is quite clear; and everyone must be brought to accept it, as a condition of better cities. It is stressed in Conservative *and* Socialist pamphlets. *At the point of development, or redevelopment, individual property rights must be extinguished and replaced by community property rights.* And in some areas, a permanent reshuffling may be necessary of the sort of property to which the rights relate: as when many small houses are replaced by a few large blocks with a lot of common open space.

The Socialist schemes outlined earlier both achieve this by putting land permanently in State possession. This may be desirable; but it is misleading to say that it is a necessary condition of good planning. It is important here to be clear about the meaning of ownership, which is two-fold. One is physical control of the use to which the property is put: we can destroy it, or use it to provide income, or use it ourselves. The other is the enjoyment of whatever income it yields us. Both these attributes are already tightly controlled and limited in application by the State, and may be further limited if the State so desires. It is on these limitations that political action should concentrate; not upon the outward forms of ownership. Applied to the present case, this means that the community should exert decisive control when control is necessary, that is during development; and that it should make sure to get a substantial share afterwards of the increased value of the property, which it may do through taxation. These can be dealt with (though most discussions, curiously, have not done so) as separate problems; for the moment we are concerned with the first.

What then would be the simplest, least objectionable way of ensuring community development? The answer is some form of pooling. This might be temporary, or permanent; voluntary, or controlled. We can reject voluntary pooling straightaway; it would be virtually impossible to work. The other question is more difficult. In the 1930's permanent compulsory pooling was stoutly advocated by Sir Gwilym Gibbon in his book *Problems of Town and Country Planning*[1] and in his evidence before the Barlow Commission.[2] Each pool would be managed by a nominated body, selected solely for competence. In 1942 the Uthwatt Committee decisively rejected Gibbon's scheme on a number of grounds:[3]

[1] 1937; Ch. II.

[2] *Royal Commission on the Distribution of the Industrial Population, Minutes of Evidence*: 25th Day, Q.7405–18.

[3] Uthwatt Report, *op. cit.*, paras. 42–5.

1. That private landowners would object to compulsory association. (What was supposed to be their attitude to compulsory purchase, which the Committee finally advocated for developed land requiring redevelopment, was unclear.)

2. That the pool would further its own financial interests.

3. That the interest of the pool would conflict with those of the planning authority —which assumes that private interests are incompatible with public planning, thereby implicitly denying the whole basis of the 1947 Act.

4. That the pool would not solve the compensation-betterment problem because there would be shifts of value, arising from planning restrictions or directions, which extended beyond the pool. This is true; but the answer is a separate solution to that problem.

5. That a conflict of interests would arise between owners (i.e. shareholders) and occupiers. But this is simply the historic conflict of interest between landlords and tenants; pooling might merely make the relationship more remote.

6. That a commercial monopoly in land would be created. This is not necessarily true; shares in the pool would remain freely buyable and sellable. But in fact this objection does have serious force. A pool, run by nominated representatives, would be in danger of falling into the hands of large property interests. The pool would act like a large industrial corporation, where the mass of small shareholders exert no real control. The planning authority here might well find its plans being frustrated by the ingenuity of the speculators, bent on getting the maximum return. For this reason and for this reason alone, compulsory permanent pooling does not seem a satisfactory answer.

This leaves temporary but compulsory pooling. The model, which attracted great interest before the 1939 War but which has passed almost into oblivion, is the so-called Lex Adickes, invented in 1902 by the Bürgermeister of Frankfurt-am-Main, after whom it is named.[1] It consists in the compulsory pooling by the Local Authority of areas of land which are divided into plots too small to achieve good development, and the redivision of the land after replanning to the former owners, in proportion to the size of their interests.

The Uthwatt Committee rejected the Lex Adickes because in Germany it had been used only for the initial development of previously unbuilt-on land, and because they could not see how it could be applied to urban renewal:

'The responsible authority would need to take over and demolish the property in the area, presumably paying compensation for the buildings, and then hand back the bare sites to a large number of separate owners, some of whom might have neither the desire nor the capital to rebuild. The division into a fixed number of sites might be prejudicial to proper replanning, and in any event it would not provide a permanent solution to the problem which small-scale ownership creates.'[2]

---

[1] Franz Adickes (1846–1915). For an account see the *Barlow Report* (Report of the Royal Commission on the Distribution of the Industrial Population), Cmd. 6153 (H.M.S.O. 1940), paras. 257–61.

[2] Uthwatt Report, *op. cit.*, para. 143.

These objections are not really valid. The Lex Adickes can be applied to urban renewal, and indeed has been so applied with great success, in the postwar rebuilding of Kiel.[1] If an obsolescence tax operated, those who had 'neither the desire nor the capital' would already have sold out to someone who had. There would be no need for division into a fixed number of sites: former owners would get shares according to an Inland Revenue valuation of the site alone, of value say £50 each, with which they would have first preference to buy a number of new sites (with appropriate planning permissions) or developed buildings. If they wanted neither, they could sell the shares for money; preferably to a public authority in the first instance, to forestall speculative operations.

This system would demand a new approach to comprehensive development. In Chapter 7 I have already suggested a two-stage preparation of a comprehensive development plan for all areas of cities where renewal is imminent. In preparing these the planning authority would work closely with Inland Revenue officials who were making their surveys for obsolescence tax. Where large areas were reaching obsolescence simultaneously, then the authority would prepare the second, detailed stage. At this point a Redevelopment Commission would be established. This would do for our cities what the Enclosure Commissions did for our fields in the eighteenth century. It would be an independent corporation consisting of members of the Planning authority, members of the Inland Revenue, and representatives of the individual owners and any local Development Corporation. It would have large powers to borrow money from the Treasury for certain purposes. With this money the Commission would assume an obligation to pay the site value to owners of plots wishing to be relieved of them; in this way it would accumulate enough new plots so that parts of the redevelopment would take place ahead of others, and so that it could thereby offer new plots or buildings to those wanting them. In this work the local planning authority representatives would have the detailed knowledge of local conditions and contact with the owners, while the Inland Revenue would command the necessary financial expertise.

The Commission would determine, in the light of the particular circumstances of the redevelopment area, the best agency for physical redevelopment. In some cases it would carry the financial burden of redevelopment itself, though actual construction would be undertaken by a commercial firm, a local authority or by the local or Regional Development Corporation. This would be necessary wherever a large number of former owners lacked capital or expertise to carry through the rebuilding themselves; for instance, where many small shops or flats had to be rebuilt in new blocks. The Commission would then sell the development back to the old owners for shares, guaranteeing mortgages for any balance involved. In other cases they might leave it to big owners to build themselves. Most areas would contain both types of redevelopment.

[1] E. T. Greene, 'West German City Reconstruction: Two Case Studies', *Sociological Review*, New Series, 7 (1959), 231–44.

There is one remaining problem. How is the planning authority to deal with the many individual applications for development which are made, and will continue to be made, outside areas for which detailed comprehensive plans have been drawn up? In inner London there are countless applications for development, big and small, in areas where the majority of buildings still have years of life left in them. Here the local authority must make the best of a difficult job. It will have to declare the parts of the area most immediately affected as sub-areas of comprehensive development, and try to ensure that the development at least fits the projected future pattern of circulation and open space. In as many cases as possible, however, it should try to steer major developments into areas of full-scale comprehensive development, by helping in negotiations between the potential developer and a Redevelopment Commission.[1] Where permission might reasonably have been expected under the old system of permissive planning, but is now refused, it might be compensated, not as of right but on grounds of hardship, out of a new equivalent of the £300 million fund created by the 1947 Act, and abolished in 1954.[2]

When the Redevelopment Commission for a given area has completed its job—a process that may well take many years—it will wind itself up. The operation of the obsolescence tax will ensure that the solution will be repeated when needs be.

A similar Commission could be appointed for an area which was to be developed for the first time. The Regional Planning Authority or its local agents would set out, as part of their Development Plans, the areas on which new building was to take place within the period of the plan; and they would prepare as part of the plan a first-stage comprehensive development scheme. When development was imminent, a Commission would be set up at the initiative either of the developers or of the planning authority. It would contain representatives of the authority, of the Inland Revenue, of the developers, and of a local Development Corporation if interested. The precise composition of the Commission would depend on the form of the development. If a single authority—whether private or public—were to carry it through, it would have substantial representation. If the area was to be developed by individual freeholders or small builders it would be necessary to have a big Commission, with some delegation of authority, so that their views could receive expression.

A Land Gains Tax

I turn now to the other main problem. On development, and subsequently, gains accrue to individuals. How is the community to get a share? The answer is, by taxing them. It is as simple as that in principle, and as the Uthwatt Committee finally came

---

[1] A Redevelopment Commission might be enabled to buy land outside its area, offering shares in a Redevelopment area by way of exchange.

[2] Though it need not necessarily be paid out at one moment of time, as was the intention with the £300 m.

to recognize, discussion about betterment only obscures the issue. So—it must be said at the onset—does discussion about the purpose to which the revenue should be put. It may well be a good thing to earmark some of this revenue for desirable projects connected with urban renewal or other major public works in cities; although it is certainly contrary to all understood principles of public finance that tax revenue should be so earmarked. This, however, is a separate and subsidiary issue; the problem at hand is to find a workable method of collection.

The tax would evidently be a special case of capital gains tax. It is outside my scope here to discuss fully all the arguments for and against capital gains taxes, which were fully aired in the Report of the Radcliffe Committee and the memorandum of dissent to that report, in 1955.[1] The chief difficulty is that some way needs be found of setting off losses against gains, and that losses or gains tend to be bunched in particular years. For this reason advocates of capital gains taxes have usually had to settle for a non-progressive, that is a flat rate tax.[2] The precise rate of tax would have to be related carefully to the rate of tax on company profits; otherwise capital gainers would turn themselves into companies to get a lower rate.

To some extent, the special case of gains from land presents an easier problem than the general case. We have already seen that a large part of land gains arise at the point of development. Under the scheme I have advocated, at this point the land would be pooled; and in these special circumstances it would theoretically be possible to charge any rate, consistent with the need to make development attractive.[3] The Treasury would have two choices. Either it could decide—as the drafters of the 1947 Act decided—that development gains were a special case, justifying a specially high rate of tax; or for reasons of equity it could impose a general tax. This might be the tax on company profits. If we took the present rate of tax on both undistributed and distributed profits on companies with an annual income exceeding £2,000, this would give a rate of just under 50 per cent; if we accept Dr. Prest's powerful arguments for a higher rate of tax on undistributed than on distributed profits,[4] and fix the effective rate at about 20 per cent plus income tax, this would give a maximum of about 60 per cent. If on the other hand a capital gains tax were imposed, this would give a lower rate, probably the standard income tax rate. The company rate seems preferable.

Collection of this special development tax would present no difficulty. It would be paid by the Commission, which would pass it on to the shareholders when they turned their shares into money, sites or buildings. Under this system it would be easy, if it were thought desirable, to earmark some or all of the tax for community development within the area: new roads, public housing, schools, hospitals. This

[1] Radcliffe Report, op. cit., paras. 80–117; and Memorandum of Dissent, paras. 34–84.

[2] Memorandum of Dissent, ibid., paras. 60–2.

[3] Though of course the Obsolescence Tax would in itself provide a strong extra incentive to develop.

[4] A. R. Prest, Public Finance in Theory and Practice (1960), 303, 341–2.

would solve the problem created by the 1959 Town and Country Planning Act, whereby central or local authorities have to pay full market value for land compulsorily acquired for such purposes.[1] Whether this is done or not will depend on political philosophy. It could well be argued that it is bad social administration to disguise the true economic cost of any development, whether public or private; to make such development pay its true cost ceases to be objectionable once the community is fairly taxing private gains, and thereby acquiring the revenue to pay the cost. But if it is thought desirable to provide cheap or free land, this could be achieved by collecting the development tax in shares, which would be passed on to public authorities who would trade them in for land.[2] The former individual owner would get back a smaller parcel of property than he put in, but it would be worth more than his old parcel, minus the amount of the tax.

This modification should especially commend itself to the Labour Party, because it would be a better way of securing the mild form of 'creeping nationalization' of land envisaged in their official scheme. Here indeed might be the central difference in the application of the scheme between the two major parties: the Conservatives would take only the minimum amount of land necessary for public purposes; Labour would take a substantial part. But this is a detail: there does not seem to be anything in the broad outline scheme which is objectionable to the present philosophy of either party, which would mean that its continuance would not depend on the outcome of a General Election.

Whether tax were taken in land or in money, whether part were earmarked for certain purposes or not, it is evident that in practice it must perform an essential planning function: it must help, directly or indirectly, to relieve the enormous community cost of carrying through the early stages of redevelopment, before a particular scheme begins to show any profit. If the Redevelopment Commission carries this burden on behalf of the small owners who cannot themselves manage redevelopment, it is only right that it should recoup some of it from owners, both large and small, in other parts where redevelopment has reached a later stage and where land values are enhanced. So the finances of the Commission will show a continuous flow, drawing from mature schemes, passing the money to support the 'carrying-over' period elsewhere.

For this reason each Redevelopment Commission should cover a substantial area —probably not less than a square mile. Even so, it is highly unlikely that most Commissions will cover areas which are big and heterogeneous enough to give a reasonable

[1] See H. R. Parker, 'The Town and Country Planning Bill, 1958', *Town Planning Review*, 30 (1959), 139–44, and P. Ash, 'The Town and Country Planning Act 1959', *Estates Gazette*, 8 August 1959.

[2] Of course it would be possible under the scheme to exempt from development tax any land or land shares already in possession of a public authority or passing into its possession. The authority would have acquired obsolescent property at bare site value, to which only limited development value attached; if it were then free of tax liability on the enhancement of value that followed development, this would largely meet the difficulty created by the 1959 Act.

average of profitable and unprofitable reconstruction. Those in the central area should yield huge profits; those in the obsolescent inner residential ring almost certainly will not. That is why pooling, of itself, cannot solve the land value problem, as Uthwatt pointed out: the only pool that could solve it would be one covering the whole country. We must look to taxation to take a reasonable share of the increased values and to redistribute the proceeds on the most desirable public projects. That taxation must be central taxation if the redistribution is to be truly equitable.

The remaining land gains—those which accrue more slowly during the life of the development—would be taxed as ordinary capital gains to the individual owners, at whatever rate was deemed appropriate for this tax: probably not more than 40 per cent[1] (as implied in the Radcliffe memorandum of dissent) compared with the 75 per cent which the Uthwatt Committee recommended for its periodic levy in 1942. In contradiction to that levy, the tax would be levied on realized gains only: that is, on the seller at the point of sale.

The Need for Action

In this chapter I have examined various solutions to the problems of land development and land values, most of which bear political labels. I have rejected schemes with Conservative labels because they seem ineffectual or unjust, which means unacceptable to large numbers of people. Similarly I have rejected schemes labelled Socialist because they appear ineffectual or dogmatic—which again means unacceptable. These are the criteria by which we should judge any scheme: it must be effectual, and it must be acceptable to most people, which means acceptable to the major political parties. I have proposed a scheme which bears no label: it could be called pragmatic or eclectic, and it is certainly radical in that it limits the freedom of the individual to the enjoyment of his property, first by imposing restrictions on its use, and secondly by taking some of the profits of ownership. What is important is to find, and impose, a solution quickly. For unless we do, most of the other concrete proposals of this book, and most of the many thousands of words written about planning in the last few years, are quite abstract ideas, incapable of realization. The plan for land is the cornerstone of any effective planning policy for London.

Postscript, 1969

The Gordian knot has been cut. The official Labour party proposals to set up a Land Commission, which *London 2000* rejected in favour of a different solution, have been carried into law by the Land Commission Act 1967. But in the process they have suffered a profound change.

The original Labour proposal, in *Signposts for the Sixties*, was for a process of creeping land nationalization. Unless a proposed development were too small to

---

[1] i.e. a marginal rate of 7s. 6d.–8s. 0d. in the £.

worry about, the Land Commission would buy up any land coming up for development or redevelopment, and lease the site back to the developer. It would buy at existing use value, plus a *douceur* to cover contingent losses and encourage willing sale; it would lease back at market value, with a rent revision clause to cover appreciation in value over the life of the development. This had been the Uthwatt Commission's 1942 proposal in the case of land being developed for the first time; twenty years later, Labour revived it and applied it to all land. But in practice the Land Commission Act has emerged differently.

In fact it contains two separate sets of arrangements, though both are administered by the Land Commission. The first, following the original Labour proposals, allows the Land Commission to buy land, either on the open market, or compulsorily. To this end, on its setting up the Commission received a £45 million floating fund from the Treasury. The power to buy land, to quote the words of the Government White Paper on the Land Commission, is to ensure the original objectives for which Labour proposed setting it up: 'to secure that the right land is available at the right time for the implementation of national, regional and local plans'.[1] Here an important definition emerges: the Commission may buy land suitable for 'material development', that is all development save for certain cases where there is an automatic right of development without need to ask for planning permission.[2] Since the operative phrase is 'suitable for material development', the Commission can buy land up well in advance of the time when it is actually needed. This is to fulfil an object of the exercise: to see that the Commission has enough land to release on to the market, to ensure that shortages do not drive land values up. There is an important distinction between the Commission's powers to buy voluntarily and compulsorily. For purchases by agreement, the Commission has virtually unlimited powers from the beginning. This means that within the financial limits set by the Treasury fund, it can begin to build up the all-important land bank. Sir Henry Wells, the Commission's Chairman, has already made it clear that he expects most of the Commission's profits to come from large new allocations of land needed to meet the rising demands of industry and housing to cope with the overspill from London and the other great conurbations, not covered by the plans for new towns. As soon as the broad pattern of land needs is settled as between Regional Planning Councils and local authorities, Sir Henry suggests, the Commission can move in—and it is clear that in many cases, the Commission will be able to buy in the market.

For compulsory purchase, the Commission's powers are more restricted. First, for several years while it is building up its organization and its expertise, it is limited to certain defined cases of problem. For instance, to deal with a shortage of land for the housing programme, or to buy land for a new airport, or to ensure comprehensive planning. Secondly, even after that time it can only buy compulsorily where there is a planning decision that the land is suitable for 'material development'. It might be

---

[1] *The Land Commission* (Cmnd. 2771, H.M.S.O. 1965), para. 7, p. 4.
[2] *Ibid.*, footnote, p. 6.

noted, though, that an outline planning permission will be enough—and that the Commission can apply for planning permission itself.[1] In the longer run, therefore, the Commission will have very extensive powers of compulsory purchase, backed by the ability to hurry through the purchase and argue about the financial details later, at leisure; certainly, as Desmond Heap points out, some of the greatest powers ever given to a Government body has yet possessed in peacetime.[2]

When the Land Commission gets rid of land, it can do so virtually as it wishes—subject to Government directions. To local authorities, it will normally sell the freehold. To others, it can either sell or lease—generally on long lease. It will also be able to dispose on a new system: Crownhold. Under this, it will be able to repurchase when development is due again, at a price which allows it to recoup all future development value. This will be a particularly useful device in areas with high and rising values and short building cycles, such as the commercial central area of cities. It can also sell houses direct to the public on this basis. Alternatively, to organizations like housing associations or local authorities willing to build houses for sale, the Commission will be able to sell land at less than market value if it decides this is justified.[3] In these ways, the Commission could clearly operate a discriminatory pricing system on a very large scale. It could wring the maximum amount of development value out of commercial developments like central area schemes, using some of the proceeds to sell land for residential development at less than market value. In this way it could, theoretically, reduce the cost of building land for housing. Doubtless, however, defenders of *laissez-faire* will point out that the only certain result will be an excess of demand over supply.

When it buys compulsorily, the Commission will pay a sum based on current use value; in effect, it will take part of the development value for itself, leaving part to the seller. (The details of this are explained below.) It will then lease, of course, at market value. If these rules were to apply only to land which the Commission bought compulsorily, there would clearly be inequity, as there was between 1954 and 1959; people whose land was bought compulsorily would get less than those who sold in the open market. The other part of the Land Commission Act remedies this, by applying the same principles to private sales. It imposes a levy on development value, which will be charged alike to purchases by the Commission, and to transactions between private individuals. In the case of private sales, the Commission calculates the amount of levy and charges the seller. (It can also charge the developer at the point of development, if extra development value has accrued since he bought the land.) In the case of its own purchases, the Commission simply pays a price for the land net of levy. It thus should become a matter of indifference to the individual whether he is selling his land to another private individual, or the Commission; he gets the same amount in the end.

The actual rules for calculating the amount of levy are slightly complicated. Levy

[1] Desmond Heap, *Understanding the Land Commission Act* (London 1967), pp. 108–9.
[2] *Ibid.*, p. 106.   [3] *The Land Commission, op. cit.*, paras. 22–24, pp. 7–8.

is charged as a percentage (40 per cent at first, rising quickly to 45 and then 50 per cent, perhaps more later) on the net development value. This development value is basically the difference between the market value of the land, and the current use value. But the current use value is allowed to be increased, in three ways. First, it is inflated 10 per cent, to provide a special incentive in the case of urban land being redeveloped. Secondly, a special allowance is made for any fall in the value of adjacent land held by the seller, because of severance. And thirdly, an allowance is made for any expenditure on improvements or ancillary rights.[1]

There is a critical distinction in the Act, which will surely provide fruitful wrangling ground for lawyers in years ahead. It is that the levy applies to development value only, and is not to be charged on increases in the value of land for current use. Thus, to quote Desmond Heap's example, a house which appreciates in value is not liable to levy; but if it has a very large amount of potential building land attached and its value has risen disproportionately because of that fact, then there is development value, and this is liable to levy. All will turn, therefore, on what a house can reasonably be expected to have in the way of grounds.[2] Any country house within 50 miles of central London, for instance, might well excite the Commission's suspicion—unless, presumably, it were in the Green Belt or some other place where development permission was virtually unobtainable.

Levy will be the only tax on development value; development value will be excluded from capital gains for the purpose of calculating tax on long term gains, or corporation tax. Thus there will be no double taxation, though there will be a higher rate of taxation on gains in development value, than on other types of capital gain.[3] This is presumably justified by a notion that capital gains in land accrue from a monopolistic position on the part of the owner of land. Local authorities do not pay levy on any land they develop or sell. (Originally the exemption was to apply only to land developed for 'social service' purposes,[4] but in practice this distinction would have been virtually impossible to make.) Similarly statutory undertakers, like nationalized industries, will not pay when they develop or sell operational land; for instance, when British Railways release London land to local authorities for housing.[5]

The Land Commission was bitterly attacked by the Conservative opposition, and they have promised to repeal it when returned to office, as they repealed the financial provisions of the 1947 Act in 1954. Then, they had good reason, though they could have modified the provisions without repealing them; now, they will have far less reason. There seems no reason why the Commission should not become a permanent British institution, though with varying limitations on its powers (especially those of purchase) as different governments come and go. The one thing to be said now is that though the Land Commission Act was not the only way of doing it, it has cut

---

[1] Cf. Desmond Heap, *op. cit.*, pp. 64–70. Alternatively, the seller can elect to use a formula based on the previous sale, if this gives him a lower rate of levy.

[2] *Ibid.*, pp. 21–2.   [3] *The Land Commission, op. cit.*, para. 30, p. 9.

[4] *Ibid.*, para. 33, p. 10.   [5] *Ibid.*

the Gordian knot. Betterment, defined as an arbitrary rate of levy as Uthwatt suggested, is being collected for the community; at the same time, a device exists for physically assembling land when that is needed for good planning. The critical question is how much this power of assembly will be used, and for precisely what ends.

Here, a good deal of help has been given by Sir Henry Wells. In a talk to the Town Planning Institute, he has defined five cases in which the Commission would consider buying. The first is to get hold of land which the planning authority has decided should be developed but is not being put on the market. This should not be a very important category. The second is land allocated for development but which the planning authority does not want developed just yet—for instance, because there are no roads or sewers. The third case is analogous to the first: it is land the planning authority would like to see developed, but has not yet been marked for development in the plan. Fourthly is a group of difficult cases, for instance land in fragmented ownership. And fifthly, and most importantly, there are the large new allocations to meet the growth of population around the big conurbations.

This, clearly, is where the Commission is going to play its greatest role. Sir Henry Wells, who is a member of the South East Planning Council, has said quite specifically that in these cases, the Commission should step in as soon as the broad pattern of development had been determined among the national, regional and local authorities. Put concretely in terms of the contemporary South East, that means that as soon as an agreed regional strategic plan can be determined by the government departments, the Economic Planning Council and the Standing Conference of Local Authorities, then the Commission will start buying (voluntarily or compulsorily) in the areas earmarked for development, releasing the land as it is needed. However, it is clear that the Commission will simply not have the money to buy all the land that is needed; it will step in only when it is reasonably sure it is needed to serve the interests of planning. It will tend, then, to wait for others to take the initiative: either the local authorities, or private developers who can quite properly ask the Commission to act as middleman for them. The important point, in all this, is that the Commission sees its role as an *intermediary*: between the regional plan on the one hand, and the small local authority or small developer on the other. It can help bridge the gap between the need for an overall strategic plan, and the desire of the small authority or builder to get on with the job. If it is successful in this, it could prove to be the greatest single contribution to positive planning that has been seen in this century. At least, this is the explicit hope of the Commission's Chairman.

CHAPTER 9

Administering London 2000

Most books and pamphlets about planning start with sweeping reforms of the system of administration. I have left this question till last, because I do not see how you can devise a satisfactory system of government till you know what you want it to do. As a good Colonial administrator wrote: 'in social, as in civil, engineering, form does not determine function, but function determines form.'[1]

Here I must limit myself to planning functions, using the word in its widest sense. First I look at the functions of planning under the permissive system, established by the 1947 Town and Country Planning Act: I show how they have been allocated up to now among the organs of local government, and how they are likely to be re-allocated in the current period of local government reform. Then I ask whether the resulting system will meet the needs of 2000; looking at present social and economic trends and at the necessary jobs of present-day planning, I conclude that it will not; and I outline the system that I think the future problems of London will demand.

Planning since 1947

The system of permissive planning, established by the 1947 Act, and still in existence, has depended on a threefold division of powers, among the central Government (the Ministry of Town and Country Planning, later the Ministry of Housing and Local Government); the 'top-tier' (County) or 'all-purpose' (County Borough) authorities, who have the main job; and, playing a subordinate role in considering applications for development, the 'second-tier' (Borough or County District) authorities.

This system essentially did its best with the available structure of English local government. From experience of earlier attempts at planning, the 1947 drafters knew

[1] J. S. Furnivall in Phillips Talbot (ed.), *South Asia in the World Today* (Chicago, 1950), 20.

242

the weaknesses inherent in administration by small weak authorities. So basic planning control was given to the biggest authorities available, the Counties and the County Boroughs (who could hardly be left out since they controlled virtually all the other local authority functions). The only alternative would have been that adopted for hospital administration in the 1946 National Health Service Act: Regional Boards for areas larger than counties, chosen by the responsible Minister of the central government after rather perfunctory consultation with local health authorities. But the 1947 Act did provide for central co-ordination, by obliging each authority to prepare (and quinquennially review) a Development Plan, which must be submitted to the Minister for his approval. This was evidently necessary, for in the case of the Greater London Conurbation the responsibility for preparing a Development Plan was shared among no less than nine authorities—six Counties and three County Boroughs; while in the wider London Region no less than eighteen authorities—thirteen Counties and five County Boroughs—were involved.

Planning administration—the consideration routine of applications for development—was, everywhere outside the County of London, soon delegated by top-tier to second-tier authorities; difficult cases were left with the top-tier authority. In Kent, the second-tier authority was allowed to judge what was routine.[1]

When the Herbert Commission on Local Government in Greater London investigated the structure of planning administration in the Conurbation[2] in 1958, they were perturbed. The Ministry of Housing and Local Government told them:

'The mere statement of the planning aims for London makes it obvious that the problems are problems of Greater London[3] as a whole, or at the very least of its concentric rings—viz., the congested or exporting area, the suburban ring, the green belt ring, and the area for reception of overspill. In theory, therefore, one might hope to expect to find in planning a strong argument for some authority with powers over the whole region. But in practice the plans of the various authorities have been on the whole well co-ordinated—largely through reference to the Abercrombie Plans but partly through informal contacts with the Department . . . it would have been extremely difficult if not impossible to achieve a consistent planning policy for the region without the Abercrombie Plans; and it is a question whether some machinery is not required for continuous review of the whole region, and perhaps also for carrying through some of the work needed to implement planning.'[4]

In this statement the Ministry were evidently suffering from a conflict of loyalties. On the one hand, they seem to have thought (they were probably right) that they did

[1] Herbert Report (*Royal Commission on Local Government in Greater London, Report, Cmnd. 1164*, H.M.S.O. 1960), Part II, Item 12.

[2] Not strictly the Census Conurbation area; but very similar to it.

[3] i.e. the London Region; the Ministry used this confusing nomenclature until 1959.

[4] *Royal Commission on Local Government in Greater London, Memoranda of Evidence from Government Departments* (H.M.S.O. 1959), Ministry of Housing and Local Government, Part III, paras. 14–15.

a good job of central co-ordination; on the other they recognized that they were supposed to stand up for local government, and that the system as it stood simply would not function without their help.

The New Pattern of Local Government

In the event the Herbert Commission decided that the vice of local government in Greater London was precisely this last: that it had, in many ways, become so ineffectual that it was in danger of being, in all but name, paternal central government: '. . . we are convinced that the choice before local government in Greater London is, in truth, to abdicate in favour of central government, or to reform so as to be equipped to deal with present-day problems. There are great and growing problems to be solved and the present machinery of local government is inadequate to solve them. Unless this machinery is made adequate, the problems are so great and intrude themselves so obviously on public attention that they will be taken out of the hands of local government.'[1]

The Government had given them, the Commission conceived, a brief for London, as it had given the Local Government Commission a brief for provincial England—to make local government work again.

In London they proposed to do this, first, by giving the traditional functions of local government—housing, personal health, welfare, children's service, environmental health, roads (other than main roads), and libraries—to new authorities: the fifty-two[2] London Boroughs. These would have minimum populations of 100,000—the size which, elsewhere, would qualify them to ask for county borough status. They would be what Peter Self had called for a decade earlier—powerful 'most-purpose' authorities.[3] But to perform the new functions thrown up by a twentieth-century conurbation—physical planning, main roads and traffic planning, educational planning—the Commission proposed a completely new type of authority, without precedent in the history of English local government: a Council for Greater London, which would govern a population larger than that of many European states. This was no longer a 'top-tier' authority in the traditional sense: it was a regional government, exercising very wide powers in a limited number of fields.

Some of its functions, the new regional authority would take over from the existing top-tier and all-purpose authorities—thus the preparation of the development plan, educational planning. But some it would take over from second-tier authorities—for instance, the maintenance and lighting of main roads, which had become a matter of much more than local concern. More important, it would receive some functions from central government—for instance, traffic management, which, as a *pis aller*, had been developed by a group within the Ministry of Transport. But this last principle

---

[1] Herbert Report, *op. cit.*, para. 707.

[2] Since reduced to thirty-two in the Government's modification of the plan (London Government Bill, 1962).

[3] Peter Self, *Regionalism* (1949), 58. He was calling for this status for towns *outside* conurbations.

went wider than the mere transfer of formal functions: the tradition, which had developed by slow degrees since 1920, of weak local government supported by powerful central government, was to be replaced by a system of strong regional and local governments, in whose management the central government need intervene far less. This was the essential philosophy behind the Herbert Report.

Since the appearance of the report, the Government have modified its educational proposals very considerably, so that the Council for Greater London has become much more exclusively a one-purpose authority, a Council for Planning Greater London. Nevertheless, if the reform is carried through, 1 April 1965 will be a significant date: Britain's first regional government will be born.

The Greater London Council and the Future

At its demise the London County Council will have lived its three-score and ten; seventy-seven years to be precise. Will the new system prove viable as long? Will the Greater London Council still serve our needs in 2040? I would argue no. The English have an extraordinary knack for devising pieces of administrative machinery for London which are admirably suited to the conditions of a quarter-century back. In 1835, when they were administering a gentle dose of middle-class democracy to the ancient boroughs, nothing was done for London. In 1855, when this middle-class democracy had worked smoothly on the national level for twenty-three years, they created a creaking piece of indirectly elected machinery which had to be hastily dismantled, thirty years later, after a history of unbridled corruption. In 1888 they created the body they should have created in 1855, to govern the area of London which had been designed for poor law purposes in 1834: an area which, with the rapid growth of suburban railways, had already ceased to be an adequate definition of London.[1] In 1963, they are creating the London authority that was desperately needed in 1937 to control suburban sprawl, but which ceased to be adequate for the management of London as soon as the Abercrombie Plan became accepted policy.

The important question about the Herbert Commission's report, in fact, is not: why did they create the system of government they did?—the logic behind that was almost inescapable—but: why did they refuse to carry that logic to its 1960 conclusion? Why did they not propose a regional government that would function over a really effective area?

The Commission themselves raise this question, but avoid it.

'We accept the view that the problems of Greater London are inextricably concerned with the problems of south-east England as a whole, but it is a *non-sequitur* to argue from that that no attempt should be made on the part of local government to organise planning, housing, transport, and some other services within the Review Area[2] as a whole.'[3]

[1] For the full story, see W. A. Robson, *The Government and Misgovernment of London* (1948).
[2] Approximately the Conurbation.   [3] Herbert Report, *op. cit.*, para. 720.

True: but if that is a non-sequitur, what is the sequitur? Here the Commission, suddenly and unpredictably, stand their own logical premises on their heads:

'It is no doubt the business of central government to hold the balance between Greater London and the rest of south-east England, as it is also the business of central government to hold the balance between south-east England and the Midlands, some of whose problems are beginning to converge.'[1]

But if the problems are inextricably connected, what part has the central government to play? Surely no more, on the Commission's premises, than it has as between the L.C.C. area and the suburban part of the Conurbation. The job is one of regional government; and having stated the principle, the next step is to define the region and extend the government to cover it.

The question then becomes: what led the Commission to decide that the Conurbation was a more meaningful region than the wider London Region? The answer is curious and not very clear. In the first place the Commission were obviously circumscribed, in fact if not in theory, by their brief. They were to consider an area roughly equal to the Conurbation: to argue a solution for an area six times the size would have raised major technical difficulties. So their doubts about boundaries are all small matters. Secondly, given this limitation, there was no difficulty in finding that their review area was a reasonably well-defined one. Research material prepared by the Ministry of Housing and Local Government showed that in the extent of the built-up area, or the proportion of urban land use, there was a reasonably sharp boundary corresponding to the boundary of the review area. The difficulty is that since the establishment of the Green Belt, these static indices have become merely formal indications; for a functional definition of London, it is now necessary to look at the dynamic relationships between one area and another. Here the Commission were less well-served. Maps of journey-to-work patterns, which showed a sharp falling-off just outside the Conurbation in the proportions of workers travelling daily to central London, were based on 1951 Census figures, then eight years old, while in the intervening period there had undoubtedly been a dramatic growth in long-distance commuting across the Green Belt; the Commission themselves regretted that they had nothing more recent to work on.[2] Other indices—dependence of manufacturing industry on London sales, of retailers on London wholesale markets; contacts with central London for shopping or entertainment; ties of kinship or friendship with the inner districts—were all difficult if not impossible to devise; and the Commission apparently did not consider them.

The Commission did the most thorough job they could with the available information. But on an even moderately long-term view it is difficult to avoid the conclusion that their area was defined for them much too narrowly. Perhaps for this reason, it is not at all evident from their report that they understood fully the implications of the rapid growth of population in the nineteen-fifties in the Outer Ring, and the slow decline in the inner districts, coupled with the great increase of employment at the

[1] *Ibid.*   [2] *Ibid.*, para. 987.

centre. Indeed they nowhere recognize that the area they were planning for had actually suffered declining population for eight years when they reported:[1] a fact which alone will make the Greater London Council, from its inception, more obsolete than was the London County Council.

Given the basic limitation, the interesting question is: what sort of solution did the Commission envisage for these rapidly growing areas outside the Conurbation? Writing about Watford, they concluded that it was representative of the wider problem of the Outer Ring; towns like it were likely to grow fast, and to become more closely bound to London along the main spines of communication:

'. . . the case must be regarded as a difficult one which will set a precedent for the future development of local government in the whole of this very large region. There are already a number of towns in it approaching the size of Watford: others are likely to grow: is the pattern of county and bounty borough, regarded as appropriate in the provinces outside the conurbations, to be applied also in the Home Counties?'[2]

But they refused to commit themselves; they had completed their half-brief, and it was for the recipients of the other half—the Local Government Commission for England—to come up with the answer:

'We must however give our colleagues an opportunity to consider the wider issues which are their responsibility.'[3]

But if this was intended as a gauntlet, the Local Government Commissioners have shown no signs of hurrying to pick it up. Nine months after the Greater London Report, they published their final proposals for the first of these 'problem towns'— Luton—following draft proposals which had already appeared before the London Report. The final report deals with Luton's growth by saying merely that

'It has grown rapidly since the beginning of the century and is continuing to grow. . . . Luton is primarily an industrial town. The traditional industry was the making of hats and this remained the chief employer of labour up to 1931, but the manufacture of vehicles now has pride of place.'[4]

There is no recognition of the problem of metropolitan overspill, save in relation to details of boundary questions, though both Luton Borough and Luton Rural District are 'Expanding Towns' under the 1952 Town Development Act; nor of the potential growth of Luton as a dormitory suburb for London consequent on improved train services. The final recommendation to make Luton a County Borough is based entirely on the book of rules:

'Section 34 of the Act lays it down that a population of 100,000 is to be presumed sufficient to support the functions of a county borough council. Luton is the largest non-county borough outside the Metropolitan area (*sic*), with a present population

---

[1] Though it is noted in the statistics accompanying the Report.
[2] *Ibid.*, para. 997.   [3] *Ibid.*, para. 998.
[4] Local Government Commission for England: *Report and Proposals for the East Midlands General Review Area* (1961), paras. 229–30.

of 123,000 and the prospect of further growth. The claim to become a county borough was not opposed by Bedfordshire County Council, and it is clear that Bedfordshire without Luton would continue to be an effective county.'[1]

It seems clear from this that the Commissioners did not intend to be impeded in their work by any pause to examine fundamental dogmas. Yet these dogmas, embodied in the brief the Commission were given, are extraordinarily rigid ones. England is divided into special review areas—broadly the Conurbations—and general review areas, the clear assumption being that each will require a different solution. And certain rules of thumb are handed down, notably for the general review areas, where it is assumed that the right pattern will be one of strong counties and strong county boroughs. These assumptions, I would argue, ignore the one unmistakable trend in population within England since 1950: the trend away from the Conurbations, which can no longer be regarded as significant economic or social units.

The Conurbation: An Adequate Concept?

The term 'Conurbation' was invented by Patrick Geddes about 1910[2] to describe a phenomenon which was then relatively new. Nineteenth-century industrial development, based on coal, railways, and primitive or non-existent urban transport, had created the compact mid-century industrial town, of which the archetype is the Lancashire cotton town or the Yorkshire woollen town. But in the later nineteenth century, with the growth of specialized business functions, the improved methods of urban transport (suburban train, tram, bus), increasing prosperity and the demand for space, cities had spread; in doing so they had swallowed up smaller village or urban centres, or had amalgamated with other large centres, to form bigger urban complexes, or 'super-cities'. These Conurbations were further defined by C. B. Fawcett between the two wars; and after a suitable time-lag, the concept was officially recognized. Our Census statistics, since 1951, have contained special sets of figures for Conurbations; and the present system of local government reform is evidently to be based on a Conurbation solution.[3]

But official forms, as usual, are being outrun by economic and social facts. Between 1951 and 1961, all the official major Conurbations showed slow rates of growth, or actual declines. But the areas immediately outside them—their Green Belts, where these existed, and their Outer Rings—grew at a phenomenal speed. This process was most striking in the case of London, where the Conurbation fell by 176,000 but the Outer Ring increased by 964,000. But the same thing was happening on a smaller scale elsewhere. Thus while the West Midlands Conurbation increased by only 107,000 (5 per cent), the area outside it, and up to 30 miles from central Birmingham, but excluding Coventry, increased by 153,000 (15 per cent). While

---

[1] *Ibid.*, para. 246. [2] *Cities in Evolution* (published 1915), Chap. 2.

[3] For the development of the Conurbation concept, see *Census* 1951: *Report on Greater London and Five Other Conurbations* (H.M.S.O. 1956), xiii.

the population of the Merseyside Conurbation fell by 406 people, the area 15 miles around rose by 96,000 (26 per cent).

Because of the operation of post-1947 land-use planning, however, it is no longer adequate to talk of these increases as 'expansions of the Conurbations'. The Conurbations themselves are now frequently hemmed in by Green Belts, as in the case of London or the West Midlands. Their overspill has to leapfrog the Green Belt, and even then its distribution is tightly controlled. The new standard pattern of the urban parts of England is that of a Conurbation, broadly static in population; a Green Belt; and a mixed urban and rural zone outside, in which well-defined towns are separated by wide areas of countryside. A new term is needed for this sort of complex: we can borrow from one of Wells' uncanny prophecies, and call it an 'Urban Region'.[1]

Because the phenomenon has occurred at such speed, and because our statistics lag so far behind events, we do not know nearly enough about what is happening in these Regions. We need to know how people circulate between the outer parts and the centre, to work, to shop, to play. It is clear that while the centres of the Conurbations are losing resident population, they are tending to gain extra workers; so long-distance commuting must be on the increase. There is every evidence that the magnetic attraction of the centres for shopping, entertainment and culture is growing: witness the reconstruction of provincial shopping centres by powerful speculative interests, the continued growth of the big department stores and retail multiples there, the expansion of professional and business services and other sorts of office jobs, the unprecedented development of regional centres of higher and further education of all sorts. It appears—but we need the statistics to prove it—that the new Urban Region is no less a coherent functional unit than was the Conurbation in the interwar years.

The Jobs of Planning in the London Region

For London and for the planning function, at least, I hope that this book has proved the truth of the assertion. *The jobs of planning concern the wider London Region.* If the various proposals in this book came to be, the planning machine would have the following main functions.

1. To prepare a Development Plan covering the whole region. This is vital because the progress of development in the main area of residential growth—the Outer Ring—must be closely co-ordinated with the expansion of jobs in this ring, and elsewhere; with the development of transport facilities, especially between home and work; and with the progress of reconstruction in the older parts of the Region.

2. To guide the growth of employment within the region, on the basis of the plan, so as to minimize social costs, through a new system of financial incentives and disincentives.

---

[1] *Anticipations*, Fifth Edition, page 61.

3. To plan the main communications network, in consultation with those responsible for the national network. If the public transport system continues in the hands of a nationalized corporation with broad responsibility to Parliament, to work in close consultation with it, preferably with formal links.

4. To plan in detail housing for the extra population in the Outer Ring.

5. To play a big part, in areas currently being developed or redeveloped, in the creation of the Redevelopment Commission, which will manage the necessary pooling of property and will supervise or carry through construction; to help contribute, through local knowledge, to that Commission's work.

6. To continue to operate, outside the areas where large-scale development is currently occurring, the 1947 system of development control, but strengthened with much more radical plans for the eventual reconstruction of the area than are now attempted.

These functions have to be allocated among the central government; a regional government; big 'top-tier' or 'all-purpose' authorities; and smaller 'second-tier' authorities of all sizes.

The New Planning System

To create a viable new system, only gentle change is needed. This is because the Herbert Commission have given us the administrative model we want. It is merely necessary, in the first place, to extend it to the wider London region: to make the Greater London Council an effective regional authority. Outside the Conurbation, this will mean modifying, to a minimal extent, the solution which the Local Government Commissioners seem bent on. Here, both Counties and County Boroughs would be shorn of their highest planning functions, which would pass to the regional authority; thus towns like Reading, Southend and Luton would have the same powers and status as the Herbert Commission proposed for the new London boroughs; they would be 'most-purpose' authorities.

To compensate the County Boroughs for their loss, it seems right to allow them to participate, in a more formal way, in preparing the Regional Development Plan. And this may be administratively necessary, for a top-tier authority preparing a plan for 4,000 square miles could hardly do it all from the centre. So members of the G.L.C. Staff should be seconded to the offices of the 'most-purpose' authorities to do the necessary preparatory work on the relevant section of the plan: and if then, in preparation, the 'most-purpose' authority disagreed on a point of substance in the plan —as might happen about zoning for overspill, or redevelopment of a central area of a town—they could be given the right to refer it to the Minister of Town and Country Planning as a last resort.

In areas where large-scale development was currently proceeding, the Redevelopment Commission would contain representatives of both the Greater London Council and the 'most-purpose' authority planning staffs. Outside these areas, responsibility for considering routine planning applications would rest with the 'most-purpose' authority, as proposed by the Herbert Commission. I would favour leaving the decision as to what is routine with the regional authority; this as opposed to the Government's present proposals for the Conurbation, which give it to the lower-tier authority with provision to refer to the Minister.

The difficult question is not the division of powers but the areal extent of London. Throughout this book I have taken the Ministry of Housing and Local Government's London Planning Region as a definition of London, and in this chapter I have argued for it as a more meaningful unit than the Conurbation. But that is not to say that I would argue for the exact present boundaries of the region. They are quite openly arbitrary, and likely to remain so, wherever they are placed and whatever research is done to try to delimit the 'natural boundaries' of the New London. While the book was being written the Ministry made a minor extension of the region; and before long it may bring in whole new areas in East Anglia, the South Midlands and Hampshire. This problem is likely to be less difficult, though, if we visualize not a London regional authority in isolation, but similar administrations centred upon all the big Conurbations and forming a major chain up the industrialized middle of England, plus other authorities to group the less industrial counties with their often strongly-defined regional consciousness. In such a scheme London might be bordered by a West Midlands authority to the north-west, by a Central England authority to the west, by a Wessex authority to the south-west, by an East Anglian authority to the north-east and by an East Midlands authority to the north. The precise boundaries of these Regions would have to be based on close study of regional ties, which could be founded on the invaluable work done many years ago by the geographer, C. B. Fawcett.[1]

Towards a Structure of Regional Government

In the previous paragraphs I have been writing only of the planning function. But there are many other fields of social administration where a system of regional authorities would be invaluable. Such a system would have spared the creators of the National Health Service the necessity to create *ad hoc* Regional Hospital Boards. For higher education, in the Fabian Society group's evidence to the Robbins Committee we concluded by suggesting a system of Regional Higher Education Authorities which, under a National Authority, would provide a unified regional system of higher education embracing university institutions, colleges of advanced technology and teacher-training colleges; again, because no system of government existed, an *ad hoc* solution had to be proposed.[2] John Vaizey has gone further and proposed that all education should be provided by strong regional planning authorities, if possible directly elected:

[1] C. B. Fawcett, *Provinces of England* (revised edition by W. G. East and S. W. Wooldridge: 1961).

[2] *The Structure of Higher Education* (Fabian Tract No. 334: 1961), 18–19.

'There is little doubt that only a big authority can provide special schools, a variety of secondary schools, and other services in sufficient quantities to enable realistic and adequate decisions to be taken about the satisfaction of the vastly diverse needs of the children.'[1]

Again, the general tendency of recent years has been to decentralize the administration of nationalized industries onto regional boards. These boards might be given formal responsibility to the regional authority in matters of broad policy, similar to the responsibility each industry now bears to Parliament at Westminster. There might be scope for further development here, in particular the combination of all short-distance public transport in and around the main Conurbations under regional boards.

These are only among the most obvious suggestions for the functions of regional authorities. There are many others that are quite feasible in the long term—regional broadcasting, the public control functions of the Home Office, many matters of public health. If we started with only the most urgent—probably planning and the higher levels of education—we could gradually, as we gained experience of the new system, extend its scope. Then it would be within our power, if we wished it, to give the regional authorities the same powers and status as the States of the American Union, or the West German *Länder*: a structure that would admirably meet the needs of any future European Union. But that may take us beyond 2000.

Postscript, 1969

London 2000 looked at the London government reforms while they were still proposals, and predicted that in their turn they soon would be out of date. A conurbation solution, I argued, was right for the 1930s, not for the 1960s; the great zones of population growth, above all around London but to some extent everywhere, were no longer the conurbations but the areas outside and around them. The solution that was now needed was a unit of government based on the city region; a region that took in London, and all its sphere of influence, perhaps for forty or fifty miles around. Five years later, there is a Royal Commission on Local Government in England, under Lord Redcliffe-Maud. It will report in spring 1969, before publication of this edition, and it is confidently expected to recommend a city regional solution for the whole of local administration, all over England. It cannot change the government of London, but it can recommend an extension of the Greater London Council's boundaries, to cover the city region if needs be. The irony, in this, is that the London city region now seems much less clear a concept than it did back in 1962 and 1963.

There is a good reason for this: factual evidence, which throws doubt on the original concept of the city region as defined in the late 1950s and as used in *London 2000*. But before this evidence is examined, the historical record should be brought up to date.

[1] John Vaizey, *Britain in the Sixties*: *Education for Tomorrow* (Harmondsworth, 1962), 102.

In the event, the recommendations of the Herbert Commission on London local government were carried into effect, with due major modification and one minor one. To take the minor one first: several peripheral authorities, chiefly in south and south-west London, complained that the Commission had wrongly included them in Greater London, and asked to be excluded. Their wishes were granted. The effect of this was to make the London boundary less tidy than Herbert had proposed, since most of these areas did include obvious extensions of the built-up area of London (for instance: Staines, Sunbury, Esher, Walton-on-Thames, Caterham, Chigwell, Cheshunt) and the new boundary thus runs through developed areas rather than through the inner part of the Green Belt, as the Herbert Commission had intended.

The major change concerned internal organization. Herbert had recommended 52 boroughs in addition to the City, with populations ranging from 81,000 to 249,000. It also recommended a division of powers for education as between the Greater London Council and the boroughs, which everyone—including the then Ministry of Education—said was unworkable. To the government the alternative solution of handing over all education to the GLC seemed to represent an inconceivable degree of centralism; therefore, education must go to the boroughs, and therefore, in turn, the boroughs must be big enough to take on the job. The boroughs were therefore amalgamated and compressed, after the wishes of the existing authorities as to grouping were taken into account, to 32 plus the City, ranging in population from 147,000 to 345,000. But even this did not satisfy the Department of Education: and therefore the old L.C.C. Education Authority survived for the inner boroughs, in the form of the Inner London Education Authority. Originally, this was to be subject to a review after five years; the Labour government struck this proviso out shortly after its return to power, and it now seems inconceivable that inner London education will ever be handed over to the boroughs.

As it emerged from the Statute Book, the London Government Act of 1963 was by no means the tidy reform which the Herbert Commission had conceived. In particular, there were several important respects in which Parliament failed to make the critical distinction Herbert had insisted on: between the powers of the GLC, and the powers of the boroughs. Thus for the first three or four years of existence, both the GLC and the boroughs (which came into formal existence in May 1964, and into formal power on the unfortunate date of 1st April 1965)[1] found themselves involved in boundary disputes on matters of responsibility—some of them, ironically, on just those matters where Herbert had insisted on clear powers for the GLC. Thus the Greater London Council failed to get unambiguous powers over large-scale redevelopment in the central area, though this was clearly a critical element of any development plan for London; over the control of the most important roads ('metropolitan roads') which were inadequately defined in the Act; or over traffic management, where the GLC in effect shared powers with the Ministry of Transport,

[1] The GLC chose this day to announce its proposals for the controversial London Motorway Box. Cynics, and opponents of the Box, have not been slow to exploit the fact.

the Metropolitan Police (who are of course answerable to the Home Secretary) and the Boroughs.[1] This is to name only the chief problems in the sphere of planning and transportation; there are plenty of other ambiguities, for instance, in the education and child welfare services.[2]

As regards transport, some of the most important of these anomalies will be removed under the proposals in the Government's 1968 White Paper. There the Ministry of Transport set out their unambiguous view that eventually all important roads in the GLC area shall be a GLC responsibility; meanwhile, all so-called principal roads in London will go to the GLC, though on some the boroughs will still exercise development control, within a framework handed to them by the GLC.[3] At the same time the GLC's traffic powers will be strengthened and streamlined, so as to centralize in the Council some powers now exercised by the Ministry of Transport and some powers exercised by the boroughs. As regards planning, there are indications at least that the GLC and the relevant boroughs are reaching some sort of co-operative *modus vivendi*. The critically important and imaginative proposals for Piccadilly, issued in the summer of 1968, were a joint enterprise of the GLC and the Westminster City Council, the GLC concentrating on broad systems of pedestrian and vehicle movement, Westminster on the detail of the site.

Three years after the new system of government came into complete responsibility for London, it is clear that in most respects it is beginning to do the things that Herbert hoped it would do. Even within the present limitations, the GLC is at last providing London with the overall transportation authority it so long lacked. And the overall GLC development plan, which will lay down the critical policy guidelines for the boroughs' own development plans, is rumoured to be a powerful and imaginative document—at any rate in comparison with the early statement of principles issued by the GLC to the boroughs, which was an alarmingly vacuous document.[4] The Greater London Group of the London School of Economics, at the end of a detailed study of the lessons of the Greater London reforms for the Royal Commission on Local Government in England, came to the conclusion that the new system 'has some clear advantages over the systems it replaces'.[5] They concluded too that the GLC area was viable but should be extended to take in the wider areas of Surrey recommended for inclusion by the Herbert Commission.[6] They admitted that there was a case for a wider area for planning and highway functions, but found it difficult to delimit what this area should be.[7] And here, almost without doubt, is the nub of the problem which must now confront the English government reformers.

[1] *Royal Commission on Local Government in England, Research Studies, 2. The Lessons of the London Government Reforms*, by the Greater London Group, London School of Economics and Political Science (H.M.S.O. 1968), pp. 7–8.

[2] *Ibid.*, p. 9. The Seebohm Committee has added a weighty voice to these criticisms. *Report of the Committee on the organization of the Social Services* (H.M.S.O. 1968), para. 249 (p. 74).

[3] Ministry of Transport, *Transport in London* (Cmnd. 3686, H.M.S.O. 1968) pp. 15–16.

[4] These were wrong: the Plan was utterly vacuous.

[5] Royal Commission on Local Government, *op. cit.*, p. 49. [6] *Ibid.* [7] *Ibid.*

There are really two closely related questions here. One is: on what principles should local government be reconstructed in England as a whole? The second is: how does such a principle apply in the particular, and very special, case of London? On the first question, the agreement is so general as to be unanimous: the present local government units are too small, and need replacing by something bigger. The critical question is how much bigger; and here there are two views. The first is that of virtually all the central Government departments in their evidence to the Royal Commission—and, in modified form, of the County Councils Association. (The modification is that the Association, understandably, wishes to avoid breaking up existing units as far as possible;[1] the Government Departments would probably do so cheerfully. But on broad questions of size, they are at one.) It was also the declared view, before the setting up of the Commission, of one prominent member: the planning journalist Derek Senior, who wrote about it.[2] This notion is that the basic unit of government, outside London, should consist of 30 to 40 city regional authorities. They should normally have between half a million and 2 million people, though this latter figure might be exceeded round the big conurbations. They should comprise one urban core or (this is important) a group of urban areas, and their sphere of influence on the surrounding countryside. They should be responsible for long term structure planning, including the planning of the main structure of communications.[3] From the evidence of the other departments, it is clear that they could also be perfectly capable of running education, the children's welfare services, police, fire services and ambulances[4] (Fig. 10A).

The second and contrary view, which can be called the planning region-district solution, has the support of the Association of Municipal Corporations.[5] This suggests that certain top level functions—such as structure planning, highway and transportation planning, and further education—should go to a number of provincial authorities covering very large areas. These provinces would be smaller than the present planning regions, but bigger than most counties. Other functions should be given to local authorities, which would be based on a town and the surrounding countryside which is related to it. It may well be, according to the Association

[1] County Councils Association, *Royal Commission on Local Government in England, Memorandum of evidence as proposed improvements in the structure of local government* (London 1966), p. 6.

[2] Derek Senior, *The Regional City* (London 1966), p. 19. See also T. W. Freeman, *Geography and Regional Administration* (London 1968), pp. 28–9.

[3] Royal Commission on Local Government in England, *Written Evidence of the Ministry of Housing and Local Government* (H.M.S.O. 1967), p. 64. 'Structure Planning', a term introduced by the report of the Planning Advisory Group (H.M.S.O. 1965) was made into the statutory responsibility of planning authorities by the Planning Act 1968. It involves long term strategic planning of a broad overall nature, essentially over large areas. It therefore presupposes local government reform.

[4] Cf. Royal Commission on Local Government in England, *Written Evidence of the Department of Education and Science, Home Office*, etc. (H.M.S.O. 1967).

[5] *Municipal Review*, Supplement December 1966, p. 332.

of Municipal Corporations, that a single structure for local government is not applicable equally to all parts of the country. Nevertheless, there is an important point here: it consists in saying that the city region solution is too small for certain purposes, too big for others.

In all the evidence submitted by the Government Departments, by the County Councils Association) and by the Association of Municipal Corporations, we look in vain for detailed justification of the case. This is perhaps most surprising with the Government departments. From their evidence, it is clear that in planning and transportation, there is an unanswerable case for units of at least city-regional size. But two critical points still remain strikingly unclear. The first is exactly why the city region is so preferable, on planning grounds, to a rather larger unit. The Ministry of Housing deals with this in a curiously circular fashion, by saying that bigger units must be too big because they are bigger than city regions:

'They are bigger than necessary for planning purposes . . . since they encompass several areas or city-regions, which are virtually distinct; and for the most part they would be too large in area and population to constitute effective units of local government responsible for the planning functions discussed above.'[1]

Curiously, even the Department of Economic Affairs fell in with their colleagues at the Ministry of Housing on this argument, arguing rather curiously that:

'It is clear from the experience of DEA's present regional organization that areas the size of the present regions are too large for the purpose of executive local government and that some sub-division into smaller units would be needed.'[2]

Not surprisingly, this led to the familiar conclusion that 30 to 40 units was the right number. But in neither of these two pieces of evidence, nor in that of the Ministry of Transport, is there any discussion of just what sorts of jobs strategic planning involves, on what scale. The evidence nowhere discusses in any detail the actual problems of strategic planning like motorway lines, the location of overspill housing projects like new or expanded towns, the location of major investments like power stations, or the evolution of recreational planning policies. Had departments done this, they might have had increasing doubts about their city regional concept—at any rate in the more densely-populated parts of the country. For there they must have seen that most of these critical planning problems could only be seen on a scale far greater than any one typical city region.

This failing goes with the second: that nowhere does the Government Departments' evidence actually try to define in detail what a city region is. It might be thought that the essence was simple: a city plus its surrounding sphere of influence. But on a not particularly restrictive definition, considering each conurbation, and in addition all freestanding towns over 100,000, as city regions, that would give at least something like 50 regions in England—not 30 to 40. But looked at more closely, the densely-

---

[1] R.C. Local Government, *Evidence Ministry of Housing, op. cit.*, pp. 65–6.

[2] R.C. Local Government, *Written Evidence of the Department of Economic Affairs* (H.M.S.O. 1966), p. 4.

populated parts of England prove to have many well marked-city regions round quite small towns, of between 50,000 to 100,000 people; and because of this density, such regions may often number 200,000 or more people—an adequate size, on the analogy of the London government reforms, for the exercise of a wide range of local government functions. In other words, the 'city region' in its simple, pure form is a much more common, and therefore a smaller phenomenon than the government departments imagine. This may well be the reason why the Department's evidence specifies that in some cases a city region is built up around a *group* of free-standing towns. But how this is to be done, and still more why it is to be done, are never discussed.

In the research evidence of the Greater London Group at the London School of Economics, submitted to the Commission in summer 1967,[1] we tried to fill this gap by considering what, in practice, a city region was. Our technique, as we originally conceived it, was this. The administrative experts among us would use two different methods to try and discover whether there were critical minimum and maximum limits of size for the efficient performance of the various local authority functions. First, they would develop purely statistical indices of performance, based on readily available material; secondly, to try to fill the gaps in that material, they would conduct an intensive interview study of a few differently-sized authorities. When they had reported back to the Group on their findings, the geographers would try to give expression to their ideas in terms of natural social groupings of people. In other words, if the administrative experts said that half a million people was the size to aim at, we would try to discover cohesive units of half a million. All this was to be done within the limits of the South East Region, which was our area of study given to us in the remit from the Royal Commission.

In practice, it turned out rather differently. This was because it proved very difficult to establish any optimal size for the performance of functions, though sometimes it proved possible to establish a minimum. For education the conclusion was that 200,000 was a minimum;[2] for personal health services, welfare, and children's services, somewhere between 200,000 and 4–500,000;[3] for maintenance of minor roads, anywhere between 100,000 and 500,000.[4] There was occasionally evidence, of a not very definite kind, that a maximum size operated too; beyond this, diseconomies of scale began to operate. Thus in education, the bureaucratic organization probably became too complex and remote at much above a million people.[5] But for some of the most important functions, like strategic planning and communications planning, it was clear that a rather large unit of government was needed; certainly an authority bigger than the 200,000 or so specified as the minimum for some of the more personal functions. On the other hand some functions could work

---

[1] R.C. Local Government in England, *Research Studies 1, Local Government in South East England*, by the Greater London Group, London School of Economics and Political Science (H.M.S.O. 1968).

[2] *Ibid.*, pp. 7, 25.   [3] *Ibid.*, pp. 8, 26.   [4] *Ibid.*, p. 27.   [5] *Ibid.*, pp. 26–7.

well with much smaller minima; for instance housing, where there was no evidence to suggest that an authority with 30,000 people could not operate effectively.[1]

The evidence then was inconclusive, and it was particularly inconclusive on the main question which formed in the minds of the Group. This was the essential question posed earlier in this section: should local government be reformed on the basis of large city regions of approximately county size (the county solution, giving units of between half a million and a million people), or on the basis of provincial authorities plus small city regions (the district solution, giving top tier authorities of several million and second tier authorities of between 150,000 and 500,000)? Quite clearly, either type of solution was theoretically applicable to the evidence of performance we had produced. We had to find another answer; and we found two.

The first was to use our personal expertise, such as it was, to fill in the gaps in the evidence. It seemed clear to us that in the circumstances of South East England, strategic and communications planning needed integrated control over rather wide areas. Elements like the main communications network, or the distribution of new and expanded town developments, or a new national airport, or the designation of zones of special landscape protection—all these should be determined by an authority that covered either the whole region, or a very large sector of it. That this is the case is proved by the fact that two special *ad hoc* bodies had to be created for the purpose, covering the region: the Economic Planning Council, and the Standing Conference. It would be inconceivable that their strategic studies should have covered an area much smaller than the planning region. On the other hand, it was equally clear that a whole range of personal services could be most effectively performed by much smaller local government units which could be in more immediate touch with the populations they had to service; these included education (except further education), personal health and welfare services. This indicated a two-tier structure, with the provincial region at one level and the small city region at the other.

The second, and critical, piece of evidence came from the geographical research. This assembled all the evidence that was readily available about the socio-geographic areas within which people live most of their everyday lives. The most important evidence, because the fullest and most reliable, was about commuting. It was possible not only to identify the commuting areas around the major employment centres with a high degree of accuracy, but also to analyse changes in these areas over a forty-year period, between 1921 and 1961. This led to some surprising conclusions. If one adopts American practice, and defines a Standard Metropolitan Area as a substantial employment centre (either 5 workers per acre, or 20,000 jobs) plus a zone of contiguous areas around the centre all of which send 15 per cent or more of their resident employed population into it, then the result in south-east England is a large number of rather small commuting areas: to be precise, London plus 24 others, ranging in size from Portsmouth (410,000) down to Colchester (89,000).[2] The London commuting area, which numbered 9,561,000 people in 1961, was much more restricted than might

[1] *Ibid.*, pp. 424–5. [2] *Ibid.*, pp. 27–8.

be supposed, especially in certain directions: though it stretched half-way to the Sussex coast in the south and beyond Southend to the east, it hardly reached beyond the green belt to the west. And it had shown much less extension since 1921 than would have been thought. The reason for this was that its growth had been impeded, in effect, by the formation of the many small commuting areas all around, in a belt approximately 20–30 miles from central London; it was because no such centres had appeared due south of London that the London commuting zone had extended more widely there. In other words, put into Royal Commission terminology, the London city region was much smaller in extent than the definition usually quoted, extending at most about 30 miles from the centre, and sometimes less than 25; while there were a great number of rather small city regions occupying the so called Outer Metropolitan Area.

This immediately created a difficulty. First, because some of the commuting areas were almost certainly too small for the efficient performance of even the personal welfare functions. And secondly, because though the commuting zones showed remarkably little overlap as they were defined, they did still leave large tracts of the South East region unincorporated into any city region. This conclusion was only fortified when we came to consider the second main piece of evidence: that of shopping for durable goods. Here the data were much less direct and less reliable: they consisted of evidence of shopping patterns in Kent in 1962/4, which was used as the basis of a theoretical gravity model for application to the whole of the South East.[1] The result, which has to be treated with some caution, is a mosaic of very small shopping areas based in many cases on quite small towns. For instance, centres like Winchester, Newbury or Andover all form the nodes of quite well developed shopping areas. Further statistical evidence, about the hierarchy of shopping centres in the region, only provided confirmation: for the moderately sized centres, commonly called '3B' centres in the literature, had markedly increased their role as central service places between 1950 and 1961.[2] In other words: if one reformed local govenment solely on the basis of the patterns of people's everyday movements, one would get a pattern of units too small for efficient performance of functions. This may seem odd; the fact is that even in the supposedly mobile and dynamic South East, most people live their lives within a very restricted geographical framework.

Clearly, we had to seek some compromise. We did it by aggregating up the city regions we had discovered; by taking into account not merely direct flows of commuters and shoppers, but also indirect patterns of movement, we managed to incorporate the areas round the smaller centres into the areas round the bigger centres. Thus if Winchester were the local commuting and shopping centre, but if in turn sent commuters and shoppers into Southampton, the Winchester area could be incorporated into the Southampton area. By doing this all over the region, we managed at last

---

[1] *Ibid.*, pp. 537–44.

[2] *Ibid.*, p. 548. The terminology is drawn from W. I. Carruthers, Major Shopping Centres in England and Wales 1961, *Regional Studies*, 1 (1967), pp. 65–81.

to devise a set of commuting regions which covered the whole area; and these corresponded reasonably closely to a revised set of shopping regions. This was the basis for our recommended basis system of local government; but this, it goes almost without saying, was a district system. It gave, in addition to Greater London, a set of 30 districts (three of which would later be split, giving 33), ranging in 1961 populations from 619,000 (Portsmouth) down to 164,000 (Ashford). (Map 10B). Such a system of 30 units in the South East, with about one-third of the country's population, is hardly compatible with the notion of 30–40 units covering the whole country; though, it should be noted, districts in the rest of England might well be larger than in the densely populated South East. The best rough estimate that can be made is that over the whole country, such a solution might involve 60 to 70 authorities.

Axiomatically, the district solution demanded also a regional solution for the performance of the high-level planning functions. Here, the Group differed as between two alternatives. The first was to take the whole region as the unit, but then to exclude peripheral areas which in planning terms would and should be self-contained. In view of the accepted policy of developing the counter-magnets, 60 or 70 miles from London, as separate centres well outside London's commuting range, this suggests that they logically should be split off. Because of the relative self-containment of the Oxford region, and its economic links with the Midlands, that solution is also applicable there. The result is to take out of the South East the Southampton-Portsmouth-Bournemouth region; the Oxford region; the Milton-Keynes region; and the Colchester region. What precisely happens to these truncated regions is an open question; they might form enlarged city regions in their own right, but more probably they would be combined into rather larger provinces which would be the same size as, or a little smaller than, the present economic planning regions. Thus South Hampshire could be combined with Oxford, and also the Swindon region, to form a new Wessex province corresponding closely to the old Southern standard region; Colchester would form part of an East Anglian region, and Milton Keynes part of a South Midland (or East Midland) region.

The other regional planning alternative is in a sense more radical, and depends on an acceptance of the Economic Planning Council's *Strategy for the South East*: namely that future growth in the region will be concentrated into sectors following the main radial transportation lines outwards from London. This would allow a sectoral system of sub-regional authorities, running outwards from the edge of the Greater London Council, and logically incorporating the counter-magnets which terminate the development sectors at their outer ends. Logically, then, these sub-regional sectors would incorporate certain counter-magnet areas now not part of the South East region, such as Swindon, Northampton, Ipswich, and perhaps even Peterborough.

Finally, the Greater London Group were careful to point out that South East England was not necessarily typical of the rest of the country. The explosion of the area around London into many small city regions was perhaps a phenomenon

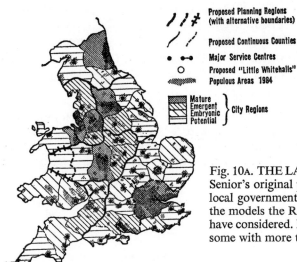

Proposed Planning Regions (with alternative boundaries)

Proposed Continuous Counties

Major Service Centres

Proposed "Little Whitehalls"

Populous Areas 1984

Mature
Emergent
Embryonic
Potential } **City Regions**

Fig. 10A. THE LARGE CITY REGION SYSTEM. Derek Senior's original proposal for 30–40 city regional units of local government in England and Wales, which is one of the models the Royal Commission on Local Government have considered. In the south east it gives very large units, some with more than one obvious centre.

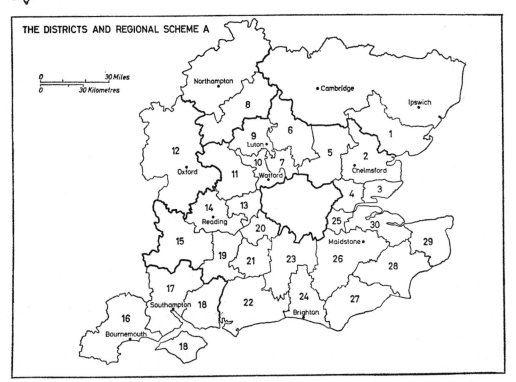

THE DISTRICTS AND REGIONAL SCHEME A

Fig. 10B. THE SMALL CITY REGION ALTERNATIVE. The Greater London Group's detailed analysis of commuting and shopping, coupled with administrative considerations, led them to propose much smaller basic units of government, to be called 'Districts'. In one of the Group's alternative proposals to the Royal Commission, these Districts are grouped into a new south east England unit which excludes the major planned counter-magnets.

261

associated only with the growth of a very large metropolis. Certainly, later work at Political and Economic Planning (PEP), which has extended the concept of the metropolitan area to the rest of England, has found no such tendency round a major provincial conurbation like Birmingham. Here, the city region solution may well prove to apply; though it is notable that the PEP study has identified no less than 100 metropolitan areas in England and Wales.[1]

[1] Written before publication of the Royal Commission's Report in summer 1969. Its recommendation of 58 nearly-all-purpose authorities for England outside the major conurbations is based primarily on the need for big units to perform services, not on the facts of social geography. Derek Senior's memorandum of dissent seizes on this last point, but does not come nearer defining what a city region is.

Part V · LIVING IN IT

CHAPTER 10

London 2000

Planning involves the manipulation of the bricks and stones and concrete and glass, which make up cities. But these things are in themselves meaningless. What matters is that people feel easy in moving around their cities, that they are at home in them, that they like them and even come to love them. The important thing, finally, is the lives lived within cities; and planning can go only some way in improving the quality of those lives.

This book has concentrated on the bricks and stones. And it has seen them in separate compartments: bricks for houses, concrete for roads, glass for offices. In this last chapter, I want to try and bring them together, and imagine the London of 2000 as a living city. That means, finally, that I shall have to conceive the life in and among the bricks and stones. But I must first enter a reservation. Planning should provide a better physical shell, within which people can better live the sort of life they want to live. The most grievous sin of the planner is to try to plan life rather than places: to plan for some concept of life, which the planner wishes to impose on the planned. To imagine the life in London 2000, we should first be asking: what life will Londoners then want for themselves? And then put the shell round that image.

Certainty and Choice

The sort of life people will lead in 2000, the way London will look and feel and work then, will depend on the interaction of three sets of variables. The things we are to all intents and purposes certain of; the things that are practicably unknowable; and the element of human choice, the things that might go one way or another, on which planning can exert an influence.

The certainties, I have tried to argue, occupy a much larger part of the planners' calculations than they have generally cared to admit in the past. They set close limits to what planning can do. I assume, almost as a matter of certainty, that by the end of the twentieth century there will be in the London Region one and three-quarters to two million extra jobs[1] and nearly four million more people, in one million extra households.[2] The planning of London Region must start on the assumption that these people will be here, not that they can somehow be diverted into other regions of the country. Unless the British economy suffers complete long-term stagnation, the 16 million Londoners of 2000 will be on average richer than Londoners now, and will demand more of certain consumer goods, the most important of which for planners are homes and vehicles. By 1980 nearly 30 per cent of these people might be able to afford to buy their own house out of income, and very hazardously we might project this to about 45 per cent by 2000; another 30 per cent may be able to buy out of capital, giving a total of three in four.[3] By 2000 the great majority of the rest of the population should be able to afford the economic rent of the homes they live in. But however, they, or the community, pay for their homes, it will be cheaper for them and society to build one-family homes on previously undeveloped land in the Outer Ring of the London Region, or beyond, rather than to try to redevelop the inner parts of the Region at higher densities. So—again almost certainly—the planners should be thinking of finding in these outer parts of the Region at least one million extra homes in the next forty years.[4]

Also certain is that people will own very many more private vehicles, and (barring some technological revolution) that most of these vehicles are likely to be motor-cars. Current estimates give over eight million vehicles in London Region by 2000, against two and three-quarter million in 1961.[5] Though Londoners may not wish or be able to use their vehicles for all things, they will certainly use them as much as now, if not more, for purposes like visits to friends, to restaurants, to shops, to get away for the day or week-end. This will demand radical replanning of the road system and a big increase in the area of London given over to the parked vehicle.

A last certainty is that the total volume of commuting will almost certainly increase and that the average commuter's journey will increase in length. This is a matter of arithmetic. The extra people will almost all have to be accommodated in the Outer Ring of the London Region, while it is almost certain that not all the new jobs will occur there and that some extra jobs will be at the very centre.[6] Because parts of the commuters' public transport system are already overstrained, the planners will have to provide for large expansions and improvements to the system; which will almost certainly prove expensive.

The unknowables have been ignored in this book because it is unprofitable to speculate on them. If we could devise a cheap private helicopter, our chief concern in London 2000 would no longer be to fit new highways into the existing structure of London, but to control the airlanes. If the pipeline could be developed to transport bulky low-value solids, or if we could develop the synthetic production of bulky

---

[1] See Chapter 3, page 67.
[3] See Chapter 4, page 96.
[5] See Chapter 5, page 106.

[2] See Chapter 4, page 103.
[4] See Chapter 4, pages 103–4.
[6] See Chapter 4, page 104.

primary foods,[1] London's dependence on its port would be greatly reduced, and this would alter its whole economic geography profoundly. If we developed revolutionary new methods of building high, we might make high-density development more economic than low-density housing on undeveloped land. But we cannot plan for speculations; we can merely alter our plans if they become certainties.

Most important are the areas of choice, where the actions of the planner can make a difference for good or ill. In this book I have defined five such areas of choice, and have recommended specific planning policies for them. They are:

1. *Employment*. I have argued[2] that though we cannot hope to divert the growth of jobs out of the London Region altogether, we could affect their internal distribution to some extent by financial means. Directly, we could place a payroll tax on employers in the centre and out of the proceeds give subsidies to those willing to move to the outer edge of the region. Indirectly, by charging for the use of congested roadspace in the centre, we would also make location there more expensive. Both measures would cause employers, in considering the location of their businesses, to take account of the social costs which their decisions impose on others. The result would be that employers who needed less to be at the centre would leave it; while those who remained would be compensated for their payments by the extra efficiency resulting from the decrease in congestion.

2. *Homes*. Given that very large numbers of extra people must be housed in the Outer Ring of the London Region, I have argued that the places they live in ought to be more effectively planned. I have suggested that many more people should be accommodated in a series of New Towns;[3] that the expansion of existing towns needs more comprehensive methods of control and higher standards of design;[4] and that these objects require a totally new sort of public development agency.[5]

3. *Transport*. I have said that we cannot plan transport until we know how much transport, of each sort, people are going to want. I have argued[6] that the most effective way to find this out is through a new charging system, which will cover use of the road system as well as the existing public transport. I have postulated that on this basis, people by the year 2000 should be willing to pay more for more and better transport. The public transport system, under a rational price system, will still carry the vast majority of commuters; but as there will be more of these, it will have to be extended, improved, and better integrated physically than it is today. But because there will be so many more private vehicles, the road system, and parking facilities, should be expanded so far as people are willing to pay for the expansion.

4. *Redevelopment*. We need to find a way of ensuring that the redevelopment of obsolete property—whether in the central business core or in the Victorian Inner Ring—takes place according to a comprehensive plan which remakes the system of circulation around the buildings and provides for their satisfactory massing. In

---

[1] Cf. R. L. Meier, *Science and Economic Development: New Patterns of Living* (1956), Ch. 2.

[2] See Chapter 3, passim.   [3] See Chapter 6, pages 137–57.   [4] See Chapter 4, page 78.

[5] See Chapter 6, page 134.   [6] See Chapter 5, pages 109–15.

addition some way needs to be found of taking for the community at least a part of the gains that accrue to private individuals from the profitable developments. I have suggested means whereby these aims might be achieved.[1]

5. *Administration.* If London is destined to grow so greatly by 2000, and if in particular the Outer Ring of the Region is approximately to double its present population, I have argued that the system of government which is currently proposed for London will prove inadequate and should be replaced by a completely new type of regional government, as yet unknown in this country, and analogous to the status of an American state or German *Land*.[2]

Whether, within the areas of choice, we take the steps to plan effectively, will depend on some very large and imponderable conditions: political, economic and social. Because a lot of the proposals cost money, they demand a dynamic economy with the habit of high investment. Because others involve new interferences with the freedom of the individual, they demand a capacity for rapid adjustment on the part of British society. Because they nearly all require abandonment of cherished dogmas, they postulate a period of serious self-criticism on the part of both planners and politicians. We have no right at all, on present form, to be sanguine that any of these conditions will obtain between now and 2000. But supposing they did, after all; what sort of London might we expect then? What sort of life would representative Londoners be living in it?

The Dumills: Londoners 2000

The Dumills are these representative Londoners, though they are not the average Londoners; an average, in a city of sixteen million people, would be a meaningless statistical abstraction.

Edward Dumill. 54. University Administrative Officer.
Mary Dumill. 51. Public Opinion Consultant.
Sebastian Dumill. 24. Trainee Works Manager, Electronics.
Chloe Dumill. 20. Student in Catering Technology.

By even the most generous standards of the early nineteen-sixties, the Dumills would not have been called Londoners. They live sixty-one miles from Charing Cross, at Hamstreet in Kent, only eight miles from the English Channel. Hamstreet is the farthest from London of all the New Towns built under the ten-year programme announced in 1968. It received its first family in 1973; by 1980 it had 20,000 people— including the Dumills, who had moved there in 1976, three years after their marriage; by 2000 it had nearly reached its target population of 95,000; and plans were in hand to raise the target to 120,000 to house a first generation of Hamstreet sons and daughters, who were beginning to marry.

From the Dumills' window, you have the immediate impression that Hamstreet is a tight, enclosed, compact town. So it is: 70,000 of its 95,000 people can walk to the

[1] See Chapter 8, passim.

[2] See Chapter 9, passim.

central shopping district within a quarter of an hour: as quick as driving and parking a car there. At the front, the Dumills' house is grouped with four others round a small, irregular cul-de-sac court, which gives off a pedestrian alley; at the back it looks at neighbours' kitchens just across the deep, narrow vehicle road which runs down at basement level, where the garages are.

Three of the four Dumills spend every working day outside Hamstreet. Chloe alone stays, though even she sometimes goes to courses in Canterbury. She is numbered among the 20,000 Hamstreet people working, or enjoying education, in the town centre. Next term, when she goes to get practical experience in a local biscuit factory, she will join the stream of 20,000 Hamstreeters who every morning make their way to the factory zones at the edge of the town, there joining 10,000 who have come in from outside by train, bus, car and scooter. Mrs. Dumill leaves every morning to travel to Canterbury. She is numbered among the 8,000 daily Hamstreet commuters to other Kentish towns. Sebastian, who works at Headcorn, twenty miles nearer London, is one of Hamstreet's weekly commuters; from Monday till Friday he lives in a hostel built by the Headcorn College of Technology. In the summer he will marry and get a job in Hamstreet; then he will take one of the Corporation's rented flats until he saves for the deposit on one of the new houses being built for purchase. And Mr. Dumill (who bought this house from the Corporation when he moved here) is one of the 2,000 remaining Hamstreet workers, who daily make the long trek up to London.

When movements like these first attracted attention in the seventies, they caused alarm and despondency among the older generation of planners. These people were violating the New Town ideal of the closed community where the problem of journey to work had been practically abolished. But as the tendency increased, the concern largely evaporated. People, the planners came to accept, were becoming more mobile. They thought as little of going twenty-five miles to work as of driving fifty miles in the evening to see friends, or going over to Brittany for a week-end. The fact was that the range of modern jobs was so wide, people's special skills so varied, their ambition and appetite for higher pay so great, their propensity to travel so high and their ownership of vehicles so great, that you could never hope to employ them all satisfactorily in a community of one hundred thousand people. And finally, the sociologists reassured the planners even about the London commuters; many of them actually rather enjoyed the two oases in their working day.

Two of the Dumills leave their house this Friday morning by the front door: Chloe walks to the College of Technology and Mr. Dumill to the station. And two habitually leave by vehicle at the back: Sebastian, each Monday, on his scooter, for a week in Headcorn; Mrs. Dumill, daily, in her car, for Canterbury. Their paths will never cross on the same level; the road system of Hamstreet, planned in a series of gigantic one-way loops, passes under and over the pedestrian alleys and paths, and finally converges on a main spine road under the quarter-square-mile of pedestrian deck which carries the town centre.

LIVING IN IT

The railway station is eighteen minutes' walk from the Dumills' front door across one corner of this great deck. The train Mr. Dumill catches there is the 8.28 semi-fast from Paris via the Channel Tunnel. It has already picked up a few London-bound commuters in Boulogne—labour mobility was already establishing that habit by the seventies—and quite a lot more in Folkestone. It will collect yet more at Headcorn, twenty miles along the line; at Bromley it will lose one-fifth of its passengers, to join the 175,000 people who work in this great shopping and office centre; and at Brixton it will lose another fifth, including Mr. Dumill.

Brixton cannot, as Bromley perhaps could, be described as a 'suburban' shopping and office centre; it is part of the central complex itself. That is not to say that Brixton was swallowed up in a mighty sea of offices, that washed down from the South Bank via the Elephant and Castle. It remains a separate entity, and the Brixton of 2000, apart from the new tall buildings near the station, looks curiously like the Brixton of 1960, or the Brixton of 1910. There are the same rows of Early Victorian porridge-grey terrace houses; the same bright, brash, gay, vulgar shopping centre, huddled under the elevated railway arches. But on a closer look the whole has been subtly remodelled. All that was good is there still; but the problems of the sixties have been mitigated, or cured. The terrace houses have been rehabilitated and modernized; their road pattern has been broken up and sealed off from the main traffic streams. The shopping centre, likewise, is no longer bisected by a stream of through traffic; some has been diverted to a new through motorway, the rest to an inner loop. On a pedestrian deck above part of the inner loop, and carrying the motorway at high level, are the new shops and offices and campus of higher education, which bring 200,000 people into the middle of Brixton every working day. But they do not destroy the character of the old Brixton; they have made it even livelier and more bustling.

All this is the result of sympathetic replanning under the Town Planning Act of 1970. Through taxes on obsolescence and pooling schemes, this at last gave the possibility of comprehensive renewal in areas like Brixton. When Brixton's turn came, in the seventies and early eighties, a school of planners trained up in the decades 1960–80 were conscious of the terrible truth, that failures of urban renewal in North America had taught: in rebuilding, you must not destroy the qualities that make cities live. You must keep the old buildings people like: you must mix up land uses; you must not let the place go dead at night. In these aims the planners succeeded.

Edward Dumill is an administrative officer with the University of South London. 'SL' is the result of the crash programme for higher education introduced in the early sixties. The planners then had just realized that one of the fastest-growing 'industries' in the central area was education; and under the crash programme it would grow yet faster. So the programme diverted the growth of the University of London into separate institutions, of which SL was only one result. In 2000, students are a much commoner sight than in 1960, not only on the streets of Brixton, but in any British town; twenty-seven per cent of our young people between eighteen and twenty-one are receiving whole-time education, and another forty-four per cent are attending courses for part of the day or week. And educational buildings are a much more important feature of the urban landscape. SL spreads out beyond Brixton; some departments are in Battersea, Clapham, and Tooting; halls of residence are in Streatham and Wandsworth. There are separate University centres in Rochester, Dartford, Woolwich, Croydon, Kingston and Guildford.

Edward Dumill's job takes him to one of these other centres of SL and often he has to get there quickly. So he takes a pool car. SL's underground garage always has some; others are in open public parks. All London's cars, whether they are public pool cars or privately owned, are metered and their driver has to pay for his use of the road, according to the amount of congestion on it. But the pool car driver puts shillings in the slot; the owner has to rent his meter, and in addition pays a quarterly bill. Most people find it cheaper, and less trouble, to pick up a pool car; few private cars are seen on London streets till meter time ends, at half-past six every working evening.

So Mary Dumill, who is bringing the second family car up to London, has to wait till that time to cross the border into inner London on her way to Brixton. Tonight the Dumills are celebrating their twenty-seventh wedding anniversary with dinner by the river in Hammersmith. Since the sixties, London's restaurant belt has spread wide afield: after 1945 it had reached Knightsbridge, Chelsea and Kensington, but it was not till the seventies that it got to Hammersmith and only in the eighties that it affected Strand-on-the-Green and Kew. The process was part and parcel of the explosion of London's West End, which the planners had guided. By 2000 the West End spreads along the arterial roads to London Airport. But the centres of shops and offices are highly concentrated. 200,000 people work in Hammersmith, 150,000 in Ealing, 100,000 at Shepherd's Bush and Wood Lane. Hammersmith was the earliest of these major 'sub-centres', as planning jargon described them. Superficially, it looks like Brixton; there are the same tall office blocks and shops gathered around the station, though here the rebuilders swept away most of the old Victorian Hammersmith. But functionally it is different. Its bigger shops are West End shops, drawing customers from all over the country. Its offices house prestige headquarters for national companies, and two big advertising agencies. Education is less important there. And in character Hammersmith is smarter, more brittle, less earthy and uninhibited than Brixton. But it shares with Brixton some of the same advantages. It is not just a place that attracts commuters by day, and goes dead at night; it brings in each evening a new flow of people to eat and drink and visit its specialized theatres and cinemas. And besides, people still live there; by night, they throng the shopfronts and arcades and riverside walks too.

At 11.30, as the Dumills drive out of London by the New Kent Motorway, the expressways of London are a brilliant sight. When the first ones were built, back in the late sixties, the pessimists confidently predicted that they would wreck London. By 2000 most people admit that they gave it a new dimension, now trenching by the sides of railways, now flying over rooftops, now burrowing through the heart of the reconstructed shopping and office centres. In these centres, on average three to four miles across London, are the sharp concentrations of very tall buildings, grouped around railway stations and reachable direct from the motorways through special car parks. Each of these concentrations houses between fifty thousand and three hundred thousand workers; Brixton and Hammersmith are only two out of a score.

Between these new concentrations, the London of 2000 is still the recognizable old London. No cataclysm has swept away the rows of terrace houses or the corner pubs, the busy shopping centres, the miles of suburban semi-detached. Even in the dynamic economy which Britain has become, change does not occur in a day. Nor would we welcome it if it did.

There is heavy traffic on the New Kent Way, though it is now past midnight. It is Friday night, and apart from a few special lorryloads moving to the continent, the private car dominates the road. Most of these cars are moving out, from theatres and cinemas and restaurants and parties in central London. But not a few are coming in, from country eating places or visiting friends or going to parties in places up to sixty miles from Central London. For the Londoners of 2000, distance is no longer an object. They learned to do without cars for much of their working day, but for living their own lives the car has become part of themselves. Just as they no longer can work in isolated communities, so they can no longer form their friendships and their social lives within bounds of space. For them Hammersmith to Dover has no more significance than would Hammersmith to Hampstead in 1960.

Most of the towns you see from New Kent Way, towns like Maidstone and Ashford, are big old-established towns, important centres for the areas around them. Maidstone has 150,000 people and Ashford 100,000. All these towns have complex functions. They have their contingents of London commuters; their local factory, shop and office staffs; and their quotas of workers who emigrate to factories in other towns. The lights over there belong to a new town: Headcorn, built in the same ten-year plan which produced Hamstreet. Twenty miles up the line to London from Hamstreet, Headcorn rapidly became a big commuter town, and most of its houses are owner-occupied. Its architects, finding they had to build a town on ill-drained Weald Clay, made a virtue of water. They built the town along canals and designed its houses in the neo-formal style which had become popular in American architecture by the sixties.[1] The canals turn Headcorn into a series of islands, and effectively channel the motor-car into its proper place, as in any old Dutch town. The rival school of architects—the uncompromising functionalists who had designed Hamstreet—condemned Headcorn's formalism as 'escape architecture'; but it proved popular with the commuters, and soon had plenty of imitators. Now, it is only the very old-fashioned people—Mr. Dumill counts himself one—who faintly disapprove of it.

And so back to Hamstreet. It seems strange for people who move so easily across

[1] Cf. William H. Jordy, 'The Formal Image: USA', *Architectural Review*, 127 (1960), 157–65.

the face of southern England and northern France, but the Dumills think of themselves quite unconsciously not only as Londoners, but also as Hamstreeters. Hamstreet is their town, and when they stroll next morning along its pedestrian alleys and paths, pushing their big wire trolleys, to do their weekly shopping in the big central supermarkets, they will feel as much at home in it, and part of it, as they felt themselves Londoners on the banks of the Thames last night.

Last Questions

The Dumills are us—or our children—forty years on. We must ask whether the picture I have drawn of their lives is valid. Our answer will depend on whether we accept the essential thesis, which I have tried to argue throughout this book.

First: do we accept that the present course of economic and social evolution will make many features of their lives inevitable, whether we like them or not? I mean the facts that by 2000 London has grown so big, and that many Londoners live so far from the centre of it; that they commute in different directions so far each day to work, and that some of them still travel very long distances to the centre each day; that they depend so completely, for an important part of their lives, on the motor vehicle; that though they have loyalties, these are complex ones, and that they cannot live their lives within the social and economic bounds of a small enclosed community.

Second: accepting these things, is the London which I have described the best we can devise, for them to live the lives they want to live? This London is the result of a set of positive planning actions by the community, which it need not have taken. It need not have built these New Towns; these motorways; these new shopping and office sub-centres. Indeed, it would have been easier to turn the blind eye; to prepare wholly specious and impracticable alternatives on paper, and to fail to make plans where plans would be effective. In that case we should have a different London 2000. It also would be recognizable; but chiefly through the ugliness and frustrations which have been maintained, and intensified, from the London we know now. We could have formless, inadequately planned sprawl of offices out from central London, as suburbs sprawled between the wars; traffic gradually congealing to a stop in the centre and along the main arteries; ugly, dispiriting, demoralizing suburbs sprouting like fungi from every old town within sixty miles of St Paul's. These things are not possibilities; if my argument is correct, they also are certainties, unless the community acts soon, to recognize the practicable limits of planning, and within those limits to devise a new concept of planning, more total and effective than that which it produced in those intense wartime and early postwar years.

Which?

London 2000

For any author foolhardy to offer a blueprint and a vision of the future, there is finally only one test: whether the vision was right. He may in the meantime amass Ph.Ds., research grants, professorships in predictive science; but sooner or later, his sins will find him out. I was doubly foolhardy, in making my vision actual; and, if out of curiosity anyone turns back to this book in the Year 2000, they will surely turn to this concrete picture first.

Looking at it again, six years later, I resisted all temptation to modify it or qualify it. It may fail to come right in some details; I still think it will prove on target in most of them. Indeed, the only detail I would happily change is the date: this may prove to be less a picture of London 2000, than of London 1984. Here at the end, as elsewhere through the book, the real mistake I made was to be far too conservative about the pace and the possibility of change.

But planners still have to make it happen. I think they are better placed, and better armed, to do it now in 1969 than when I wrote in 1962. But planning is subject to strange whims of fashion: it reached an apogee in Britain in the late 1940s, a nadir only a decade later. For the probable lifetime of this second edition, the moral should be: planners beware.

Beware, above all, of ignoring the basic message of *London 2000*; that planners must remain aware of their limitations. In any economy but a Maoist one (and, perhaps, even there) no one planner controls all the levers of power. Certain tendencies in the economy, certain developments in society, must be regarded to all intents and purposes as outside the planner's control. His job, then, is to achieve certain objectives within the limits of his competence. Too often, this message has been ignored.

There is an extra reason for heeding it now. One of the most remarkable changes in Britain, since *London 2000* was first published, is the rise of the consumer protest movement. The consumer pure and simple, the ratepayer as consumer of local authority services, the student as consumer of education; all are interesting themselves in the product as never before, and are rightly insisting that their voice be heard when it comes to discussing the quality. In this changed world, the planner can no longer feel free to impose standards because he feels they are professionally right; he has to find out what the public wants (if that is discoverable) and then to enter into public debate, to try to persuade the public of his professional viewpoint.

In many cases, this will mean that the planner will have to redefine his role. He will need to be much less concerned with aesthetic minutiae. In detail, he will have to allow people much more freedom to express their own tastes and preferences. In order to find out what those tastes and preferences are, he may have to settle for experimental zones where individuality is allowed to run riot. 'Nonplan', which a group of us advocated in *New Society* early in 1969, is first an educational tool for planners. But used in the right places, it could also provide a great deal of room for exciting experiment and initiative, which the existing system now suppresses.

If planning is no longer concerned with the old image of the city beautiful, what is it concerned with? With what society decides. Planning is an activity that can embrace most human actions. Basically, it means taking foresight; considering the consequences of one's actions before taking decision. This attitude of mind can be applied to economic policies, to putting a product on the market, to making love or war. So the emphases of planning may change from time to time. In the late Victorian age, it was small wonder that the main concern was with public health and public beauty. In this age, the main concerns are far more likely to be with economic regulation, with the management of complex systems like traffic and transportation, with providing for the casualties of the welfare state.

This suggests some basic aims of planning—though it does not suggest the means, or solutions. At national level, planning will be much concerned with the optimal level of allocating resources among regions. Thus it will be concerned with different and perhaps competing objectives of economic policy—with maximising growth, with minimizing disparities between regions, with reducing disparities between groups and with how far regional policies in investment, and control, can affect the achievement of these objectives. At regional level, it will be much concerned with the geographical location of investments on the ground, and the co-ordination of those investments in time. Again, those investments will have to be considered from the viewpoint of how they contribute to the solution of different policies. This policy may encourage people to live in towns, that policy may encourage them to spread into the countryside. This policy may encourage people to commute and shop by car, that policy may tend to put them on public transport. In itself—this is the important message—planning and planners cannot say which of these policies is right. That is a political decision, which means that finally it depends on certain shared values which a majority of the population (or the biggest minority) comes to hold.

What planning can do and must do, is look farther than men can do unaided. It must say, 'if you do this, it seems that the consequences for you will be this, and for that group of people over there it will be this'. In other words, it isolates chains of consequences that flow from actions, and attempts some calculation in exact terms of costs and benefits. It may even, on this basis, presume to come to a conclusion: that one course of action is *better* than another. It can do this only if it is sure that the values it assumes are those of the society it represents, or at least of an overwhelmingly large majority of that society. If it is not sure, then its duty is to say so, and present the choice to the people and the politicians.

Finally, physical planning is only one branch of the activity called planning. Society as a whole may give physical planning at some times a higher, at some times a lower priority. It might decide for instance that it does not rank efficiency very highly as a good, in which cases it will ignore that case for planning which argues that it improves efficiency. Or, it may decide that physical appearance is not a very important consideration, and that resources for improving appearances may be better spent in other ways. I do not think either of these possibilities is very strong in Britain in the next thirty years, so I think that physical planning will still be important for us as a society. But only—the final message of this book—if the planners recognize why they are there, and who they are serving.

A Final Postscript

The day before this new edition went to the Press, the *Greater London Development Plan: Statement* came from the Greater London Council. It would have been exciting to report that the new Statement contained so radically new a vision of London's future, that it put this whole book back into the melting pot. But that is far from the case. The Statement is flat, unimaginative, unoriginal, unmemorable. It says almost nothing that was not widely known before to any Londoner who knew what was happening in his city.

The new Statement confirms the prediction that the population of Greater London is falling; in 1981 it may be as low as 7·1 million, over a million below the peak point of the 1930's. Employment in central London, too, is no longer increasing; and as the labour supplies within the conurbation contract, so employment may be driven out. London, so recently seen as suffering from congestion of the arteries, now seems in danger of losing its blood supply.

Most people had thought that the new Plan would provide the opportunity for a bold long-term vision of a new structure for London, taking the weight away from the centre, developing new nodes of activity in the suburbs, and finally regrouping the great mass of employment in the centre so as to make it more accessible to the major radial and circumferential transportation routes. But there is little hint of that vision here. There are the familiar proposals for the circumferential motorway box (now renamed Ringway One), connected to the main national motorways which radiate outwards from it. There are proposals too for new 'sector' shopping centres in the suburbs at Ealing, Brent Cross, Wood Green, Newham, Bromley, Lewisham, Croydon and Kingston. But nowhere are these two nations fused into a total picture of a new pattern of activity and of movement. Significantly, though the new centres are described as 'accessible', only two of them are at all likely to be connected to the high-speed motorway network by the end of the 1970s.

Almost the only virtue of the Statement is that it is so open, so uncommitted, so finally uncommittal, that in reality it is no Plan at all. Londoners deserved better than this. In reality, if there is to be a Greater London Development Plan worth the name, they will have to get it.

276

Index

INDEX

Payroll tax, 71–2, 267
Peak traffic, 137
Pedestrians, 219
PEP, 138
Peripheral development, 112
Personal health, 244
Peterborough, 120, 122, 169, 170, 171, 185, 189, 260
Petersfield, 181, 203
Pevsner, N., 136 n., 170 n.
Physical planning, 22, 244
Piccadilly Circus, 210, 213, 254
Pick, F., 139
Pimlico, 107
Pipeline, 266
Planned and unplanned population growth, 88–91
Planning: *see* separate heads; function, 245, 249–50; object of, 265; system, since 1947, 242–4; Act 1963, 77
Planning Advisory Group, 255 n.
Planning Act 1968, 255 n.
Planning and Communication Committee, 157 n.
Planning permissions, 239
Plumpton, 181–201
Political and Economic Planning, 138
Pool cars, 271
Pooling of land, 231–4, 237
Poor Law, 142, 245
Population: changes, 75; distribution, 74 n.
Population, density of, 260
Population growth: past, 74, 85–93; future, 94–5, 116–17, 121, 266; London, 35, 252; and employment, 76 n.
Population, Royal Commission, 92
Port (London), 267
Portsmouth, 121, 122, 159, 169, 186, 188, 192, 258, 260
Postwar economic growth, geography of, 49–59
Postwar, urban renewal of the, 216
Potential households, 103
Powell, A. G., 20 n.
Precincts, precinctual solution, 28, 208–10
Prest, A. R., 235
Price, in transport, 133–9, 267
Prices and Incomes Board, 158
Princes Risborough, 181, 196
Printing and publishing, 58
Private builder, 165
Private costs, 60, 61–4
Private vehicles, 131, 132, 133, 138
Productivity, 64

Professional organizations, 59
Professional services, 47, 52, 53, 57, 58–9
Progressive traffic lights, 144
Pro-London, 40–1
Proudlove, J. A., 148, 149
Provincial culture, 39–40
Prussia, 152
P-solution, 208–10
Public Building and Works, Ministry of, 167
Public Health, 37, 252
Public Transport, 137–9
Public Services, 183

Quarters, industrial, 60, 66, 72
Quasi-dwellings, 104–5
Queenborough-Minster (Sheppey), 181, 199–200
Quendon, 181, 198

Radcliffe, *see* Taxation of Profits and Income, Royal Commission
Radial roads, 146; tangential plan, 147
Radio industry, 62
Rail services, 83, 153, 172
Railways, motorway lines along, 149
Rate deficiency payments, 112
Rates, differential, 76
Reading, 31, 32, 121, 169, 250
Redcliffe Maud, *see* Local Government.
Redevelopment Commission, 233–4, 236–7, 250
Redhill, 67
Regent Street, 218
Regent's Canal, 149 n.
Regional analysis, 45–6, 64
Regional Boards, 243
Regional Government, 244–52, 268
Regional Higher Education Authorities, 251
Regional Plan Association (New York), 132 n., 140 n.
Regional Planning, Standing Conference on London and South East, 190 n.
Registrar-General, 92, 94
Reith, Lord, 31
Renewal, 66, 204–16
Rents, 66, 67, 72
Research in industry, 62
Retail trade, 58, 132, 246
Reversible flows, 144
Review area, 245–6
Reynolds, D. J., Wardrop, J. G., 134 n.
Ring roads, 147
Road accidents, 206
Road Research Laboratory, 130 n., 138, 144 n.

284

Vehicles, 47, 52, 53, 247, 265; numbers of, 130, 266
Vertical segregation (solution), 151, 210–15
Vickrey, W., 137 n.
Victoria, 67, 69, 80, 82, 160, 206
Victoria Line, 140, 160
Volpe, J. A., 132
V-solution, 210–15

Wages, 67
Waiting bans, 144
Walkaways, 218–9
Walker, G., 135
Wallingford, 181–196
Walsall, 38
Walthamstow, 140, 160
Walton-on-Thames, 253
Wandsworth, 150
Wandsworth Road, 208
Washington, D.C., 137
Water supply, 174
Waterloo, 82
Watford, 247
Watson, L. K., 32
Weber, A., 59–60
Weekend Telegraph Magazine, 192
Welfare, 244
Wells, H., 227, 238, 241
Wells, H. G., 206 n., 249
Welwyn Garden City, 31
Wessex, 260
West Cross Route, 143 n., 156, 159
West End, 148, 218

West Ham, 86
West Middlesex, 53
West Midlands, 62, 248–9, 251
West Side, 26, 125, 206
West Suffolk, 122
West Sussex, 181
Western Avenue, 217; extension, 143 n.
Westminster, 38 n., 96, 209; City Council, 254
White, P. A., 133 n., 141 n.
Wholesale markets, 246
Wibberley, G. P., 111
Willesden, 82, 86, 110, 125
Wilson, C. H., and Reeder, W., 61 n.
Wimbledon, 110
Wimpole Street, 213
Winchester, 171, 193, 259
Wollheim, R., 40 n.
Women's Clothing, 208
Wood Lane, 271
Woodham Ferrers, 181, 199
Woodrow, T., 126
Woolwich, 67, 136, 271
Work journeys, 129–30, 153, 161
Working class, 99
Worthing, 169
Wren, Sir C., 116
Wycombe, 32, 33, 34
Wyllie, J., 111
Wythenshawe, 206 n.

Yorkshire, 248
Young, M., and Willmott, P., 114–15